— CALMING THE FERGHANA VALLEY —

The Center for Preventive Action's Preventive Action Reports

A series sponsored by
the COUNCIL ON FOREIGN RELATIONS and
THE CENTURY FOUNDATION,
formerly the Twentieth Century Fund

Volume I: *Toward Comprehensive Peace in Southeast Europe: Conflict Prevention in the South Balkans* (Report of the South Balkans Working Group)

Volume II: *Cases and Strategies for Preventive Action* (Papers from the Center for Preventive Action's Third Annual Conference)

Volume III: *Stabilizing Nigeria: Sanctions, Incentives, and Support for Civil Society* (Report of the Nigeria Project)

Volume IV: *Calming the Ferghana Valley: Development and Dialogue in the Heart of Central Asia* (Report of the Ferghana Valley Project)

Center for Preventive Action
Council on Foreign Relations
58 East 68th Street
New York, NY 10021
tel: (212) 434–9400
fax: (212) 517–4967
www.foreignrelations.org

The Century Foundation
formerly the Twentieth Century Fund
41 East 70th Street
New York, NY 10021
tel: (212) 535–4441
fax: (212) 535–7534
www.tcf.org

To order any of the Preventive Action Reports,
please call 1 (800) 552–5450

PREVENTIVE ACTION REPORTS
VOLUME 4

CALMING THE FERGHANA VALLEY

Development and Dialogue in the Heart of Central Asia

Report of the Ferghana Valley Working Group of the
Center for Preventive Action
Senator Sam Nunn, Chair of the Working Group
Barnett R. Rubin, Director, Center for Preventive Action
Nancy Lubin, Project Director and Principal Author

SPONSORED BY THE COUNCIL ON FOREIGN RELATIONS
AND THE CENTURY FOUNDATION

1999 • The Century Foundation Press • New York

THE CENTURY FOUNDATION

The Century Foundation, formerly the Twentieth Century Fund, sponsors and supervises timely analyses of economic policy, foreign affairs, and domestic political issues. Not-for-profit and nonpartisan, it was founded in 1919 and endowed by Edward A. Filene.

Library of Congress Cataloging-in-Publication Data

Lubin, Nancy.
    Calming the Ferghana Valley : development and dialogue in the heart of Central Asia / Nancy Lubin and Barnett R. Rubin ; with a foreword by senator Sam Nunn.
        p.   cm. — (Preventive action reports ; v. 4)
    "Sponsored by the Council on Foreign Relations and The Century Foundation."
    Includes bibliographical references and index.
    ISBN 0-87078-414-5 (alk. paper)
    1. United States—Foreign relations—Uzbekistan. 2. Uzbekistan—Foreign relations—United States. 3. United States—Foreign relations—Tajikistan. 4. Tajikistan—Foreign relations—United States. 5. United States—Foreign relations—Kyrgyzstan. 6. Kyrgyzstan—Foreign relations—United States. I. Rubin, Barnett R. II. Council on Foreign Relations. III. Century Foundation. IV. Title. V. Series.
JZ1480.L83   1999
958.7—dc21   99-30898
                                                                        CIP

COUNCIL ON FOREIGN RELATIONS

The Council on Foreign Relations, Inc., a nonprofit, nonpartisan national membership organization founded in 1921, is dedicated to promoting understanding of international affairs through the free and civil exchange of ideas. The Council's members are dedicated to the belief that the nation's peace and prosperity are firmly linked to that of the rest of the world. From this flows the Council's mission: to foster America's understanding of other nations—their peoples, cultures, histories, hopes, quarrels, and ambitions—and thus to serve our nation through study and debate, private and public.

The Council takes no institutional position on policy issues and has no affiliation with the U.S. government. All statements of fact and expressions of opinion contained in all its publications are the sole responsibility of the author or authors.

Century Foundation and Council on Foreign Relations Books are distributed by Brookings Institution Press (1–800–552–5450). For further information on Council Publications, please write the Council on Foreign Relations, 58 East 68th Street, New York, NY 10021, or call the Director of Communications at (212) 434–9400. Or visit our website at www.foreignrelations.org.

— Note —

The Council on Foreign Relations takes no position on issues. *Calming the Ferghana Valley* is a report of the Ferghana Valley Working Group of the Center for Preventive Action. The views expressed reflect the general policy thrust and judgments endorsed by the Working Group, although not all members of the group necessarily subscribe to every finding and recommendation in the report.

— Acknowledgments —

This is the fourth volume in the Center for Preventive Action's *Preventive Action Reports*, a series that is cosponsored by The Century Foundation and the Council on Foreign Relations. This volume was made possible by the generous support of the Carnegie Corporation of New York and The Century Foundation. This report was written by Nancy Lubin, Keith Martin, and Barnett R. Rubin. The Center for Preventive Action is grateful to: the members of the Ferghana Valley Working Group; Arustan Zholdasov, who organized our interviews in the Ferghana Valley and provided us with the insights derived from his own research; Anthony Richter, for making available the Soros Foundation Ferghana Project description; Anya Schmemann, whose organizational skills made the mission possible and who provided indispensable assistance with early versions of the manuscript; Peter Sinnott of Columbia University for help with population and geographic data; Fiona Dunne and Katya Nadirova of the Open Society Institute for their assistance with research; and Susanna P. Campbell, whose editorial skills were invaluable in preparing the final version.

— CONTENTS —

— FOREWORD —

SENATOR SAM NUNN

The vast energy resources of the Caspian Basin, combined with Central Asia's location at the intersection of American interests in Russia, China, Afghanistan, and Iran, have heightened the strategic importance of this vast region to the United States. So, too, have other concerns, including Central Asia's role as a source and transit route for narcotics and weapons (possibly including components for weapons of mass destruction), its potential susceptibility to the spread of an anti-Western political Islam, and a political landscape characterized by fairly authoritarian governments that have brought serious economic, political, and human rights tensions in their wake. U.S. policy has focused on encouraging healthy development of these societies, both to facilitate investment there and to mitigate these other dangers. But U.S. interests are challenged here not only by pipeline routes or instability in neighboring countries but by the potential for conflict within Central Asia itself.

With this in mind, the Council on Foreign Relations' Center for Preventive Action convened a working group to examine the sources of instability in Central Asia through the prism of one of its most volatile regions, the Ferghana Valley. Often viewed as a potential Islamic hotbed in the region, this valley straddles three countries: Uzbekistan, Kyrgyzstan, and Tajikistan. It is a major source of food and water for all three states but is also the site of serious and growing economic and political pressures that have led to violence and bloodshed in the past. The purpose of the working group was to develop recommendations for U.S. policy to help prevent further conflict.

The working group included both Council on Foreign Relations members and nonmembers from diverse disciplines. Various members of the group had extensive U.S. policymaking expertise, practical, on-the-ground experience in the region (as lawyers, foundation donors, consultants, etc.), experience in other parts of the world in conflict prevention and resolution, and extensive, prior scholarly expertise on

Central Asia. Some members of the group were already deeply familiar with Central Asia; others had long-term experience working with these issues in other regions of the world, but this marked their first attempt to apply that experience to Central Asia.

During the past two years, the working group met twice and sponsored two visits to the region: the first, in February 1997, by the project director and staff; the second, by eight members of the group one month later. Numerous interviews in the region and among policymakers and specialists in the United States supplemented the reams of documents the group received in Central Asia. Uzbekistan's and Kyrgyzstan's government officials provided extensive information for the report as well as logistical support and hospitality during the trip there, and the many nongovernmental actors who assisted us throughout Central Asia also played an invaluable role. Active participation on the part of the working group members themselves was vitally important during the research and drafting of the report and was greatly appreciated.

Special thanks are also due to Les Gelb, president of the Council on Foreign Relations, whose support was so important to the working group's realization. Barnett R. Rubin, director of the Council's Center for Preventive Action, conceived of the project and made it happen. Nancy Lubin, president of JNA Associates, Inc., was brought on as project director and principal author, working with JNA's senior research associate, Keith Martin. Nancy has traveled to Central Asia on numerous occasions, and her experience and expertise were invaluable. Funding was provided by The Century Foundation and the Carnegie Corporation, which have provided much-needed funding for work on Central Asia in general. Indeed, this working group report was designed to complement a parallel report on U.S. policy toward the Caspian region and Central Asia sponsored by the Carnegie Corporation's Commission on Preventing Deadly Conflict. It is my hope that, taken together, these analyses will provide greater insights into how to improve the formulation of U.S. policy in Central Asia, a region where our national interests are great, but where critical gaps in our understanding remain large.

— PREFACE —

THE CENTER FOR PREVENTIVE ACTION

Director: Barnett R. Rubin

Chair: Gen. John W. Vessey, USA (Ret.)

The Center for Preventive Action (CPA) was established by the Council on Foreign Relations in 1994 to study and test conflict prevention. CPA is chaired by General John W. Vessey, USA (Ret.), former chairman of the Joint Chiefs of Staff, and directed by Barnett R. Rubin. CPA has operated under the guidance of a distinguished advisory board representing a wide range of disciplines and expertise (see Appendix E for a list of members). CPA has been funded by the Carnegie Corporation of New York, The Century Foundation, the United States Institute of Peace, and the Winston Foundation.

Many of today's most serious international problems—ethnic conflicts, failing states, and humanitarian disasters—could be averted or ameliorated given effective early attention. CPA defines preventive action as those steps that can be taken in a volatile situation to prevent a crisis.

In order to study the prevention of such crises, CPA selected four case studies: the Great Lakes region of Central Africa, the Ferghana Valley region of Central Asia, Nigeria, and the South Balkans. For each case study, CPA assembled diverse and experienced practitioners and experts in working groups and sent a delegation on a study mission to map out strategies for preventing, settling, or managing the conflicts in the region.

CPA draws on the knowledge gained from all four case studies, the experience of others, and previous studies to determine what strategies are most effective in the field of preventive action. In order to disseminate the recommendations of its case studies and its other findings, CPA has established, in collaboration with The Century Foundation (formerly the Twentieth Century Fund), a series of Preventive Action Reports. *Calming the Ferghana Valley: Development and Dialogue in the Heart of Central Asia*, is the fourth volume in this series.

CPA PROJECT ON THE FERGHANA VALLEY

Of all the regions of the former Soviet Union, Central Asia is potentially one of the most explosive and certainly one of the least understood. It is also a region that is growing rapidly in importance to U.S. national security, commercial, and foreign policy interests for a variety of reasons: its vast oil, gas, gold, and other resources; its role as a source and transit route for narcotics and possibly nuclear and other materials; its proximity and historical ties with the Middle East; the fierce conflicts that have already occurred there and continue; its ties to international organized crime; its vast size (larger than Eastern and Western Europe combined); its rapidly growing population of more than 50 million people; and the persistence of relatively corrupt and authoritarian governments that have brought new economic, political, and human rights challenges in their wake. All of these characteristics suggest that increased instability and conflict in the region could have severe repercussions locally, regionally, and directly for the United States.

The purpose of the Ferghana Valley project of the Center for Preventive Action is to assess the potential for conflict in Central Asia by studying one of its most volatile areas and to provide recommendations to offset these dangers. The fertile Ferghana Valley intersects the three troubled states of Uzbekistan, Tajikistan, and Kyrgyzstan and includes a mix of ethnic, religious, and social groups. A key premise of the project is that tensions in Central Asia stem not only from these schisms but from a range of economic, political, social, organized crime, environmental, security, and other factors that have long proved incendiary in this part of the world.

CPA Ferghana Valley Working Group

CPA's Ferghana Valley Working Group was assembled to study the sources of potential conflict in the Ferghana Valley region of Central Asia. The project is directed by Nancy Lubin, president of JNA Associates, working closely with CPA director Barnett R. Rubin. The working group, chaired by former Senator Sam Nunn, consists of people who represent a variety of fields and areas of expertise. The project aimed to pool various kinds of expertise rather than gather scholarship strictly on Central Asia, in order to broaden the discussion and develop new approaches to questions of conflict prevention in this region. The working group comprises a mix of policy experts, business executives, members of the media, national security specialists, and representatives of the nongovernmental community. A full list of the working group membership is included in Appendix C.

CPA Study Mission to Central Asia

A delegation of the working group traveled to the region in March 1997, visiting Moscow; Tashkent, Namangan, and Andijan in Uzbekistan; Osh and Bishkek in Kyrgyzstan; and ending in Almaty, Kazakstan. Owing to the unstable situation in Tajikistan, the group did not travel to the northern part of that country, though several members of the working group visited Khujand, in the Tajikistan part of the Ferghana Valley, in May 1998 on a project for the Open Society Institute. The group met with a wide variety of figures in these cities, including government officials, businesspeople, human rights monitors, journalists, scholars, activists, religious leaders, and representatives of international and nongovernmental organizations. Several members of the working group took additional trips to the region. Nancy Lubin also conducted numerous interviews in Washington, D.C.

— EXECUTIVE SUMMARY —

After several years of viewing the former Soviet Union primarily through the screen of Russia, U.S. policy has now developed differentiated approaches to other regions of this vast landmass. The Caspian Sea basin, including Central Asia and the Caucasus, which by some (probably exaggerated) estimates contains fuel reserves equivalent to up to 200 billion barrels of oil, is now attracting particular attention. Yet access to these riches is threatened not only by the lack of transport and pipelines connecting this landlocked area to world markets but by current and latent conflicts in adjoining territories.

In a major speech on U.S. policy to the region, Deputy Secretary of State Strobe Talbott pointed out:

> If economic and political reform in the countries of the Caucasus and Central Asia does not succeed—if internal and cross-border conflicts simmer and flare—the region could become a breeding ground of terrorism, a hotbed of religious and political extremism, and a battleground for outright war.
>
> It would matter profoundly to the United States if that were to happen in an area that sits on as much as 200 billion barrels of oil. That is yet another reason why conflict-resolution must be Job One for U.S. policy in the region: It is both the prerequisite for and an accompaniment to energy development.[1]

The Ferghana Valley, spanning parts of Tajikistan, Uzbekistan, and Kyrgyzstan, is a vulnerable area where the signs of possible conflict are clear. Only about one hundred kilometers from the region's largest city, Tashkent, it includes only 5 percent of the territory but nearly 20 percent of the population of the five post-Soviet states of Turkmenistan, Uzbekistan, Kazakstan, Kyrgyzstan, and Tajikistan. The Valley is a major source of water and food for all three states of which it is a part. It has a higher population density and more economic distress than most other parts of Central Asia (war-torn southern Tajikistan is also in great need).

The countries of Central Asia have the potential to contribute to either stability or turmoil in the vital regions they straddle, the former Soviet Union and Southwest Asia, including the Caspian. United States policy has not reconciled effectively the sometimes competing goals of economic and political reform and conflict resolution and promoting access to oil and gas. Accountable politics and dynamic economies provide the best institutional framework to channel strife into peaceful competition, a necessary condition for investment.

In dealing with conflict, however, concentrating on resolution of existing or past confrontations leaves us with a reactive policy in a region where new violence is likely, indeed, almost certain. Reforms will not succeed in heading off trouble unless they are targeted to the most vulnerable and tense areas like the Ferghana Valley that may otherwise be left behind. Policy must aim to prevent new conflicts. The outbreak in 1997 of assassinations of officials followed by massive police repression in the Uzbekistan part of the Valley, the brief November 1998 uprising in the Tajikistan parts, and the well-coordinated bomb explosions in Tashkent on February 16, 1999, allegedly by Islamic militants from the Ferghana Valley, are only the most recent indications of the urgency of the task.

Long-standing social tensions have increased as a direct result of the political developments of the 1990s. With independence, the former Soviet republics partitioned the Ferghana Valley, which despite republican borders and ethnic differences has always been a common economic unit, among three sovereign states. Each of these states, Uzbekistan, Kyrgyzstan, and Tajikistan, has pursued a different political and economic path and attempted to integrate its part of the Valley into the new nation. While the inhabitants of the Ferghana Valley share their compatriots' national pride and hopes for an independent future, this division has imposed special hardships on them, as it has disrupted economic exchange, educational and cultural ties, and even family relations. In each state, the Valley regions have lost power to national governments dominated by other regions, adding to a feeling of resentment. And these changes have taken place in an overall situation marked by economic decline and insecurity bred by the continuing wars in Tajikistan and Afghanistan, perceived by Central Asian leaders and secular elites as posing the threats of Islamic extremism, drug trafficking, and weapons proliferation.

The risk of conflict in the Valley is not hypothetical. In 1989 and 1990 violent ethnic clashes in both the Uzbekistan and Kyrgyzstan parts of the Valley took hundreds of lives. An Islamic movement took control of portions of the administration in one district of the Valley in Uzbekistan in 1991–92. The government suppressed the movement, but it shows signs of revival in a more violent form. While the main fighting of the Tajikistan civil war originally occurred elsewhere, riots and a violently repressed prison uprising in the Tajikistan part of the Valley during 1996 and 1997 led to hundreds of deaths and an attempted assassination of that country's president. In 1997 assassinations of police and other officials in the Uzbekistan sector of the Valley led to a massive crackdown, including hundreds of arrests of suspected Islamic extremists, one of whom has been sentenced to death and others to prison. The government of Uzbekistan has charged members of this same movement with responsibility for the bombs that killed nine people in Tashkent on February 16, 1999, in an alleged attempt to assassinate President Karimov. And in November 1998 a rebellion by a fugitive military leader took control of key installations in the Tajikistan part of the Valley for several days and also caused hundreds of deaths before being suppressed.

If, as Deputy Secretary Talbott said, it would "matter profoundly to the United States" if the region became "a breeding ground of terrorism, a hotbed of religious and political extremism and a battleground for outright war," the United States should integrate conflict prevention into its policy in Central Asia. This report mainly offers recommendations targeted on the Ferghana Valley itself, but these should form part of a broader regional policy, to which we also turn our attention.

With regard to the Ferghana Valley, we recommend the following measures:

- Creation of cross-border institutions to promote economic development and interethnic cooperation and to monitor potential conflict; in particular, an information clearinghouse on the Ferghana Valley as a whole is needed to assist both investment and foreign aid;

- Support for institutions of civil society and human rights, especially those that span borders;

- Support for efforts at intercultural dialogue, including both ethnic and religious issues; extremists who engage in violence must be punished as criminals, but the religious freedom of the many Muslims in the Ferghana Valley who are reconnecting with their faith in peaceful ways should be protected, and they should be integrated into the political and social mainstream;

◆ Concentrating foreign assistance on regional programs in the valley that cross borders while maintaining bilateral aid; such programs could be funded through USAID's Central Asian regional program or through other, independent mechanisms;

◆ Support for foreign direct investment in the Valley by pressing Uzbekistan to relax its border and currency restrictions and then establishing incentives for cross-border projects.

We recommend, therefore, that the United States promote regional frameworks for the social and economic development of the Ferghana Valley. It should back indigenous efforts toward this end, including relevant programs of the Central Asian Union, formed by Uzbekistan, Kazakstan, and Kyrgyzstan to encourage economic cooperation, and nongovernmental organizations with projects that further regional cooperation and dialogue in the Ferghana Valley. The United States should also support efforts by international organizations to establish regional conflict prevention programs. The United Nations has established a Ferghana Valley Development Program, proposing measures for economic growth and equity, interethnic peace, transparency of boundaries, languages and education, and revival of cultural heritage and cooperation. Kyrgyzstan and Tajikistan have joined the program, while discussions continue with Uzbekistan. Some integrated regional approach of this nature would offer additional prospects for ameliorating today's harsh realities in the Ferghana Valley. The United States should work with all the countries of the region, the Central Asian Union, the UN and other international organizations, international financial institutions, and private organizations to take into account objections and develop a regional proposal to address the challenges of peace and prosperity.

A particularly important focus of such activities would be efforts to promote direct investment, the major potential source of capital to increase employment in the Ferghana Valley. Uzbekistan has two major projects located in the Valley, a Coca-Cola bottling plant and a Daewoo vehicle assembly plant. Kyrgyzstan and Tajikistan have agricultural and mining projects on the Valley's outskirts. Each part of the Valley is separated by high mountains from the rest of its state, and open borders and transactions within the Valley are important to attracting capital. Such openness is mainly limited by Uzbekistan's more restrictive policies in the Ferghana

Valley and across the country as a whole. With a relaxation of such policies, financial institutions and aid organizations could then offer incentives to investors, who might then find it more advantageous to establish projects that would provide an economic boost to all parts of the Valley and encourage greater integration across borders. The goal is not to re-create the Soviet Union or limit these countries' newly won independence (as some in the region fear) but to create a freer open economic and social space that respects the political sovereignty of each country.

A long-term strategy of conflict prevention requires region-wide policies toward Central Asia as well as policies focused on the Ferghana Valley. While we have some recommendations to improve elements of current U.S. policies, the basic thrust is already in place. What we find inadequate is how these policies are implemented on the ground. Attention focused too single-mindedly on Caspian oil may ignore potential conflicts that could undermine the rest of U.S. policy, and enunciation of broad policies without careful design of implementation can be counterproductive. The regionwide policy should include:

◆   Support for political reform to promote government accountability through respect for human rights and civil society;

◆   Support for reform that opens up these economies, protects property rights, limits corruption, and provides a basic social safety net;

◆   Efforts to resolve the conflicts in Tajikistan and Afghanistan, especially through pressures on outside governments that continue to supply weapons;

◆   Engagement with Iran if it moves toward reform in the hope that it can help open Central Asia to world markets; and

◆   Cooperation with Russia, without ceding Central Asia to its sphere of influence.

Carrying out such a policy will require improving the processes through which policies are developed and implemented. We recommend:

◆   Requiring full, written assessments of the impacts on conflict potential of all aid projects and other U.S. policies;

◆ Inclusion in major projects of regional experts who understand the political and social context;

◆ Inclusion of requirements for follow-up and accountability in projects; and

◆ Better coordination among major donors.

Economic crisis in Russia, increased tension in Afghanistan after U.S. air raids and Taliban victories in the north, continued obstacles to implementation of the peace process in Tajikistan, the outbreak of violence in both the Uzbekistan and Tajikistan parts of the Ferghana Valley in 1997 and 1998, and the tensions in Uzbekistan after the February 1999 bombings all make these tasks more challenging. Despite this region's remoteness, the stakes for the United States, including not only oil and gas but peace and security of American citizens around the globe, are high. The Ferghana Valley is in a sense a link in a chain of conflicts across the former USSR and Southwest Asia. Without early intervention, there may be no alternative to belated attempts at conflict resolution. But prevention of such simmering and flaring "internal and cross-border conflicts," in Secretary Talbott's words, should be the United States' real "Job One."

— Part I —

Mission and Recommendations

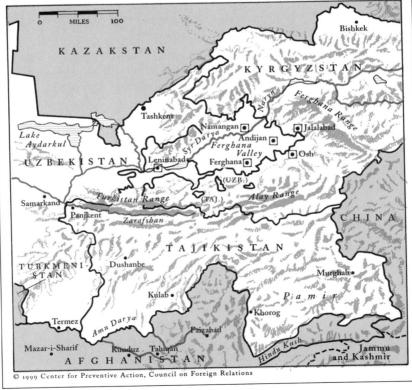

— 1 —

MISSION TO THE FERGHANA VALLEY

A s the male members of our delegation from the Council on Foreign Relations' Center for Preventive Action were ushered into a side precinct of the Central Mosque in Namangan, an industrial and market town in Uzbekistan, we thought we would be witnessing a local cultural event, not an early sign of a violent crisis. We had arrived in this city by air from the capital, Tashkent, the night before. Crossing the mountains that separate the rest of Uzbekistan from the Ferghana Valley, we touched down in that small but fertile area watered by the Syr Darya, one of the two rivers that flow (or flowed) into the now desiccated Aral Sea. The Valley is a natural ecological unit now divided among three newly independent states, eastern Uzbekistan, northern Tajikistan, and southern Kyrgyzstan. This relatively small area covers only 5 percent of the land of post-Soviet Central Asia but is home to 20 percent of the region's people. Several times in the past decade it has been the scene of ethnic or political violence; its states have repressed Islamic leaders and movements; and the security of the whole region is at risk from the long-standing wars in Tajikistan and Afghanistan.

Central Asia has long been isolated from the international community and particularly from the West. The least visited or studied part of the Soviet Union, its newly independent states are suddenly the focus of great interest. According to some (probably exaggerated) estimates, the energy equivalent of up to 200 billion barrels of oil lies beneath the Caspian Sea basin, and all the major powers of Eurasia have begun to maneuver for a share. Access to these anticipated riches is blocked not only by the lack of transport and pipelines connecting this landlocked area to world markets but by conflicts in many countries of the area. These countries have the potential to contribute to either stability or turmoil in the vital regions they conjoin, the former Soviet Union and Southwest Asia, including the Persian Gulf.

The emerging strategic and economic importance of this area influenced the decision of the Council on Foreign Relations' Center for Preventive Action to send a fact-finding mission to the region. But we were motivated as well by our overall goal: to learn how the members of the international community could act more effectively to prevent the violent conflicts that seemed to have broken out in so many areas, notably in parts of Africa and the former Communist states. Precisely because our mandate was to explore how to prevent conflict before it becomes intractable, because the Ferghana Valley is in many respects the heart of Central Asia, and because that region had been the scene of violent outbreaks that had not—or not yet—developed into full-fledged wars, we decided to undertake a visit to the Valley and the capitals of Uzbekistan and Kyrgyzstan in March 1997.

On March 25, therefore, we found ourselves in the mosque in Namangan, guests of a former chief engineer in a Soviet arms factory that had closed in 1991. He and a few other former workers now made ornamental knives and swords for tourists. They had found a small export market in the Middle East and Southeast Asia, as Central Asia renewed its contacts with the broader Muslim world. In the partly reopened factory a fraction of the former employees had also started to manufacture agricultural implements for the densely populated, irrigated plains of the Valley.

Retired on a disability pension worth about $20 per month on the open market (and about $45 at the official exchange rate forced on the country's fuming foreign investors, whom we had met in Tashkent), he also served on a council of elders in his neighborhood, dealing with community and religious matters. Before walking to the mosque we sat with him on floor cushions around the traditional *dastakhan*, a mat for communal meals, in the *mehmankhana*, or guest house, that is an essential part of every traditional Central Asian dwelling. Such houses are built around a courtyard where the owner cultivates some kind of greenery, however meager. Gardens are prized in this land of little rain, where agriculture depends on channeling the water of rivers fed from mountain snows that are visible, at times, on the horizon.

As we discussed our impending visit to the mosque over tea and candies, our host emphasized that while most of the people of Namangan were Muslims—surveys show this area to be the most observant in all of Central Asia—only a few "Wahhabis" wanted to turn

Uzbekistan into an Islamic republic. "Wahhabi," a term we heard repeatedly, is a derogatory reference to the puritanical brand of Islam that rules Saudi Arabia, or to more radical versions. Our host may have insisted on this point precisely because Namangan had been the scene of an Islamic political movement (called Adolat, "Justice") during the confused months of 1991–92 when Uzbekistan became independent, and there were still rumors that hundreds of that movement's supporters had joined Islamic fighters in Tajikistan and Afghanistan.

As we walked to the mosque, we learned we were to attend the funeral of a prominent person. Men filed in, washing their hands, feet, and mouth before moving to the covered central area of the mosque to await the start of the midday prayers. Out in the open, we sweltered in the hot, dry sunlight, though it was only a few days after the Navruz holiday marking the start of spring. The newly independent states had begun to celebrate this ancient festival of the Persian new year publicly as part of the revival of national customs. The boulevards were still decked out with lights, as they are also at that season in Iran and Afghanistan—or were, until the conquest of most of the latter by the Taliban (Islamic students) movement. That puritanical group, the very image of the type of movement that many feared in Uzbekistan and about which we had already heard such concern in Tashkent, had banned public celebration of this feast predating Islam.

That morning the sun had warmed us against the cool breezes of early spring as we wandered through Namangan's market streets, filled with stalls of vegetables, meat, bread, spices, rice, electronic and household goods, Central Asian and Western-style clothing, and books, including many offering instruction in the beliefs and rites of Islam. Though goods seemed plentiful, actual buyers were few, except at stalls selling basic necessities. In a stark difference from most of the rest of Central Asia, a few women were fully veiled with the face-covering *burqa* that the Taliban had imposed on all women in areas they controlled a few hundred kilometers to the south. In Uzbekistan voluntary adherence to this personal form of piety indicated allegiance to a form of Islam that the government considered a threat.

After the noonday prayer service, we followed the several hundred men who had assembled, mostly dressed in the Central Asian long robe and embroidered skullcap, as they paraded out to the street behind the coffin. We learned from our female colleagues, who had been speaking to law enforcement officials and others waiting outside the mosque, that the deceased was a high-ranking police officer killed in the line of duty. Details of how he had died remained sketchy.

That afternoon, in a mostly empty restaurant pavilion in a well-swept municipal park, we spoke to a few representatives of the area's once active dissident movement—some from human rights organizations and some from Birlik ("Unity"), which had spearheaded the call for Uzbekistan's independence, only to find itself banned in independent Uzbekistan. According to them, the officer had been killed with his own pistol by an escaping prisoner. (Others later intimated that the officer may have been involved in infighting among criminal groups.) Earlier in the month the deputy hakim (governor) of Namangan province had also been assassinated. As usual in Uzbekistan, it proved difficult to ascertain details of these incidents or to determine if they resulted from official corruption, common crime, or political tensions.

Driving that evening from Namangan to the nearby city of Andijan, we passed police checkpoint after checkpoint. We counted ten within a few kilometers. Despite security concerns, however, life was continuing. We took advantage of the breakdown of one of the aged cars we had rented to visit a collective farm, where, even as evening wore on, we found farmers at work trying to overcome some of the economic problems that made this region so tense. The chairman perched on a tractor, instructing the farmers in a new technology for cotton planting imported from China. By planting the seeds through holes in clear plastic strips that cover the furrows, the farmers could improve the yields, prevent the growth of weeds, and conserve water, that precious, dwindling resource.

The next day in Andijan we heard about more violent events. American development workers living in the city told us that the deputy provincial head of GAI (the traffic police, who also deal with smuggling, including the mounting traffic in drugs from Afghanistan) had been killed along with his family. A journalist from a local newspaper confirmed that story and added another, the killing of the director of a local alcohol factory under unclear circumstances. His wife had also been shot but survived. The newspaper had been forbidden to report either event, so the journalist had tried a subterfuge: asking the police officer's colleagues to place an announcement offering condolences for his death.

Later that day, when we tried to put our interpreter on a flight back to Tashkent, we learned that all flights had been filled by the security agencies, who were sending men back and forth from the capital. There were rumors of arrests taking place in Namangan. Was the violence simply a criminal incident? Was it connected to the "Wahhabis," whose leaders were reported to have fled to Afghanistan, where they trained with the Islamic fighters from neighboring Tajikistan? Did the killings involve organized crime, which, we were told, Uzbekistan's President Islam Karimov himself had said could hardly be distinguished from the police in Namangan?

Answers to such questions are hard to come by in Uzbekistan, where public discussion remains strictly controlled. After several more police and government officials were assassinated in Namangan in December 1997, including one case in which a police official's severed head was displayed on a gate, the government responded swiftly and publicly. The events were widely reported, and the president accused "Wahhabis" of being responsible. The police arrested suspected activists, and the government banned the use of loudspeakers on mosques. Tohirjon Yuldashev, leader of the once active Adolat, told the BBC from an unidentified place of exile that his movement had nothing to do with these killings. Hundreds of people were arrested in police sweeps through the city as security forces once again descended on the town from Tashkent. In July 1998, one alleged leader of the killers was condemned to death and others to prison.

In what may have been a sequel to these events, on February 16, 1999, five bombs exploded in the center of Tashkent, directly in front of a government building at a time that President Karimov was scheduled to arrive at a cabinet meeting. Though the president was not harmed, nine people lost their lives and many more were injured. The reputation of Uzbekistan as an "island of stability" was another casualty. Government television broadcast the photographs of a couple from the Ferghana Valley, members of the Islamic movement, whom the authorities were seeking as the main planners of the crime.

These incidents had followed many others. During the last days of the Soviet Union the Ferghana Valley had seen outbreaks of mass violence that were sparked by seemingly minor incidents. In 1989, the city of Ferghana, Uzbekistan, witnessed violent attacks by Uzbeks against Meskhetian Turks in which hundreds were killed. As a result, nearly all of this small ethnic group, deported by Stalin from the Caucasus, had left Uzbekistan. In 1990, in the so-called Osh events, named for the Valley district in Kyrgyzstan, a dispute over the allocation of land for housing led to massive bloodletting between Uzbeks and Kyrgyz, including scenes of rape and torture and the deaths of hundreds. Only Soviet troops managed to calm the fighting. In early 1992, Adolat, which had started collaborating with the authorities to control crime in the city of Namangan, occupied some government buildings and made several demands. After an attempt at negotiation with

President Karimov, many militants were arrested, while others fled to Afghanistan, where they joined the Tajik Islamic fighters. The Tajikistan part of the Valley escaped the violence of that country's civil war in 1992 but saw mass demonstrations and a prison uprising in 1996 and 1997, in response to the increasingly exclusive domination in Tajikistan of elites from the southern region of Kulab. More violence occurred during a 1998 uprising.

Despite the latter incidents, linked to the particular circumstances of Tajikistan, up to the time of our visit, Ferghana had seen neither massive ethnic clashes nor open Islamic militancy since the early days of independence. Indeed, the morning of our visit to the mosque, the deputy governor for industry of Namangan had told us over a lavish breakfast that, despite problems during the transition period, Namangan, like the rest of the Ferghana Valley, now was calm and engaged in economic development, prominently symbolized by the establishment there of a Coca-Cola bottling plant. In Tashkent an official of the Ministry of Foreign Affairs had described Uzbekistan to us as an "island of stability" in a troubled region. The U.S. Embassy echoed these remarks, while noting that, if trouble did occur, it would most likely be in the Ferghana Valley. The depiction of Uzbekistan as a rock of stability in a neighborhood that included the violent wars in Tajikistan (since 1992) and Afghanistan (since 1978) was central to the message that Uzbekistan's official representatives wanted to convey through our group: "Recognize our importance, and trust us" was how one of the country's leading strategic thinkers summarized the message he wanted to send to President Clinton.

As we drove from Uzbekistan to Kyrgyzstan, we saw more evidence of how that stability was maintained. At the same border that some members of our group had crossed on earlier visits while hardly noticing it was there, we were stopped and searched by Uzbekistan's border guards, who took our passports. We were allowed to proceed after about a half hour with as little explanation as we had received for being stopped for so long in the first place, despite our possession of valid visas. In subsequent days, we often heard how such border controls, as well as Uzbekistan's complex regulations on currency conversion, made life more difficult for the inhabitants of the Ferghana Valley, which had been a common economic and social area for centuries, under the Soviet Union and before.

Once across the Kyrgyzstan border, the atmosphere changed remarkably. If restrictions on information and the repression of opposition movements made it difficult to judge the potential for the outbreak of violent conflict in the Uzbekistan part of the Ferghana Valley, the multiplicity of views in more democratic Kyrgyzstan made the consensus that did emerge even more convincing.

Conversations made it obvious that the "Osh events" were still fresh in people's minds. At a sometimes tense meeting with leaders of newly established "cultural centers" of Osh's various ethnic groups, a Kyrgyz official of the Communist Party repeated what seemed to be a quasi-official public position. The violence, he said, had been inspired by an unnamed "black force" coming from "outside" (Moscow? Uzbekistan? the Middle East?) and therefore would not recur in independent Kyrgyzstan. At other meetings government officials frankly admitted that problems in interethnic relations persist but outlined a set of programs they were trying to implement to meet some of the grievances and improve communications. Nuriyla Joldosheva, deputy governor of Osh, also argued that people had learned from experience: "The events of 1990 convinced us that we don't need a war here."

Nonetheless, a broad range of interlocutors felt that tensions between Uzbeks and Kyrgyz remain high, especially against the background of economic decline overall. One international official, a native of a country that has recently suffered interethnic war despite a history of coexistence, observed that perhaps his own experience with violence has taught him "how quickly it comes." In the Kyrgyzstan part of the Ferghana Valley, he said, "It's here and present. There is a clear and imminent danger." If there were one incident of violence, he thought, "there will be a big war. All you need is a spark to trigger it. You need just one maniac with a Kalashnikov, and they have a lot of Kalashnikovs."[1]

In Kyrgyzstan's mountain-ringed capital, Bishkek, both an ethnic Uzbek parliamentarian and an ethnic Russian peace researcher told us that surveys showed varying but significant proportions of the population in southern Kyrgyzstan (35 to 70 percent) believed the conflict might begin again. Furthermore, no existing police or military force might be able to halt the violence. As we were told by the deputy head of the Institute for Strategic Studies in Bishkek, "there is no security architecture in Central Asia."

Member of Parliament Alisher Sabirov, an Uzbek from the Kyrgyzstan part of the Ferghana Valley, put it more concretely. We discussed the problems of his community over lunch in a pastel-tinted room in one of the elegant restaurants that have sprung up in Bishkek catering mainly to the Westerners working on Kyrgyzstan's numerous reform programs and the small Kyrgyz elite these programs have helped to spawn. When we asked him if the Osh events could happen again, he recited a list of grievances about discrimination against Uzbeks in access to credit, education, state employment, and positions in the bazaar. Of course, as a member of the opposition and a proponent of the rights of the Uzbek minority in Kyrgyzstan, Sabirov had political reasons to make these arguments. He was seeking help with his own plans to establish independent, Uzbek-language publishing and television in Osh. But many others of various ethnic backgrounds echoed his remarks:

> Now if something happens, there will not be 300 corpses, there will be thousands. I don't want to speak about it at the dining table, but I worked at the high command of the MVD [Ministry of the Interior— police] in Osh oblast. At the time [1990] the only people who halted the fighting were Soviet airborne troops who took up positions on the border of Uzbekistan and Kyrgyzstan. This was the only thing that stopped a mob [of Uzbeks] coming from Andijan to Osh. If it happens again, they will come. There will be no one to stop them. The UN will have nothing to do when it arrives but to bury the corpses.

This view was widespread in Kyrgyzstan. Uzbeks and Kyrgyz are locked in a situation found elsewhere, where both peoples feel they are threatened minorities, Uzbeks in a Kyrgyz-dominated country, Kyrgyz in an Uzbek-dominated region. People told us of many signs of trouble and discontent: continuing fears and hatred resulting from the still unresolved Osh events; growing Islamic activism among unemployed Uzbek youth; the spread of weapons among the population, encouraged by the drug trade, for which Osh was a major entrepôt; the decay of security agencies under the impact of the drug trade; and the hardships caused by the division of the Ferghana Valley into independent states, and particularly by Uzbekistan's restrictive border control and currency conversion regimes. Kyrgyzstan's fragile and flawed democracy provides mechanisms to deal with many of these problems, but the country lacks the capacity to confront them all at once and could easily be overwhelmed by events. Many people, in government, international organizations, and nongovernmental organizations, also seconded Sabirov's conclusion: "The most important thing is to prevent conflict."

— 2 —

PREVENTING CONFLICT IN THE
FERGHANA VALLEY: RECOMMENDATIONS

After several years of viewing the former Soviet Union primarily through the screen of Russia, U.S. policy has now developed more independent approaches to other regions of this vast landmass. The Caspian Sea basin, including Central Asia and the Caucasus, which by some (probably exaggerated) estimates contains fuel reserves equivalent to as much as 200 billion barrels of oil, is now attracting particular attention. Yet access to these potential riches is threatened not only by the lack of transport and pipelines connecting this landlocked area to world markets but by conflicts in adjoining territories.

In a major speech on U.S. policy to the region, Deputy Secretary of State Strobe Talbott argued:

> If economic and political reform in the countries of the Caucasus and Central Asia does not succeed—if internal and cross-border conflicts simmer and flare—the region could become a breeding ground of terrorism, a hotbed of religious and political extremism, and a battleground for outright war.
>
> It would matter profoundly to the United States if that were to happen in an area that sits on as much as 200 billion barrels of oil. That is yet another reason why conflict-resolution must be Job One for U.S. policy in the region: It is both the prerequisite for and an accompaniment to energy development.[1]

The Ferghana Valley, spanning parts of Tajikistan, Uzbekistan, and Kyrgyzstan, is a vulnerable area where the signs of possible conflict are clear. Only about 100 kilometers from the region's largest city, Tashkent, it includes only 5 percent of the territory but nearly 20 percent of the population of the five former Soviet newly independent states of Kazakstan, Kyrgyzstan, Tajikistan, Turkmenistan, and Uzbekistan. The Valley is a major source of water and food for all three states of which it is a part. It has a higher population density and more economic distress than most other parts of Central Asia, with the possible exception of war-torn southern Tajikistan.

The countries of Central Asia have the potential to contribute to either stability or turmoil in the vital regions they straddle, the former Soviet Union and Southwest Asia, including the Caspian. United States policy has not reconciled effectively the sometimes competing goals of economic and political reform and conflict resolution and promoting access to oil and gas. Accountable politics and dynamic economies provide the best institutional framework to channel strife into peaceful competition, a necessary condition for investment.

In dealing with conflict, however, concentrating on resolution of existing or past confrontations leaves us with a reactive policy in a region where new violence is likely, indeed, almost certain. Reforms will not succeed in heading off conflict unless they are targeted to the most vulnerable and tense areas like the Ferghana Valley that may otherwise be left behind. Policy must aim to prevent new conflicts. The outbreak in 1997 of assassinations of officials followed by massive police repression in the Uzbekistan part of the Valley, the brief November 1998 uprising in the Tajikistan parts, and the well-coordinated bomb explosions in Tashkent on February 16, 1999, allegedly by Islamic militants from the Ferghana Valley, are only the most recent indications of the urgency of the task.

Long-standing social tensions have increased as a direct result of the past decade's political developments. The independence of the former Soviet republics partitioned the Ferghana Valley, which despite ethnic republican borders and differences has always been a common economic unit, among three sovereign states. Each of these states, Uzbekistan, Kyrgyzstan, and Tajikistan, has pursued a different political and economic path and attempted to integrate its part of the Valley into the new nation. While the inhabitants of the Ferghana Valley share their compatriots' national pride and hopes for an independent future, this division has imposed special hardships on them, as it has disrupted economic exchange, educational and cultural ties, and even family relations. In each state, the Valley regions have lost power to national governments dominated by other regions, adding to a feeling of resentment. And these changes have taken place in a context marked by economic decline and insecurity bred by the continuing wars in Tajikistan and Afghanistan, perceived by Central Asian leaders and secular elites as posing the threats of Islamic extremism, drug trafficking, and weapons proliferation.

The risk of conflict in the Valley is not hypothetical. In 1989 and 1990 violent ethnic clashes in both the Uzbekistan and Kyrgyzstan parts of the Valley took hundreds of lives. An Islamic movement took control of portions of the administration in one district of the Valley in Uzbekistan in 1991–92. The government suppressed the movement, but it shows signs of revival in a more violent form. While the main fighting of the Tajikistan civil war occurred elsewhere, riots and a violently repressed prison uprising in the Tajikistan part of the Valley during 1996 and 1997 led to hundreds of deaths and an attempted assassination of that country's president. In 1997 assassinations of police and other officials in the Uzbekistan sector of the Valley led to a massive crackdown, including hundreds of arrests of suspected Islamic extremists, one of whom has been sentenced to death and others to prison. The government of Uzbekistan has charged members of this same movement with responsibility for the bombs that killed nine people in Tashkent on February 16, 1999, in an apparent attempt to assassinate President Karimov. And in November 1998 a rebellion by a fugitive military leader took control of key installations in the Tajikistan part of the Valley for several days and also caused hundreds of deaths before being suppressed.

If, as Deputy Secretary Talbott said, it would "matter profoundly to the United States" if the region became "a breeding ground of terrorism, a hotbed of religious and political extremism and a battleground for outright war," the United States should integrate conflict prevention into its policy in Central Asia. This report mainly offers recommendations targeted on the Ferghana Valley itself, but these should form part of a broader regional policy, to which we also turn our attention.

The forms the conflict might take, as well as the triggers that might set it off, differ in the three states. In Uzbekistan's part of the Ferghana Valley, the most evident political tension today seems to be between a small, militant Islamist movement, linked to a much broader trend toward Islamic revival, and a state that both fears the spread of violence from its neighbors and looks with suspicion upon movements it does not control. The government charges Islamic movements with responsibility for acts of terrorism in the Valley. In southern Kyrgyzstan ethnic tensions between Uzbeks and Kyrgyz remain high, and Islamic revival, especially among Uzbeks, also poses a challenge to old relationships between state and society. In northern Tajikistan, resentment festers not only over the domination of the government by an elite from the southern province of Kulab but over a peace agreement signed only by the Kulabi-based government and the Tajik Islamic and democratic opposition, also hailing from the southern part of the country. In northern perceptions, this agreement excludes from power the leaders of that formerly dominant and still most populous, educated, and economically developed region.

Focusing on conflict prevention does not require belief in the most alarmist or bloody predictions. While this report outlines how the legacies of past disputes and current tensions could lead to war in the future, we do not consider such an outcome inevitable and have tried to avoid sensational scenarios. In their very different ways, the governments of Uzbekistan and Kyrgyzstan have sought to deal with the problems analyzed in this report. Indeed, the mass violence both republics experienced during the collapse of the Soviet Union has not been repeated since they became independent countries. The people of the region also evince a strong desire not to repeat the events of the past and to avoid the bloodletting their neighbors have suffered. Whatever proposals or criticisms we may offer in the rest of this report, we recognize that both the authorities and the people deserve credit for maintaining public peace, by and large, under difficult circumstances.

Hence, the purpose of this report is not to sound an alarm about the "tinderbox" of Central Asia. It is rather to urge that, given the combination of risk and opportunity, both international and local organizations and leaders should take steps to minimize the dangers and promote the development of policies and institutions that can nurture the Ferghana Valley, and by extension all of Central Asia, toward greater stability and prosperity. It should not be necessary to await more bloodshed to take measures to remove some of violence's root causes. Unlike in other areas studied by the Center for Preventive Action, notably the South Balkans (Kosovo and Macedonia) and the Great Lakes region of Central Africa (Rwanda, Burundi, and the Democratic Republic of Congo), there is no need to divert energies at present into managing or trying to resolve conflicts that have already become civil and international wars.

PRINCIPLES OF PREVENTION

The Center for Preventive Action has drawn a number of conclusions about conflict prevention, some of which are directly relevant to thinking about how to settle problems through peaceful development in the Ferghana Valley.[2] They are:

◆ *All prevention is political.* While conflict has disastrous humanitarian consequences, conflict prevention and resolution require political, not humanitarian, responses. Humanitarianism requires neutrality among all and a concern for the alleviation of immediate suffering. A political approach recognizes that prevention of violent conflict is an ambiguous goal in itself: it does not specify which potential outcome should be pursued, only that violence should be avoided. Hence, it should be interpreted as complementary to other political goals and principles, such as respect for basic human rights and the pursuit of equitable development. Such goals provide a long-term foundation for the prevention of violence by establishing institutions for dealing with conflict without bloodshed. Pursuit of such aims may, in fact, require some clashing with political leaders who oppose them. Furthermore, the necessary policy measures require the commitment of resources by interested parties. Policy aimed at the prevention of conflict must be integrated into a strategic political framework. Just as prevention must be part of a general policy informed by basic objectives such as security, welfare, and respect for human rights, strategic approaches that ignore the impact of policies on the potential for conflict, including so-called domestic conflict within states, may be self-defeating. Hence, we situate our policy recommendations within a broadly sketched vision of U.S. interests and strategy in Central Asia. This vision is informed by overall goals and values, not just the avoidance of conflict or violence.

◆ *A regional approach is necessary.* In all the cases we have studied, including this one, the separation of domestic from international issues of conflict is difficult if not impossible. Ethnic or religious groups in one state have kin or fellow believers elsewhere; international economic networks of smuggling or money laundering that support political or military activity show scant regard for borders; guerrilla groups often use neighboring states as sanctuaries or form alliances with similar groups there; states and rulers, too, despite their use of the claims of sovereignty to insulate themselves from pressures, show little reluctance to cross borders in pursuit of their goals. Economic and social development, environmental issues, and other concerns similarly involve resources and social networks that cross political frontiers. Therefore, a comprehensive regional approach, possibly including the creation of new institutions, is needed to complement bilateral programs. As outlined below, we believe that the Ferghana Valley

Development Program of the UN could lay the foundations for developing such a framework.

◆ *Independent organizations that monitor governments and hold them accountable and that bridge social divisions are key to preventing conflict.* Unaccountable governments often provoke violent reactions. Elements of an active civil society are essential to defusing potential conflict; most important are human rights organizations, independent media, independent business associations and citizens' groups that span ethnic or other boundaries to define common interests. Nongovernmental organizations and various sectors of society have indispensable roles to play in monitoring government and upholding the rule of law. International efforts should take this into account by attempting to strengthen private institutions, not only the state. Kyrgyzstan illustrates the potential of such organizations to prevent conflict, even in situations of economic deprivation and political upheaval.

◆ *Foreign assistance can help prevent conflict and promote civil society organizations.* But such aid is likely to be effective only if donors target aid carefully, coordinate among themselves, and assess realistically the political, social, and economic context in which they are operating. Aid programs that derive from domestic concerns of the donor rather than carefully analyzed needs of the recipients often leave important gaps in some areas while overemphasizing others. Excessive spending in one area may be harmful, as when several countries or agencies decide to support human rights groups. In some countries CPA has studied this has led to a proliferation of small, competing, ineffective organizations founded in response to donor priorities. Finally, the most common error in aid is expecting technical assistance to do the work of political reform. Technical assistance to legal institutions, for instance, does not promote genuine rule of law if the political leaders have not reached agreement with their own society to govern by law rather than arbitrary power. Such processes are more difficult for outsiders to affect.

◆ *Foreign direct investment can help promote stability by providing employment and transferring needed skills and technologies.* Much conflict is exacerbated or even caused by lack of economic opportunity. Capital flows that create jobs can be critical to alleviating the scarcity that incites unrest. Not all profitable projects, however, promote stability and greater economic equity. Investments in extractive industries such as oil, for instance, may enrich unaccountable governments without spreading benefits to the population and may cause greater resentment. Such investments can also easily promote corruption. Foreign participation in manufacturing of finished products for the local market and export, while still susceptible to nurturing corruption, can be more beneficial in producing employment. Such investments can also provide multiplier effects that are vital to further growth and can create incentives to open borders and build confidence.

POLITICAL FRAMEWORK

As noted above, a few months after our mission to the region, the U.S. government announced a policy toward Central Asia that could provide an appropriate political and strategic context for our recommendations. In a July 1997 speech, Deputy Secretary of State Strobe Talbott outlined a new policy for the region. He defined U.S. interests and described conflict prevention as a priority of U.S. policy:

> The Euro-Atlantic community is evolving and expanding. It stretches to the west side of the Atlantic and to the east side of the Urals. The emergence of such a community represents a profound break with the past for all the peoples involved, but for none more than those of the Caucasus and Central Asia, who have, for so much of their history, been subjected to foreign domination.
>
> Today, they have the chance to put behind them forever the experience of being pawns on a chess board as big powers vie for wealth and influence at their expense. For them, genuine independence, prosperity, and security are mutually reinforcing goals.
>
> The United States has a stake in their success. If reform in the nations of the Caucasus and Central Asia continues and ultimately succeeds, it will encourage similar progress in the other New Independent States of the former Soviet Union, including in Russia and Ukraine. It will contribute to stability in a strategically vital region that borders China, Turkey, Iran, and Afghanistan and that has growing economic and social ties with Pakistan and India. The consolidation of free societies, at peace with themselves and with each other, stretching from the Black Sea to the Pamir mountains, will open up a valuable trade and transport corridor along the old Silk Road between Europe and Asia.[3]

Talbott noted that, while energy and other material interests may provide much of the motivation for U.S. involvement, long-term economic cooperation requires political stability of the newly independent states. The recognition that interest in Central Asia's riches and location demands balanced attention to the entire region, and a focus on conflict prevention rather than a narrow concern for drilling rights and pipeline routes, is welcome. Conflict prevention and resolution in Central Asia as a whole requires a number of policies:

◆ Consistent support for human rights and institutions of civil society, especially in states with potential oil riches; in such states oil wealth may only further empower unaccountable ruling elites that may provoke conflict, as in Nigeria;[4]

◆ Policies to address many sources of discontent, such as the economy, environment, widening inequality, and the loss of physical and economic security;

◆ Efforts to support resolution of the ongoing conflicts in Tajikistan and Afghanistan, including pressure on those states that continue to supply arms, money, and fuel to the combatants;

◆ Positive response to favorable developments in Iran, which could eventually help Central Asian nations escape from their isolation; and

◆ Economic and security cooperation with Russia in the region without ceding it as a Russian sphere of influence.

Talbott's speech recognized most of these points. What it did not mention, however, is that concern for stability must lead not only to America's "Job One" of conflict resolution but also to another task, conflict *prevention*. And the Ferghana Valley is the area of Central Asia (other than the parts of southern Tajikistan affected by civil war) where tensions are most palpable. Furthermore, the Ferghana Valley is economically and demographically significant to all the countries in the region.

Two other conclusions deserve particular attention. First, U.S. policy in Central Asia and the Ferghana Valley should seek a balance among the states in the region, despite the differences in size and power among them. Second, particularly in designing assistance programs, we should pay attention not only to the capital cities and dominant regions but also to important regions that may be less influential in the councils of these new states but whose grievances could be particularly destabilizing.

In all three states, the part of the country that is in the Ferghana Valley is in a sense a loser in the country's internal political battles. This is key to understanding the sources of grievance in the Valley because regionalism, the dominance of politics by patronage networks based on territorial units, is pervasive in Central Asia.[5] In some places it is inter-related with the politics of clan. In the cases of Uzbekistan and Tajikistan, the Ferghana Valley was formerly the dominant region. It was displaced in Uzbekistan after the cotton scandals of the 1980s and in Tajikistan as a result of the civil war. Competition for power and assets among regions in the context of economic collapse was the fundamental cause of the civil war in Tajikistan and of continuing strife today. Hence, in order to promote conflict prevention and resolution, international policy and assistance programs should try to help to overcome rather than reinforce the regional divisions of these countries. Peace efforts in Tajikistan should now focus more on bringing the disgruntled leaders of northern Tajikistan (and their supporters in Uzbekistan) into the process. Programs on political reform in Kyrgyzstan should examine the practice of appointing akims (provincial administrators) from northern Kyrgyzstan to the south. And, as part of the programs for regional cooperation proposed below, Uzbekistan should consider allowing local communities in the Ferghana Valley more leeway in working out relations with their neighbors across the new international borders.

Some assistance programs should be specifically targeted on distressed but peripheral regions such as the Ferghana Valley. The Soros Foundation, for instance, has proposed a comprehensive program for the Kyrgyzstan part of the Valley (see Appendix B). This approach could be duplicated in the other states of the region and, even better, enlarged to create a genuinely regional approach to the Valley. USAID has already established a regional program of assistance, noting that "particularly in energy and the environment, many of the development challenges facing Central Asia are regional in nature, and require a coordinated response by USAID."[6] This program thus far concerns itself only with energy and environmental problems. These are indeed among the central preoccupations in the Ferghana Valley, but an effective approach will require integrating more attempts at resolving broader issues into a common, transborder framework.

Investment promotion policies should aim at creating more incentives for investment in the Valley and other neglected areas. Investments that plant complementary facilities in different parts of the Valley would be particularly useful, as they would help to create the necessary frame-work for regional cooperation. Attracting such investments, however, would require establishment of a regional program that broke down economic barriers and ensured access to an enlarged market.

NEED FOR A REGIONAL APPROACH

Efforts to address any of the difficulties of the region—economic, social, or political—would be strengthened by regional cooperation. All of the Valley's underlying problems, which were serious enough to lead to some incidents of mass violence at the end of the Soviet period, have only been aggravated by the consequences of the region's division among several states. The most urgent need is investment for employment creation. Open borders and currency policies allowing access to larger markets is essential to attracting such investment. Interethnic peace requires arrangements to reassure Uzbek minorities in Tajikistan and Kyrgyzstan, Kyrgyz minorities in Uzbekistan and Tajikistan, the Tajik minority in Uzbekistan, and Tajik refugees in Kyrgyzstan. This demarche will require cross-border dialogues and negotiations among states and communities. Measures to combat drug and arms trafficking, manage water resources, and protect and improve the environment will likewise require regional cooperation.

These regional efforts will require the creation of appropriate institutions. It is important, though, to recognize local concerns about regional cooperation. The newly independent states are understandably sensitive about outside attempts to pressure them back into associations that seem to resemble the old Soviet Union. Analyses lamenting the consequences of the division of the Valley among sovereign states may appear in their eyes to intend to limit that new, and still fragile, sovereignty. The states themselves have begun to elaborate a framework for cooperation that they find acceptable. Kazakstan, Uzbekistan, and Kyrgyzstan have formed a Central Asian Union, and Tajikistan announced its intention to join in 1998. This Union aims mainly at promotion of economic coordination. Thus far it has dealt with the problems of the Ferghana Valley only as a by-product of broader policies.

The United Nations has also launched a new initiative aimed directly at preventing conflict in the Ferghana Valley that has already responded to some of those local objections. The UN Development Program (UNDP) first outlined its proposals in a 1996 working paper entitled "Ferghana Valley Development Programme: Draft Programme Outline."

> Despite both government and UN agency attempts, . . . there has not been a serious effort to build a comprehensive programme [of development]. There is a need to bring together these many strands and design a Ferghana Valley Development Programme which will pay equal attention to income generation and job creation, peace education, inter-ethnic and inter-country confidence building, promotion of trade (and related dialogue on the maintenance of open boundaries) and the improvement of security conditions.[7]

The UNDP draft, reproduced in Appendix A, did not propose any specific policies or programs. It outlined the problems of the valley and defined five potential areas for future projects: economic growth and equity; interethnic peace; transparency of boundaries; languages and education; and revival of cultural heritage and cooperation. The draft proposed a preparatory mission and a review in the region, to ensure that the undertaking would be "formally owned by the three countries with UNDP taking the lead in a UN system-supported process." It suggested "regional institutional building which should cover both governmental and non-governmental entities" as a central component.

Since then, although Uzbekistan thus far declines to participate, the UN has established the program provisionally, with headquarters in Osh, Kyrgyzstan. It is a first attempt at integrating different program areas and various states into a regional approach. The proposal also discussed a point we shall discuss further below, namely, the importance of extending cooperation from states to nongovernmental sectors and organizations.

Full implementation of this project has been stymied thus far by objections from Uzbekistan. Uzbekistan officials told us that this program needlessly infringed on sovereignty, as the states of the region are already handling these problems through their domestic policies and other international agreements, such as the Interstate Council. They also protested that the UNDP proposal was drafted without their participation and could instigate rather than contain unrest. In addition, a number of the implicit policy recommendations of the draft program, such as transparency of boundaries, contradict current practices of the government of Uzbekistan, which believes that security concerns now require firmly enforced border security. Other states in the region, notably Kyrgyzstan, which supported and to some extent instigated the proposal, did not share this view.

We urge, and we believe the United States and other concerned governments should also urge, that the government of Uzbekistan reconsider supporting some such framework for regional cooperation in the Valley. In discussions with Uzbekistan's diplomats, we found signs that official opinion on this question is not unanimous, and there is some scope for internal debate.

It is important to maintain a dialogue on matters of integration with Uzbekistan because its resistance is symptomatic of broader opposition to political and economic reform measures, which has blocked policies needed to reduce the potential for conflict. While Uzbekistan has avoided the economic decline of Kyrgyzstan and Tajikistan, that is largely owing to its self-sufficiency in hydrocarbons and its ability to sell goods, mostly cotton and gold, on the world market for foreign exchange. Uzbekistan has maintained apparent stability, but the increase in violence in its part of the Ferghana Valley suggests that tensions can rise quickly to the surface. Without reform, the investment that alone could bring down the country's unemployment level will not come. This is particularly true in the Ferghana Valley, where Uzbekistan's restrictive currency conversion policies and border control regime pose obstacles to improving economic life and thwart longer-term policies aimed at "preventive development" there, to use UNDP's term.

A program of regional development integrated with institutions to monitor and defuse conflict could lead to desirable consequences such as the proposed Daewoo parts plant in Osh, Kyrgyzstan, to supply the Daewoo assembly plant in Andijan, Uzbekistan, right across the border (see below in the section on investment). Investment in all parts of Central Asia is hindered by the size of the market and would increase if boundaries were more transparent. The Ferghana Valley is particularly affected by Uzbekistan's restrictive border policies, as the region is divided from most of the surrounding areas by mountains, and the border regime blocks the transport routes that are the most logical and economical.

Multilateral involvement in any regional development programs would also establish a low-level international presence in the Valley that would promote better understanding abroad of the region itself and the policies of its governments, opportunities for investment, greater integration into the world community, monitoring of tensions, and early response to problems that might arise. Such participation by those with experience in other parts of the world would also provide a framework for addressing the problems described in the body of the report in the areas of education and media access that confront ethnic groups outside of their titular republics.

We urge the U.S. government to work with the UN, the World Bank, and other appropriate agencies to encourage further discussion of regional development among both Central Asian and international organizations. Such talk must engage a large range of relevant players—

official and unofficial—in determining what the area's needs are. This dialogue should be seen as a continuous process, with no specific end-point, and it should not necessarily deal with the issue of conflict prevention directly. Rather, it should focus attention on the issues that lie at the source of conflict—economic hardship, environmental degradation, health care, civic education, and the like—so that concrete programs can be developed to resolve these on a regional as well as a domestic scale.

Such dialogue should involve many parties from all three countries in the possible formulation of regional initiatives—precisely because their goals and interests are so different. Today, meetings and conferences in the region are often based on the assumption that all of the players share similar aims, but in many instances, especially concerning the Ferghana Valley, this is not the case. The dialogue should concentrate as much on questions of how different people in each country define problems in terms of their own interests and aspirations as on developing programs to overcome them. It should also recognize that the states in the region have already established a framework for cooperation through the Central Asian Union (which also involves Kazakstan) and may want any program for the Ferghana Valley to be set up through or in collaboration with that body.

CIVIL SOCIETY AND HUMAN RIGHTS

All of CPA's studies of conflict prevention—in the South Balkans, Nigeria, and the Great Lakes—have reinforced the conclusion that prevention of violent conflict over the long haul requires more than the right policies by governments. It also requires measures to make those governments accountable, to make information about brewing tensions that could lead to trouble available, and to enable citizens to take responsibility for managing their own affairs under the rule of law. The apparent stability induced by authoritarianism can be deceptive, not only in the long run but even, as the Tashkent bombings may suggest, in the immediate circumstances.

While it would be naïve to expect or insist that the states of Central Asia would immediately come to resemble developed democracies, even the two states we visited, Uzbekistan and Kyrgyzstan, illustrate that a range of approaches is possible. Neither Uzbekistan's limited authoritarian system nor Kyrgyzstan's flawed, fragmented, and weak democracy have solved all their country's social problems or guaranteed stability. But in Kyrgyzstan now, even the representatives of some of the most bitterly dissenting groups with the most grievances appear to feel they have a stake in a system that at least allows them to participate. Kyrgyzstan's openness to the outside world, despite its geographical isolation, also offers the opposition outlets for activity and sources of support for programs such as minority-language media.

In the Uzbekistan part of the Valley, however, we sensed that the government's repressive reaction to threats, real and perceived, was a significant factor aggravating social tensions. Reports we have received from Namangan and Andijan since our 1997 trip, in particular of massive, apparently indiscriminate arrests after the series of killings of police officers and other officials at the end of 1997, lead us to conclude that the problem has worsened.[8]

In the absence of concrete facts, it is difficult to evaluate the government of Uzbekistan's claim that it faces a threat from foreign-supported "Wahhabis," though the charges are plausible. The trials in which several Uzbeks have been convicted and one even sentenced to death for terrorist acts have not provided clear evidence, and foreign observers have likened them to "show trials."[9] Islamic activists in Uzbekistan are surely not "Wahhabis" in any strict sense of that term, but several hundred of them did flee to Afghanistan and, perhaps, as Uzbekistan's foreign minister has claimed, to neighboring areas of Pakistan, where they have received religious and military training along with Tajik and Afghan guerrillas. Some Uzbek Islamic activists are active in southern Kyrgyzstan, where they are able to receive support from movements in, for instance, Turkey and Saudi Arabia. As we have noted, there are many other sources of violence in the region, notably drugs and arms trafficking, all of which involve sectors of the police and government as well as opposition movements and undoubtedly can lead to blood feuds. Certainly the movement for a revival of Islamic practice and knowledge cannot be and should not be identified with a few violent acts, even if it were proved that those who carried them out were influenced to do so by some understanding of Islam or by some extremist group.

The danger now is that the government's repression of the movement and its stigmatizing of certain forms of Islamic revival as Wahhabi may contribute to a process of escalation that drives a segment of the population of the Ferghana Valley into active and perhaps even violent opposition. No doubt the reaction to this movement inside Uzbekistan is strongly influenced by the regional security environment: the capture of Kabul by the Taliban in September 1996 and of most of the rest of Afghanistan in August 1998, together with the Russian-Iranian-brokered Tajikistan peace agreement that brings the Islamic movement back into that country's government, have increased the sense of siege in Tashkent and emboldened some activists. In Tajikistan, the civil war occurred when an Islamic political group filled a political vacuum by providing leadership to members of regional groups who felt excluded from power and opportunity. The same process is at work in Uzbekistan's Ferghana Valley. Uzbekistan's institutions, until now, have been strong enough to resist such disintegration. The corollary is that they are also strong enough to withstand a more permissive approach that would integrate Islamic activists into a more open political and social system.

The U.S. and other Western powers have indeed undertaken a number of programs in the region aimed at promoting human rights and building civil society through the training of journalists, development of new educational materials, support for independent media, human rights organizations, professional and business associations, and much more. It is important to bear in mind, however, that such assistance programs must be complemented by oversight and follow-up to help germinate a political system that protects the freedom of the institutions of civil society through the rule of law. Such institutions ultimately develop through political processes.[10]

Programs of assistance to civil society and the rule of law should be reshaped in particular to accommodate groups that have begun to establish cross-border projects in the Ferghana Valley. Some such groups, such as the Initiative for Social Action and Renewal in Eurasia (ISAR) in the United States, the Kyrgyz Peace Research Center based in Kyrgyzstan, and other small organizations consistently face precarious funding situations. Instead, these kinds of initiatives should be expanded and supported. And the experience of cross-border assistance projects in other regions of potential strife—such as those supported by the Eurasia Foundation in the conflict-ridden Caucasus region for the purpose of hosting regional conferences on conflict and sharing experiences of democratic reforms between countries—provides a useful model for replication in the Ferghana Valley as well.

FOREIGN ASSISTANCE AND THE POLICY PROCESS

Carrying out such policies will require improving the processes through which policies and aid programs are developed and implemented. U.S. assistance to Central Asia has inched up from $87 million in fiscal year 1997 (excluding food aid to Tajikistan) to an estimated $95 million in fiscal year 1998 (see Table 2.1, page 26). USAID's presentation to Congress for fiscal year 1999 called for a dramatic increase to $150 million, but the previous year's request for $148 million had to be scaled back more than a third as a result of declining appropriations for foreign aid, and 1999 is likely to repeat that experience. Even in the context of declining foreign aid, a larger proportion of technical assistance moneys should be provided to the three parts of the Valley to relieve the economic and social stresses described in this report. As noted, USAID's Central Asia Regional Program would be a particularly apt channel for such aid. Humanitarian assistance should be extended as well to both Kyrgyzstan, where the strains on UNHCR are enormous, and northern Tajikistan, where growing numbers of internally displaced persons require assistance.

More important than the quantity of aid, of course, is the type of aid and how it is given. While some Western efforts have played a useful role, directly or indirectly, in countering sources of instability in the region, others have been seriously criticized for inadvertently making these problems more difficult to resolve. This has occurred, among

TABLE 2.1
UNITED STATES BILATERAL ASSISTANCE TO CENTRAL ASIA
(MILLIONS OF CURRENT DOLLARS)

Country	FY1997 Actual	FY 1998 Estimate	FY 1999 Request
Kazakstan	35.5	34.7	46.0
Kyrgyzstan	20.8	22.0	29.0
Tajikistan	14.5 [a]	10.2	18.8
Turkmenistan	5.0	4.5	15.0
Uzbekistan	21.5	19.1	32.1
Regional	0.6	4.4	9.0
Total	97.9	94.9	149.9

[a] Includes $ 9.5 million in P.L. 480 food aid. All other funds allocated under the Freedom Support Act

For reference: the request for FY 1998 was $148m.

Source: United States Agency for International Development, "FY 1999 Congressional Presentation," http://www.info.usaid.gov/pubs/cp99/eni

other reasons, because of a poor understanding of the context in which they are operating, little follow-up or oversight, and weak accountability standards and practical benchmarks incorporated into projects.[11] We have a number of recommendations for improvement in these assistance programs. Some of the problems with foreign assistance are connected to the way policies are formulated and thus have broader implications for the policy process.

While assistance for a range of initiatives has been important and appreciated, our discussions with local specialists in Central Asia highlighted several significant gaps where support has been minimal or absent. These include on-the-ground training of journalists that goes beyond seminars to allow for joint reporting and investigations with foreign journalists; more direct support for the nascent human rights and other organizations struggling to survive in the Ferghana Valley; children's media and education in Uzbekistan and Tajikistan, similar to work being done in Kyrgyzstan; electronic media and textbook publishing for ethnic minorities; and generally encouraging those programs that help to promote greater oversight and accountability of public institutions for the benefit of citizens in the Ferghana Valley. These kinds of programs are important not only in and of themselves but also in the way that they develop a sense of stake on the part of citizens in the welfare of their own communities, which is the only way to promote stability in the long run.

"Rule of law" programs must be extended to support a public constituency as well as a community of technically competent experts. Such programs should go beyond holding judicial seminars and drafting laws to helping citizens take effective action on the full range of issues facing them and providing the vehicles to express their views. Citizen monitoring, not only government regulation, is essential for accountability.

A related recommendation is the need for more cross-sectoral programs and projects in addition to the cross-border or regional programs discussed above. In any issue area, programs directed toward the government should be complemented by programs aimed at the citizenry. For example, the tools for attacking crime in the Ferghana Valley may be found not only in the law enforcement agencies but also in the development of local media, public oversight, nongovernmental organizations, public administration programs, and the like in such a way that will enable people to work collectively on the problem.

With regard to the policy process, we recommend:

◆ *Requiring full, written assessments of the impacts on conflict potential of all aid projects and other U.S. policies.* While we have separated out the different elements in this report—economic, political, religious—none of these sets of issues can be addressed in isolation from the others. Yet most Western assistance efforts do just that. Whether supporting the government's efforts to develop a new tax code or establishing programs to encourage the rule of law, assistance providers must ensure that the potential impact of any given program or project on the stability of the region is taken into account in program design by submitting a kind of "conflict impact statement" or "political impact statement" before funding is granted.

◆ *Inclusion in major projects of experts who understand the regional political, economic, and social context.* Such context-sensitive knowledge, which functional specialists often lack, is vital to assessing the impact on conflict and stability of a variety of projects.

◆ *Inclusion of requirements for follow-up and accountability in projects.* Assistance providers and policymakers sometimes appear to fly in and out of countries without commitment to the longer-term progress that is the essential goal. Lack of such follow-up makes genuine evaluation impossible and also encourages cynicism and weakens the resolve of local partners. If we are preaching accountability, we must also practice it.

◆ *Better coordination among major donors.* Limited cooperation both among and within the various assistance agencies has been a common criticism of the aid community for many years, and it remains a deep concern with regard to the Ferghana Valley. Donors have started to hold local meetings, but proposals for joint projects and other ideas intended to coordinate better often meet with resistance from headquarters offices with different priorities. Outside evaluators should be utilized to ensure that the programs of the major assistance providers to the region—including USAID, the European Union's Technical Assistance to the Commonwealth of Independent States (EU TACIS), UN agencies, and multilateral banks—do not work at cross-purposes and that the different programs of the international donor community as a whole do not cancel each other out.

Much of CPA's previous research has dealt with the problem of coordination among multiple working parties in situations of actual or potential conflict. A multiplicity of players is necessary as states, international organizations, and nongovernmental organizations all have specific and complementary capacities. The challenge of coordination, however, like that of conflict prevention in general, is not merely technical but political. Those with primary power and resources, above all states, have to exert that power to create a framework and incentives for cooperation. The new U.S. policy toward Central Asia, defining it as an important area and emphasizing the need to prevent and resolve conflicts, should attempt to design a framework for coordination of multiple projects by multiple actors aimed at tackling different aspects of the same problem.

FOREIGN DIRECT INVESTMENT

Despite a handful of operations on the ground—such as the Coca-Cola bottling plant in Namangan, the Daewoo auto assembly plant in Andijan, and Texaco's project in the Mingbulak oil field in Ferghana— investment in the Ferghana Valley has remained limited, particularly when compared with investment in the rest of Central Asia. Uzbekistan's part of the Valley, while still receiving significantly less foreign direct investment than the rest of Uzbekistan, has gotten more than the adjoining areas of the Valley. In 1997, however, new investment dried up in response to the government's restrictive new currency regulations and continuing strict financial, border, and other controls. The February 1999 bombings will further inhibit potential investment. Investment in southern Kyrgyzstan is mainly in the agricultural sector, including forestry, fruit production, and, especially, tobacco. Locals hope this will change with the development of the Andijan-Osh-Kashgar (western China) and Osh-Bishkek roads and railways, but the obstacles, as elsewhere in the Valley, go beyond questions of infrastructure alone. Foreign investors in northern Tajikistan have largely pulled out because of the increasing tensions between that region and southern Tajikistan; Tajikistan's largest foreign project commitment to date, by Canada's Nelson Gold, is located in the northern Leninabad Oblast but is in the Zarafshon Valley, some 200 kilometers from the Ferghana Valley. Bureaucratic hurdles and corruption have also limited Western investment throughout the Ferghana Valley.

Of course, with some relatively minor exceptions, the Ferghana Valley does not have the mineral resources (oil, gold, and so on) that have attracted investors elsewhere in Central Asia. This may ultimately be a blessing in disguise as mineral wealth has proved an unreliable basis for economic and political development.[12] Despite the Valley's large and well-educated population, several characteristics make it an unattractive destination for investment, namely, its isolation from the rest of the region (and hence markets), intensified by its division into states separated by new borders and restrictive commercial and financial regulations (imposed mainly by Uzbekistan).

Yet, precisely because of their interest in reaching broader markets and expanding their base of operations, investors could be one of the forces promoting the greater regional integration that we see as key to conflict prevention through development in the Ferghana Valley. The Daewoo company, for instance, proposed building a parts factory in Osh, Kyrgyzstan, to supply its auto factory just across the border in Andijan, Uzbekistan. Despite agreement from Kyrgyzstan, Uzbekistan has not approved this project, and it remains on hold.

Investors and the government of Kyrgyzstan strongly favor a regional approach to investments, while Uzbekistan does not. (Tajikistan has been too preoccupied with conflict to develop a coherent policy.) Only in a situation where Uzbekistan's policies changed, perhaps in the context of broader interstate cooperation, would companies become more inclined to think about investments in the Ferghana Valley on a regional basis. In such a case, international or national financing or guarantee organizations, such as the International Finance Corporation or the Central Asian-American Enterprise Fund, might provide incentives such as lower-cost loans to promote cross-border investments in the Ferghana Valley.

In our view, therefore, a key task for long-term conflict prevention in the Valley, with all its implications for the stability and peace of Central Asia as a whole, is to pursue discussions aimed at encouraging all the Valley's states to plan in a regional development framework. Such a framework should include a favorable policy environment for employment-creating investment and marketing, incentives for such investment (especially those encouraging cross-border cooperation), a clearinghouse for information, and the capacity to evaluate the political, social, and environmental effects of proposed projects.

— PART II —

SUPPORTING MATERIAL

— 3 —

BACKGROUND:
PHYSICAL SETTING AND HISTORICAL LEGACIES

THE LAND AND THE PEOPLE

The short airplane ride to any part of the Ferghana Valley from the capital that governs it reveals how isolated the Valley is from the rest of Central Asia and how inextricably intertwined must be the lives of those who live within it. All of about three hundred kilometers long and between twenty and seventy kilometers wide, the Ferghana Valley is hemmed in on three sides by high mountains that are easily passable only in the summer. Although each section of the Valley is separated from the rest of the territory of the country to which it belongs, there are no natural borders between the three areas now belonging to different independent states.

The Valley includes the eastern part of Uzbekistan, the southern part of Kyrgyzstan, and the northern part of Tajikistan. These, in turn, are subdivided into the regional administrative units used by each country. In Uzbekistan, the three Ferghana Valley provinces (*hakimiyats*, or "oblasts" in Russian) are Andijan, Namangan, and Ferghana. The Kyrgyzstan part of the Valley is divided into two *akimiyats*, Osh and Jalalabad, the latter having been a part of Osh until 1991. Tajikistan's Leninabad province (*viloyat* in Tajik), also known as Khujand for its major city, comprises almost the entire northern part of the country, much of which lies in the Ferghana Valley.[1] Large but less populous mountainous areas outside of the Valley also lie within the Osh, Jalalabad, and Leninabad provinces.

Although the Valley includes only about 5 percent of the territory of Central Asia, it is home to more than 10 million people, or close to 20 percent of the population of the region's five countries (Uzbekistan, Kazakstan, Kyrgyzstan, Tajikistan, and Turkmenistan). Table 3.1 presents basic geographic and demographic data on the region. In these arid countries, where less than a tenth of the land is arable, the fertile, well-watered soils of the Valley constitute a vital breadbasket and source of cash crops, especially cotton.

The role of the Ferghana Valley differs somewhat in each state, but generally it has become an area whose economic importance is disproportionate to its political influence and where social and political tensions are higher than in the rest of the region. The Leninabad oblast that comprises Tajikistan's part of the Valley is critical to the very survival of that country. Including almost one-third of Tajikistan's population and about one-fifth of its territory, this part of the Valley accounts for three-fourths of Tajikistan's arable land and upwards of two-thirds of its GDP. It is the most industrialized region of Tajikistan and has attracted the bulk of the country's private investment. Taxes and other revenues from Leninabad account for Tajikistan's only stable source of domestic earnings.[2] The region's political importance has also been enormous, as all of Soviet Tajikistan's post-World War II leaders came from the north. Though they were on the winning side of the 1992 civil war, these leaders have now been pushed aside in favor of groups from southern Tajikistan.

With 40 percent of Kyrgyzstan's territory and 51 percent of its population, the Kyrgyzstan portion of the Ferghana Valley likewise plays a critical part in the politics and economy of that country. Half of that mountainous country's arable land is in its part of the Valley, as are its major cotton and coal resources. The two southern oblasts of Osh and Jalalabad together produce more than half of Kyrgyzstan's agricultural output and nearly 40 percent of its industrial goods.[3] Much of Kyrgyzstan's hydroelectric power is produced at the headwaters of the Syr Darya, the principal river running through the Ferghana Valley, whose water is vitally important for the region as a whole. Kyrgyzstan's leadership, however, generally comes from the north of the country.

Although only 4 percent of Uzbekistan's territory lies in the Ferghana Valley, even this small area is of great importance to Uzbekistan as a whole. It includes over 25 percent of the country's population and 35 percent of its arable land. This largely rural, agri-

TABLE 3.1
DEMOGRAPHIC AND GEOGRAPHIC DATA ON THE FERGHANA VALLEY (FV)

Geographical Unit	Percentage of State's Territory	Percentage of State's Population	Population Density (people per sq. km.)	Population (million)
Uzbekistan [1]	100.0	100.0	53.4	23.0
FV	4.3	26.9	340.8	6.2
Andijan [1]	0.9	8.7	503.6	2.0
Ferghana [1]	1.6	10.6	366.7	2.4
Namangan [1]	1.8	7.6	236.4	1.7
Kyrgyzstan [2]	100.0	100.0	22.1	4.7
FV	42.2	50.3	28.3	2.4
Osh [3]	23.1	32.0	30.7	1.5
Jalalabad [4]	19.1	18.2	25.1	0.9
Tajikistan	100.0	100.0	41.3	5.9 [5]
FV (Leninabad) [6]	18.2	31.4	66.6	1.8 [5]

Note: While the three Ferghana Valley oblasts of Uzbekistan are situated completely in the Valley, most of the territory of Leninabad, Osh, and Jalalabad provinces lies in high mountains. The population densities in the Valley districts are comparable to those in Uzbekistan, reaching as high as 2,315 people per square kilometer.

Sources: Information was supplied by John Schoberlein of the UN Ferghana Valley Development Project from the following sources:
1. *Özbekiston Respublikasi Éntsiklopediia* (Tashkent, 1997).
2. *Kyrgyzstan: National Human Development Report* (Bishkek, 1998).
3. *Oshskaia oblast' v tsifrakh 1997: kratkii statisticheskii sbornik* (Osh, 1998).
4. *Jalal-abad Regional Strategy* (Osh: Jalalabad Oblast Statistical Committee, January 1998).
5. *Naselenie Respubliki Tajikistan* (Dushanbe, 1997).
6. *Regionalnyi statisticheskii sbornik Respubliki Tajikistan za 1991–1996 gg.* (Dushanbe, 1996).

cultural area also contains five of Uzbekistan's ten largest cities. The three provinces of the Valley produce nearly a quarter of Uzbekistan's cotton and other agricultural products and are the source of most of the republic's water.[4] Mingbulak, in Ferghana province, contains Uzbekistan's largest proven reserves of oil, which have made the country self-sufficient and even an exporter to the surrounding countries. And the establishment of the Coca-Cola plant in Namangan and the Daewoo auto plant in Andijan represent an effort to expand the locale's importance as a manufacturing center for Central Asia as a whole. The Ferghana Valley's proximity to Tashkent, the capital of Uzbekistan and Central Asia's largest city (with a population of more than 4 million), adds to its significance. Tashkent is only about 110 kilometers from the closest city in the Valley and depends heavily on the Valley's produce, cotton, and water. Nonetheless, the region's political elites lost power in the Brezhnev era and have not regained it.

Economically, geographically, and politically, the Ferghana Valley has long formed a natural unit set apart from the rest of Central Asia. The kinship and ethnic ties among these districts are strong. With mixed ethnic populations on all sides of the borders, it is common to find families with relatives in one or another part of the Valley. Large numbers of ethnic Uzbeks live in Tajikistan and Kyrgyzstan, and they are the largest minority in each state (see Table 3.2). There are also significant pockets of Tajik and Kyrgyz communities in Uzbekistan, Kyrgyz in Tajikistan, and Tajiks in Kyrgyzstan, including refugees from the Tajikistan civil war.

The economy and infrastructure have also linked this area together. Trade in goods and services across what are now state borders has long been at the heart of commerce there. Owing to both the geography of the region, with its convoluted boundaries, and the unimportance of republican borders for Soviet planners, vital transportation routes linking different regions of the same state often pass through the territory of another Central Asian republic; this is particularly true of the Ferghana Valley. For example, by far the easiest road connection, and the only rail connection, between Tashkent and the part of the Valley in Uzbekistan runs directly through northern Tajikistan. The easiest road connection from Osh to Kyrgyzstan's capital, Bishkek, runs through Uzbekistan's portion of the Valley.

All of this became far more important with the collapse of the Soviet Union and the independence of these former Soviet republics. The borders drawn up by Stalin in the 1920s—lines that had little practical impact while these regions were part of one country—overnight

TABLE 3.2
COMPOSITION OF POPULATION BY NATIONALITY

Geographical Unit	Uzbecks (%)	Tajiks (%)	Kyrgyz (%)	Russians (%)	Total Population (millions)
Uzbekistan	75.8[1]	4.8[1]	0.9[1]	6.0[1]	23.0[2]
FV	84.2	5.0	3.2	3.0	6.2
Andijan	85.0[1]	1.4	4.2[1]	3.9[1]	2.0
Ferghana	83.6[1]	5.5[1]	2.1[1]	4.9[1]	2.4[2]
Namangan	85.1[1]	8.8[1]	1.1[1]	1.9[1]	1.7[2]
Kyrgyzstan	14.2	0.8	60.3	15.7	4.7[3]
FV	26.7	1.6	73.5	2.7	2.4
Osh[4]	28.0	2.1	63.8	2.4	1.5
Jalalabad[5]	24.5	0.6	67.3	3.3	0.9
Osh city	40.9	0.4	29.1	n.a.	0.2
Tajikistan[6]	24.8	68.4	1.3	3.2	5.9
FV (Leninabad)[6]	31.3	56.9	1.2	6.5	1.8

Sources: Information was supplied by John Schoberlein of the UN Ferghana Valley Development Project from the following sources:
1. *Informatsionnyi sbornik Uzbekistan 1991–1995*, Tashkent.
2. *Özbekiston Respublikasi Éntsiklopediia* (Tashkent, 1997).
3. *Kyrgyzstan: National Human Development Report* (Bishkek, 1998).
4. *Oshskaia oblast' v tsifrakh 1997: kratkii statisticheskii sbornik* (Osh province in figures) (Osh, 1998).
5. *Jalal-abad regional strategy.* Jalal-Abadskii oblastnoi statisticheskii komitet. January 1998.
6. *Naselenie Respubliki Tajikistan* (Dushanbe, 1997).
7. *Regionalnyi statisticheskii sbornik Respubliki Tajikistan za 1991–1996 gg.* (Dushanbe, 1996).

became international borders of three sovereign countries. Before the breakup, interrepublican borders were barely noticeable, almost like those between states in the United States.

Today these borders, fortified with posts and guards, are one of the main sources of friction in Central Asia. The Tajikistan part of the Ferghana Valley, for example, was historically tied more to parts of Uzbekistan than to the rest of Tajikistan, just as Samarkand, in western Uzbekistan, is considered by many Tajiks to be the historical capital of Tajik culture. Enclaves of Uzbekistan and Tajikistan in the Valley are cut off from their respective states, totally surrounded by Kyrgyzstan's territory.[5]

The division into independent countries has also made Uzbek dominance in the Valley a more sensitive issue. Of the 10 million people in the valley, close to three-fourths are Uzbeks; they are not only 85 percent of the population in the Uzbekistan part of the Valley but constitute more than a quarter of the population in the parts of the Valley belonging to Tajikistan and Kyrgyzstan as well (Table 3.2). The Uzbek share of the population is also increasing in both the Uzbekistan and Kyrgyzstan parts of the Valley. As of 1996 Uzbeks were the largest group in Osh, the largest city in southern Kyrgyzstan. They made up about 40 percent of the population, which was around 30 percent Kyrgyz and 30 percent other groups. About 60 percent of the Valley's territory is located in Uzbekistan, with 25 percent in Tajikistan and 15 percent in Kyrgyzstan. And the closer proximity of Tashkent to the Ferghana Valley than any other capital adds to Uzbekistan's influence and charges of Uzbek hegemony.

Finally, the closure of borders, along with economic policies described below, has greatly complicated cross-border trade and ethnic interaction, as each portion of the Ferghana Valley, despite the geographic barriers, is pulled to become an integral part of one of three new countries that are developing in different and sometimes incompatible directions. Indeed, while on earlier trips through the Ferghana Valley members of our group had experienced a great deal of difficulty even trying to establish where the boundaries between republics lay, on this trip we had a quite different experience: three of our four cars were held up at the Uzbekistan-Kyrgyzstan customs post for some time, along a new international border that did not exist just a few years ago.

In other words, with international boundaries now dividing this already geographically isolated area, the ethnic, economic, and other cross-border ties that once knit the region together are now increasingly sources of competition and strife. Accidents of geography and Soviet planning have themselves created an unsteady stage on which current challenges must be played out. These factors are only complicated by the long, dramatic history of the Ferghana Valley and Central

Asia as a whole, a history that has both helped provide a basis for stability and set the scene for many of the stresses and tensions that characterize the region today.

HISTORICAL LEGACIES

From the time of Alexander the Great to the nineteenth century's "Great Game" between Russia and Britain, Central Asia has been at the crossroads of invading armies. For most of those centuries, though, the region was seen by invaders more as an obstacle to reaching other destinations than as a destination in its own right. Traders, too, passed this way with other destinations in mind: a branch of the Silk Route linking China to the Middle East, the Mediterranean, and Europe passed through the Ferghana Valley. The area's rich pastures also provided famed horses to the Chinese empire. Rarely was the Valley at the political center rather than the periphery.

The Ferghana Valley was part of the empire founded by Amir Timur (Tamerlane) and passed on to his descendants. To the dismay of some of its neighbors who fear Uzbek expansionism, Timur has reemerged as independent Uzbekistan's symbolic founding father. Under his rule Central Asia, including the cities of the Ferghana Valley, became a center of international power, culture, and learning. But the capital of the Timurid empire, which at its height stretched into Europe, China, Turkey, Iran, and India, was first in Samarkand and subsequently in Herat, now part of Afghanistan.

The Ferghana Valley became a single political unit only under a khanate based in Kokand, a city in today's Ferghana oblast. Under Kokand dominion from the late sixteenth century until the arrival of Russian colonial rule in the mid-nineteenth century, the Ferghana Valley was united as a distinct political entity for the first and only time in its more than two millennia of recorded history.

Islam arrived in Central Asia in the eighth century and has played a fundamental role in the historical, cultural, and social development of "Turkistan," which the Arabs called "ma wara'a al-nahr" (that which is across the river). The term survives in Central Asia in its Persianized form, "mavrannahr." Although the Ferghana Valley contained important shrines and madrasahs (Islamic academies), Bukhara in what is now western Uzbekistan became Central Asia's most famous center of Islamic learning. Here was born Abdul Qadir Naqshband, founder of one of Sunni Islam's most important mystical (Sufi) orders. While almost all Muslims in the region are Sunni (unlike Iran's predominantly Shi'a Muslims), there have always been some differences in the mode of Islamic practice among the various communities. The sedentary peoples, today's Uzbeks and Tajiks, converted to Islam very early, and the most important centers of Islamic learning and devotion in Central Asia are in Uzbek and Tajik areas. By contrast, the nomadic peoples, particularly the Kazaks and Kyrgyz, were latecomers to Islam. Some have claimed that, as a result, their commitment to the faith was less profound, though recent scholarship has disputed this.

Throughout the pre-Soviet history of the area, ethnic and linguistic divisions played little political role. Most of the regimes and much of the population were bilingual or multilingual, and mixed marriages were common. Dynasty, religion, clan, and territory were more salient political categories. It was not until Stalin created separate Soviet republics that ethnic identity took root in its modern form.

SOVIET RULE—THE AMBIGUOUS LEGACY

While seventy-five years are a mere wink of the eye in the long history of Central Asia, the advent of Soviet rule had perhaps greater impact than any event since the arrival of Islam. Communist rule fundamentally transformed Central Asia politically, economically, socially, and even religiously, even if many cultural traditions survived and are now undergoing a renaissance. Especially by creating distinct ethnicities or nations with their own republics, the Soviet Union left a legacy in Central Asia that will mold the future of the area for decades to come.

From the beginning, Central Asians' relations with Soviet rule were ambivalent, reflecting the deep influence that Russian colonial rule had already had on the region as well as the deep suspicions about Soviet ideology in this devoutly Muslim area. While some Moscow-educated elites were active supporters of the Soviet takeover, others, who had been exposed to the modern, reformist Islamic ideals of the *jadidists*, sought a new, independent Turkistan, free of both Russian rule and the old, conservative, and at times despotic and corrupt establishment. In the Basmachi rebellion (1918–24), armed groups tried to overthrow both Russian/Soviet rule and the old political elites of the region in the name of an Islamic, independent Turkistan. As a sign of how strong political Islam was in the Ferghana Valley even then, the Basmachi rebellion continued in many parts of the Valley until 1928, four years after it had been extinguished in most of Central Asia.[6]

One of the most fundamental points that continues to shape the mind-set of the independent Central Asian states' first generation of leaders is the predominance of political interests and ideology as defined by the central government. Virtually all policies—economic, religious, agricultural, or environmental—resulted from political decisions made at the center (in Moscow).

Many in the region, as well as some Western analysts, see the authoritarian, centralized pattern of leadership from Soviet days as consistent with pre-Soviet patterns of authority in Central Asia and believe this helps explain why paternalistic rule still seems genuinely popular in these new states. Uzbekistan's President Karimov and others have argued that, in times of great social and economic upheaval, continuing tight control from the center is necessary to ensure stability and avoid conflict. Indeed, while signs of political decay and growing societal tensions were already evident in the Brezhnev era, many Central Asians (and Russians) believe that it was the reforms under Gorbachev, and in particular glasnost, that caused both the violence in the Ferghana Valley in 1989 and 1990 and the later civil war in Tajikistan. By eroding central control and allowing ethnic, political, and religious groups to air their grievances publicly, the argument goes, the stage was set for some to exploit schisms in society.

Another Soviet legacy that still affects a broad spectrum of economic, social, and political issues in contemporary Central Asia is in the classification of citizens by nationality or ethnic group. Soviet policy *created* Uzbekistan and the Uzbeks, Tajikistan and the Tajiks, and so on out of more fragmented and fluid identities that had existed earlier. When the Communists took power, Central Asians tended to identify themselves on the basis of religious practice, place of settlement (cities, villages, or nomadic encampments), locale or region, and family or clan affiliation. National states did not exist. In practice, Soviet policies precipitated nationalities from a range of less codified identities that had existed before, giving them their own distinct literary languages written in variants of the Cyrillic alphabet. Major nationalities received their titular republics, where they cemented their predominance through the policy of *korenizatsiia* (nativization) of cadres, which empowered locally born but Soviet-educated (and, hence, theoretically loyal) national elites. Similarly, under the slogan "national in form, socialist in content," education, newspapers, television, and radio were all also provided in the local languages, even if the hegemonic position of Russia and the Russian tongue was always underscored.

In certain ways, this "divide and rule" policy was successful, deflecting attention away from Moscow and enabling the titular nationalities at times to intimidate ethnic minorities, even in Soviet days. In Central Asia, where peoples were intermingled, inevitably borders were drawn so that large numbers of Tajiks, Uzbeks, and Kyrgyz were found on all sides. Examples of discrimination began in the 1920s, when many Tajiks living in Uzbekistan were "transformed" into Uzbeks for census and passport purposes, and continued through the 1990 Osh riots between Uzbeks and Kyrgyz. The design of the republican borders was no accident of history; it represented a way for the Kremlin to maintain its role as the arbiter in disputes that were, in a fundamental way, of its own making. The problems of today's Ferghana Valley offer one of the best illustrations of how the effects of the Soviet practice of sowing the seeds of conflict by creating borders and nationalisms will live on for decades after the Soviet Union itself collapsed.

The Soviet economic legacy in Central Asia has been mixed. On the one hand, as the poorest parts of the Soviet Union, the Central Asian republics received significant transfer payments and subsidies from Moscow, one of the prime reasons that the region's Communist leaders were the last to call for independence. Some of the other important benefits for the Central Asian republics were universal education, free and generally universal (albeit poor) health care, nominally full employment (until the later Brezhnev years), significant infrastructure construction (railroads, highways, electrification, hydroelectric dams), and access to services and employment for women. Even though a system of informal "fees" developed for services that were ostensibly free (such as access to higher education or basic medical care), considering that at the beginning of Soviet rule the vast majority of Central Asians were illiterate and had no access to electricity or health care, these achievements were significant. At the same time, one of their most significant drawbacks may be the expectations created by the Soviet "full-service" society. Its collapse is perhaps felt more acutely in Central Asia than anywhere else in the former Soviet Union, as these relatively poor republics had relied most heavily on subsidies from the center to fund essential programs. The Ferghana Valley may have been especially hard hit, as it is the most densely populated region in Central Asia and is not favored by the new political centers in Tashkent, Bishkek, and Dushanbe.

On the other hand, Moscow's policy of "economic specialization," in which different regions or cities of the Soviet Union were assigned the task of being the sole producers of a given product, led to the quasi-colonial exploitation of the region. Using fuel and equipment it imported from outside, Central Asia furnished raw materials and intermediate parts for an economy centered elsewhere. Its factories made few if any finished goods. This policy favored using land for a cotton monoculture, with its disastrous effects on the environment, while the area still had few textile mills or other consumer goods industries. The disintegration of the Soviet-era network of suppliers and purchasers had a profound negative impact on the economies of all the Central Asian states.

The breakup of the Soviet Union made an unfavorable economic setup for the Ferghana Valley still more dire because the Soviet trade patterns and infrastructure links crisscrossed republic borders. All of the gas pipelines, for example, and most of the electricity lines connecting the Uzbekistan part of the Valley with the rest of the country ran through northern Tajikistan. Similarly, almost all trade between northern and southern Tajikistan passed through Uzbekistan. Less than two years after independence, producers and suppliers suddenly confronted the reality of three different states with different currencies and barely functional banking systems, often making cumbersome barter one of the only ways of doing business. Customs controls and demands became sources of immense friction, particularly in the Ferghana Valley.[7]

The Soviet-era command economy also fostered two maladaptations that have continued to be a part of the newly independent states' economic reality: the creation of a parallel economy that represented an illegal but universally accepted and intricate system of payoffs and bribes for goods and services in short supply; and the expansion of what we have now termed "traditional" organized crime. The black and gray markets that arose from the Soviet economy of shortages, particularly in the late Brezhnev period, eventually accounted for a huge proportion of official production and consumption. Official corruption rapidly became deeply systemic and highly organized, starting at the top and enveloping all areas of officialdom. In the well-publicized "cotton affair" of the mid-1980s, a number of high-ranking officials, including Leonid Brezhnev's son-in-law and the Uzbekistan Communist Party chief, Sharaf Rashidov, were charged with manipulating cotton quotas and amassing huge personal fortunes. What was unusual was not the involvement of such senior officials but that they were actually charged with crimes.

These developments were of special importance in the Ferghana Valley, where the city of Margilan emerged as an unofficial capital of organized crime in the late Soviet period. Indeed, one local leader, Akhmadjon Adylov, director of the Popskii Cotton Combine on the outskirts of Margilan, became famous, if not infamous, for setting up his own fiefdom in the valley, complete with a private army, slaves, underground prison, and harem. While the harems and underground prisons may be gone today, the overall institutional arrangement of domination by chairs of collective farms and other regional officials set in place by the Soviet Union continues. For all the negative effects this authoritarian and corrupt system has had, it has given many in Central Asia experience with some of the principles of a "market economy," although not with the rule of law. But as fundamental economic and legal reforms challenge the power of officials to continue preying on the economy in this manner, the system also represents one of the most pervasive obstacles to implementing those reforms for the sake of a healthy market.

In religion, another area of fundamental importance for today's Central Asia, Soviet religious policy also left an ambiguous legacy. The official atheism led to the closing or destruction of almost all mosques and madrasahs in the region. Yet, realizing that they could not enforce atheism across Central Asia, and seeking to use Muslims as a tool in foreign policy, the Soviet leaders tried to establish a circumscribed and controlled official Islam by setting up a state-approved clergy controlled by Moscow. The official Soviet Muslim clergy answered to four *muftiyyats*; the Central Asian *muftiyyat* was headquartered in Tashkent.

The coexistence of state-controlled Islam with an official doctrine of atheism entailed constant contradictions. Islamic observance was an obstacle to career advancement, especially within the Communist Party. Yet, despite intermittent threats and campaigns from Moscow, and often with the connivance of local officials, many Central Asians continued to follow at least some Muslim rites. Mosques were few, and attendance was largely limited to the old, but practice of Islamic rituals at circumcisions, marriages, and funerals remained widespread. Many began to interpret Islam as a tradition and culture, with little understanding of the religious content. Especially in rural areas, many attended unofficial mosques operated by unregistered mullahs. Throughout the Soviet period the Ferghana Valley was known as a center of religious activity. Government efforts to crack down on Islamic activity were particularly strong in that region, even into the period of Mikhail Gorbachev's rule.[8]

While a doctrine compelling atheism is past, regimes continue to support a state-sponsored Islam. "Parallel," unsanctioned Islam burst into the open and flourished in the immediate aftermath of independence but is now coming once again under attack, especially in Uzbekistan, where the government passed a new law requiring registration of clergy and places of worship in May 1998.

The people and leaders of Central Asia's newly independent states are themselves still coming to grips with the meaning of the Soviet legacy there, just as outside observers are continually confounded by the clouded inheritance of 125 years of Russian and Soviet rule. In all areas of life where one finds potential sources of either conflict or stability in the Ferghana Valley—access to economic and political resources, ethnic and regional divisions, political Islam, and the fraying of the social safety net—Soviet policies had a profound and lasting impact.

PAST AND CURRENT CONFLICTS IN THE FERGHANA VALLEY

The threat of further clashes in the Ferghana Valley derives from both past conflicts and continuing social and political tensions. The February 1999 bombings in Tashkent may finally compel recognition of Uzbekistan's vulnerability. The charge by the Uzbek authorities that Islamic militants from the Ferghana Valley were responsible reinforces this report's warning. Although before November 1998 none of the fighting of the Tajikistan civil war had yet taken place in the Ferghana Valley, this struggle had already cast a long, dark shadow over all of Central Asia. In the aftermath of the November 1998 uprising led by renegade colonel Makhmud Khudoiberdiyev, it will have a much more direct impact on events in the Ferghana Valley itself. Khudoiberdiyev, an ethnic Uzbek military commander from Tajikistan who had found refuge in either Uzbekistan or northern Afghanistan, entered Tajikistan from the Uzbekistan part of the Valley. While the Uzbekistan and Kyrgyzstan parts of the Valley were characterized by apparent stability during the years 1992–97, a number of earlier conflicts in those zones were likewise characterized by vicious mob violence. In both Uzbekistan and Kyrgyzstan, the memory of those conflicts less than a decade ago is fresh. And in 1997 assassinations of police officials in Uzbekistan, blamed by the government on "Wahhabi" Islamic extremists, led to a police crackdown and charges that these extremists were trained in Afghanistan and Pakistan. The repression in Ferghana may in turn have provoked the attack on President Karimov in Tashkent.

CONFLICT IN FERGHANA, UZBEKISTAN (JUNE 1989)

For more than two weeks in June 1989, the Uzbekistan part of the Ferghana Valley was rocked by violence between ethnic Uzbeks and Meshketian Turks, members of a small ethnic group deported from the

Caucasus to Uzbekistan by Stalin. The fighting was said to have been triggered by a quarrel in a local market and ended in the deaths of hundreds, perhaps even thousands, of people, almost all of them Meskhetian Turks.[9] The initial dispute occurred in the small town of Kuvasi, reportedly after a Meskhetian Turk overturned the market stall of an Uzbek woman to protest the inflated price she was charging for her strawberries. This minor altercation exploded into pogroms not only there but also in Ferghana, Kokand, Margilan, and Namangan.[10] It resulted in the flight of almost all Meskhetian Turks from the Ferghana Valley and eventually from the rest of Uzbekistan.

The conflict, beyond its immediate importance, is significant for three other reasons. First, like the other conflicts, this one, too, had its roots less in ethnic hatred than in the mounting social and economic pressures, especially youth unemployment and access to land. Second, it showed how easily a small, isolated conflict can spread quickly throughout the region, often fanned by rumors and false accusations. And, third, it highlighted how deeply fellow Muslims and Turkic peoples in this region can be divided among themselves.

The economic aspect of the conflict is expressed in the words of one author who writes that "what led to this act of ethnic violence was the existing economic disparity between the relatively better-off Meskhetians and the economically deprived Uzbeks of Ferghana. . . . Many Uzbeks involved in the violence were deeply convinced that the Meskhetians' departure from the region would inevitably improve the socioeconomic conditions for the natives. It is interesting to note that Birlik [the anti-Communist opposition group] and other predominantly Uzbek organizations lent their emotional and political support to the perpetrators of these violent acts."[11]

The departure of the Meskhetian community distinguishes this crisis from the others, as "ethnic cleansing" of populations has not taken place in response to conflicts elsewhere. Nonetheless, the choice by what was then the Soviet government to resolve the troubles by helping the Meskhetians leave Uzbekistan can be considered a disturbing precedent.

CONFLICT IN OSH, KYRGYZSTAN (JUNE 1990)

In one of the most serious outbreaks of interethnic violence in the Ferghana Valley to date, more than two hundred and perhaps as many as five hundred ethnic Uzbeks and Kyrgyz were killed during riots that took place in Osh and nearby Uzgen, Kyrgyzstan, in early June 1990, with sporadic violence continuing until August of that year.[12] In this locale the division between Uzbeks and Kyrgyz seems to be relatively recent. Before the Soviet era the most common ethnonym in the area was "Qipchak." The Soviets apparently classified the lowland Qipchaks as Uzbeks and the high-land Qipchaks as Kyrgyz. Since then social and economic changes have led to settlement and migration of mountain people to cities and villages, resulting in ethnically mixed towns. Yet in this area, where the various groups lived together relatively peacefully for centuries, witnesses with whom our group spoke told of scenes of incredible brutality, including reports of bodies of dead Uzbeks in the streets bearing the sign "Uzbek Meat—Free of Charge." The main reasons cited for the riots were the strug-gle for control over land and housing, the absence of ethnic Uzbeks in the higher echelons of the local and regional administration, and demands for greater Uzbek autonomy. While the Kyrgyzstan government has made some efforts to address the political issues, the underlying competition for access to scarce resources remains and has even intensified.

In the context of Gorbachev's glasnost, ethnic Uzbeks began orga-nizing in early 1990 to demand a greater say in affairs in southern Kyrgyzstan. In Jalalabad, Uzbeks presented a petition demanding auton-omy for the Osh region (to which Jalalabad belonged at the time). That spring an unofficial organization named Adolat ("Justice"—not to be confused with the Namangan-based Islamic group with the same name) took on the issue of autonomy for the region. The organization reportedly had as many as 400,000 members in the area and sought mainly to preserve and strengthen the Uzbek culture and language in the Osh region.[13] The complaints about underrepresentation in the local and regional authorities of ethnic Uzbeks, who made up 29 per-cent of the region's population and at least 40 percent of the city of Osh, are borne out by figures from that period. Only 4 percent of the Communist Party first and second secretaries in the region were Uzbek, as were 11 percent of the leaders of the municipal and *raion* executive committees in Osh province (a *raion* is a subdivision of an oblast). By contrast, 79 percent of taxi drivers and 84 percent of workers in com-merce in manufactured goods were Uzbeks at that time. In addition to being a source of the conflict in its own right, Kyrgyz predominance in the government meant that the authorities could easily underestimate the depth of resentment felt by ethnic Uzbeks and the potential for conflict.

On the other side, "land and housing" became the battle cry of a Kyrgyz nationalist organization, Osh Aymaghi, which was formed in May 1990 with the express purpose of distributing land and housing to the eco-nomically deprived Kyrgyz. The trouble began when its leaders demanded that land belonging to an Uzbek collective farm be reallocated to build housing for Kyrgyz.[14] When the authorities agreed to distribute a small part of the land, both the Uzbeks and Kyrgyz (who had begun occupying the disputed territory) were dissatisfied with the decision, and confrontations began between the two groups.[15] Insufficient police forces quickly lost control of the situation, often shooting indiscriminately into the crowd. Only an unlikely collaboration between Soviet army units and local religious leaders succeeded in ending the riots.

The Osh riots remain a sore subject to this day. One local resident claimed that "inter-ethnic relations were good before the conflicts in Osh and Uzgen, but after that everything changed." Richard Dobson, who conducted interviews in the Osh region, found that "in Osh and Jalalabad, quite a few prospective participants of Uzbek nationality declined to take part in the focus groups, probably due to their discomfort at being in ethnically mixed groups."[16]

CONFLICT IN NAMANGAN, UZBEKISTAN (DECEMBER 1991–FEBRUARY 1992)

While relatively free of violence, the partial takeover of the Namangan regional administration in late 1991 and early 1992 by the Islamic group Adolat was the first important threat to the authority of President Karimov.[17] President Islam Karimov presents his handling of the crisis as a showcase of how he has preserved stability in the Valley as well as his own personal power.

Members of the Adolat movement took over the former regional Communist Party headquarters on December 8–9, 1991, intending to use it as an Islamic center. Many of the activists, who were led by a twenty-four-year-old university dropout, Tohirjon Yuldashev, were unemployed young men. They quickly expanded the scope of their aims, eventually implementing a form of de facto Islamic self-rule in Namangan. They also demanded amendments to the constitution to make Islam the state religion of Uzbekistan and Islamic shari'a the basis of law.[18]

The trigger for Adolat's action was apparently the indignation caused among many devout Muslims by the local official clergy's endorsement of Karimov's presidential candidacy.[19] Many religious Muslims opposed Karimov, who rose to power through the Communist Party, and considered it an affront that the official clergy had spoken on their behalf. Before this controversy surfaced, however, the militants of Adolat had already been active in the local community, where they had developed some popular support as a result of their efforts at combating crime.

So strong was the initial movement, whose supporters one estimate places at 50,000 in early 1992, that President Karimov was forced, temporarily, to accept self-rule in Namangan. After he appointed a new provincial administrator (hakim) against the wishes of the Namangan demonstrators, though, the government arrested seventy-one of the organizers and suppressed the movement.[20] Several hundred of its supporters fled the country, apparently finding refuge in Tajikistan, Afghanistan, and Iran.

Fortunately, no lives were lost in this incident, but the Namangan takeover is still important for several reasons. First, some in the area have commented on the relative absence of crime during the period of Islamic self-rule, giving the impression that many may have been favorably impressed by Adolat's actions. Second, the events warned President Karimov and others that the official clergy does not exercise full control over the Muslim community and that overt efforts to politicize the faithful for electoral gain can backfire. Finally, the situation caused President Karimov to elaborate a carrot-and-stick approach to Islam, in which he himself, a former leader of the Communist Party, has undergone a complete Islamic makeover, complete with oaths on the Qur'an and visits to Mecca, while suppressing independent Islamic movements. Karimov showed support for Islam by making or permitting (often from foreign coffers) significant financial contributions to mosque-building and allowing an ostensibly depoliticized revival of Muslim practice and tradition. The "stick" that came down on Adolat and its leaders in Namangan, however, has suppressed all forms of political Islam, especially in the Ferghana Valley. As will be seen below, simply being a popular, independent Muslim clergyman can be enough of a threat to presidential authority to warrant arrest and disappearance.

CONFLICT IN NORTHERN TAJIKISTAN (MAY 1996–MAY 1997, NOVEMBER 1998)

While northern Tajikistan largely escaped the bloodshed of the first phase of the Tajik civil war, a series of events in the Leninabad region have more recently pushed that part of the Ferghana Valley into open armed conflict, the first time this had happened in the area since the Osh riots of 1990.[21] This ongoing crisis represents a new chapter in the Tajikistan civil war, in spite of the 1997 signing of a peace agreement between the southern-based forces that fought in Tajikistan during 1992 and 1993 and continued fighting thereafter, partly from bases in Afghanistan. Since the accord violence has recurred, including uprisings in Dushanbe itself that pitted different government militias against each other, and the November 1998 Khudoiberdiyev rebellion. Furthermore, given the threat, exaggerated though it may be, of the secession of northern Tajikistan from the rest of the republic, the new tensions in Leninabad represent a potentially wider-ranging destabilizer for the whole Ferghana Valley. Any change in current borders would open a Pandora's box of irredentist claims and almost certainly lead to violence. The 1997 disturbances in the Leninabad region were the most violent to take place in the Ferghana Valley since the 1990 Osh conflict, and the November 1998 rebellion was even more bloody. Even if the violence were confined to northern Tajikistan, refugee flows and the disruption of infrastructure would have direct impacts on other parts of the Valley.

The sequence of events in 1997-98 must be seen against the backdrop of the Leninabad region's past political role. From 1943 to 1992, all leaders of Tajikistan came from the north. They channeled a large proportion of the country's resources to their home region, which was already the richest (more properly, the least impoverished) area of what had been the Soviet Union's poorest republic. In the civil war that began in 1992, however, the Leninabadis relied on militias largely raised in the southern Kulab region to defeat an Islamic-democratic alliance. Kulabis, led by President Imomali Rakhmonov, have hence dominated the central government, and the Leninabad region has been pushed ever further away from the center of power.

The current crisis began in May 1996. Demonstrators in the two largest northern cities, Khujand and Ura-Teppe, demanded the removal of unpopular local officials appointed by the southern-dominated central government and a greater say in Tajikistan's governance. The protests ended in the deaths of five demonstrators and the detention, without trial, of hundreds of demonstrators, including the organizers.[22] This followed by only a few months a series of military mutinies in the south led by ethnic Uzbek former Soviet officers and militia leaders in which many in Dushanbe saw the hand of Uzbekistan. One of those Uzbek leaders was Colonel Makhmud Khudoiberdiyev, who later led the November 1998 Khujand uprising. Khujand was part of Uzbekistan until 1929 and has always been closely linked to Tashkent.

In July 1996, together with two other former prime ministers from the north, Abdumalik Abdullajanov, a Khujand native and former Tajikistan prime minister and presidential candidate, formed the National Revival Movement (NRM) to represent the region's political interests.[23] Its demands to be included as a third, independent force in the Tajik peace talks had the backing of the United Tajik Opposition (UTO), which provides a common platform for Islamic, nationalist, and democratic groups, but the Tajikistan government refused. Abdullajanov, who maintains a residence in Tashkent, has the apparent backing of the government of Uzbekistan, even if the Karimov regime has not endorsed the secessionist option that he has publicly stated remains a possibility. In a prophetic statement to a Russian journal in December 1996, Abdullajanov said, "Unfortunately, the current regime in Dushanbe has only two methods of fighting its opponents: either to bring criminal charges or to arrange a terrorist act."[24]

In April 1997 the situation took a particularly lethal turn. In mid-April as many as two hundred prisoners, many of them leaders of the May 1996 demonstrations, were killed when Tajikistan government forces stormed the Khujand prison. The prisoners had protested against the continued detention without trial of numerous prisoners, the lack of medical care, and the planned transfer of political prisoners to the south. Eyewitnesses reported that government forces singled out and shot the political leaders of the May 1996 demonstrations in their suppression of the prison protest.[25]

Two weeks later, on April 30, President Rakhmonov was injured in an assassination attempt in Khujand; two persons were killed, while seventy others, including the head of the Leninabad region's administration, were injured.[26] The perpetrators of the attack were, according to sources in the region, relatives of killed prisoners. Groups close to the president, however, have been pinning the blame on Abdullajanov, and others have insinuated that Uzbekistan was also involved.[27] After the assassination attempt, scores of people, many of them NRM members, were arrested, with some being taken to Dushanbe for interrogation. At least ten people died in unclear circumstances while resisting arrest.[28] In another attempt to tie the NRM's leader to the assault, on May 23, 1997, Abdullajanov's terminally ill younger brother, Abduhafiz, was detained in Khujand on trumped-up drug charges and taken to Dushanbe, where he was reportedly beaten in an attempt to extract a confession concerning the assassination attempt; at last word, he remained in custody in Dushanbe.[29]

The next round of fighting took place in Dushanbe itself, in August 1997. Various government militias opposed to the peace agreement rose in revolt and were suppressed in street fighting. One of the militias was led by Khudoiberdiyev, who escaped to Uzbekistan, where he was in contact with Abdullajanov, also exiled in Tashkent. According to charges later raised in the Tajikistan parliament,

Khudoiberdiyev may also have moved to northern Afghanistan, where he and some of his fighters were protected by that country's ethnic Uzbek militia leader, Abdul Rashid Dostum.[30]

Khudoiberdiyev surfaced again on November 4, 1998. Early that morning about nine hundred armed men under his command crossed into Leninabad from Uzbekistan. They took control of security installations in the city of Khujand and at the regional airport in Chkalovsk. Khudoiberdiyev denounced the government for its corruption and pressed the case for his right to a share of power. Referring to the exclusion of Leninabadi leaders from the peace accord, he insisted on the involvement of all regions in the peace process. Specifically, he demanded a radio and television appearance by Abdullajanov and new elections.

The government, supported by units from the opposition, crushed the rebels in a week. At least 220 were killed and 500 wounded on both sides, including bystanders. The government charged that Abdullajanov masterminded and financed the operation with the complicity of Uzbekistan. Uzbekistan denied the charges. The Tajik government also charged that among Khudoiberdiyev's fighters were Afghan Uzbeks from the troops of General Dostum. According to Iran radio, quoting a Tajik news agency, Leninabad authorities charged in February 1999 that Khudoiberdiyev was planning to attack again from the territory of Uzbekistan.[31]

ASSASSINATIONS, ARRESTS, TRIALS IN NAMANGAN (1997–98)

The disturbances in Tajikistan were among several in 1997 and 1998 that increased the concern over Islamic radicalism in Central Asia as a whole. In May 1997 the Islamic movement of Taliban (religious students) of Afghanistan occupied the northern city of Mazar-i-Sharif for a few days and nearly captured it again in September. In August 1998 this group, supported by Pakistan and Saudi Arabia, finally took control of the city and most of northern Afghanistan. Mazar, close to the Afghan-Uzbek border, had been controlled by several groups, including an ethnic Uzbek Afghan militia supported by Tashkent and Moscow and a Shi'a group supported by Tehran. The killing by the Taliban of eight Iranian diplomats and one journalist during the August takeover led to a diplomatic and military confrontation with Iran.

In June 1997 the government of Tajikistan and the mainly Islamic opposition alliance signed an agreement that would bring Islamic fighters back from Afghanistan and place their leaders in a ruling coalition. In August the prospect of their return led to open warfare in Dushanbe.

By the end of 1997 a series of killings in Namangan led the Uzbekistan government to charge that "Wahhabi" Muslims trained abroad were engaging in terrorism in Uzbekistan. So intense was the fear inspired by these events that in May 1998 President Karimov warned his parliament of the danger posed by violent Islamic fundamentalists and called for harsh measures: "Such people must be shot in the head. If necessary, I'll shoot them myself."[32] Tashkent's reaction included a harsh crackdown in the Ferghana Valley, where several police and government officials had been brutally assassinated. The alleged leader of a group charged with a total of twelve killings was sentenced to death in July, while six others received prison terms.[33] Hundreds of detainees, nearly all from the Ferghana Valley, remained in jails.

As recounted in the Introduction, during the Council on Foreign Relations group's visit in March 1997 there were already cases of unsolved assassinations of police officials that rumor attributed to "Wahhabis." We attended the funeral of one of the victims in Namangan. In Andijan we heard of other recent killings as well, and we observed numerous security checkpoints on the road between Namangan and Andijan. There were rumors of security men being flown in from the capital and of massive arrests.

In December this scenario repeated itself even more dramatically. On December 2, 1997, assailants beheaded a captain in the Namangan State Motor Vehicle Inspectorate (Russian acronym GAI), a police force within the Ministry of Internal Affairs. His head was left displayed on the Inspectorate's gate.[34] GAI checks vehicles on the roads and thus potentially comes into contact with drug and arms smugglers, as well as refugees or guerrilla infiltrators. The victim in this case was reported to be related to an important local figure as well. Two other shocking incidents soon followed. On December 11 a former collective farm chairman and his wife were also beheaded. On December 19 three policemen died in a shoot-out while attempting to capture a suspect.[35]

The government reacted immediately by charging foreign-supported "Wahhabis" with responsibility. In the subsequent crackdown, hundreds of men were arrested, mainly in Namangan and Andijan. Estimates of the number run as high as 1,500; Human Rights Watch suggests 1,000 as an upper figure.[36] Arrests appear to have been arbitrary. Local police were also reported to have planted evidence of possession of illegal arms or narcotics in the homes or cars of several suspects.

Islam also became the object of repression. Some men were said to have been forced by police to shave beards. Although it was then the holy month of Ramadan, on January 8, 1998, the Muslim Board of the republic issued a decree forbidding the use of loudspeakers for the call to prayer and prescribing dismissal of imams who did not comply.[37]

Both the president and the foreign minister charged that the "terrorists" involved were trained in Afghanistan and Pakistan, though they noted the government of Pakistan was not responsible.[38] On May 6, with little advance warning, President Karimov paid a state visit to Moscow to seek support in his battle against Islamic fundamentalism. He and Russian president Boris Yeltsin joined Tajik president Rakhmonov (who participated by telephone) in announcing a joint effort.[39] This meeting suddenly reversed Uzbekistan's policy of distancing itself from Russia. In early 1999, however, Uzbekistan withdrew from military cooperation with the Commonwealth of Independent States.

BOMBINGS IN TASHKENT (FEBRUARY 1999)

Between 10:52 A.M. and 12:00 noon on February 16, 1999, six car bombs detonated in different parts of Tashkent. In an apparent attempt to assassinate the president, the most powerful bomb, set off by two men who jumped from their car and then riddled it with automatic gunfire, exploded at the entry to the Cabinet of Ministers on Independence Square, the heart of downtown Tashkent, just as Karimov was scheduled to arrive for a cabinet meeting. Though the president and his staff were not injured, these explosions killed 13 people and injured 128.

The government announced that those arrested in the incident were Islamic militants from the Ferghana Valley, and it broadcast on television the photographs of the supposed ringleaders, a married couple from the same area. It seemed evident, however, that such a sophisticated operation surpassed the known capabilities of local Islamic groups. The president of the National Security Service blamed it on "foreign extremist and terrorist organizations and people who have relations with them."[40] President Karimov admonished the public to "look around yourselves. What is happening? At a distance of 150 km from us war is continuing, people are killing each other, the war in Afghanistan has been continuing for 20 years. . . . Go and see the situation in Tajikistan, . . . shooting in the streets, killing people in the entrances of buildings, innocent people are being killed."[41] Some speculated that Moscow might be behind the incident, in order to pressure Uzbekistan to rejoin military cooperation with the Russian-led Commonwealth of Independent

States. Another theory was that the Samarkandi clan, angered by the dismissal of their leader Deputy Prime Minister Ismail Jurabekov in the fall of 1998 (an episode to be covered in greater depth in Chapter 5) had staged it. Among his followers were many with passes allowing them to enter the heavily guarded Cabinet of Ministers area.

Exiled Uzbek dissidents and others charged that the government of Uzbekistan had carried out these crimes itself in order to justify a crackdown and frighten people into supporting it in upcoming legislative elections. Abdurahim Pulatov, leader of the Birlik movement, told the Voice of the Islamic Republic of Iran from Washington that no Islamic or other group could drive six cars filled with explosives into the center of Tashkent in a country where a "totalitarian state" controls everything. He also discounted rumors of Russian involvement, claiming that Russia was pleased with Uzbekistan's role in Central Asia.[42]

President Karimov ordered a reexamination of those arrested in the crackdown on the Islamic militants in the Ferghana Valley in order to determine who had foreign connections. He claimed that the movement had organized itself in the pyramidal structure typical of underground guerrilla movements, with cells of five in minimal contact with each other. He also announced that his office had been preparing an amnesty for those of the prisoners "who lack awareness, who were led astray," and that it would continue to work on such an amnesty. He advised every neighborhood committee, however, to keep close watch on the local mosque.[43]

As this report went to press, it was impossible to be sure who was responsible for the bombings or what would be the result. If local Islamic militants carried them out, they certainly received training outside the country, and regional tensions could be inflamed further. Since the government pointed its finger at the mosques and militants of the Ferghana Valley, turmoil seemed likely to increase there in any case.

OTHER INCIDENTS

Although not of the same scope and intensity, other incidents largely unnoticed by the outside world have also marred the region's recent history. In early 1997, for example, during the first of our visits to the region, at least two violent incidents occurred along the Tajikistan-Uzbekistan border in the Valley. The two attacks, in January and February, left three Tajik policemen dead and three Uzbek customs officials injured. It is unclear if these attacks had any ethnic motivation or if they were the result of other provocations, such as armed bandits trying to run contraband across the border. But several observers on the spot believed that they illustrate the inherent potential for conflict in the establishment and enforcement of interstate border controls in the Valley, particularly when the Kyrgyzstan and Tajikistan parts of the region depend so heavily on Uzbekistan for trade and transportation of goods to outside markets. Such incidents, observers noted, could also be used by Tashkent to intervene, directly or indirectly, in northern Tajikistan.[44]

Small-scale conflicts over land and water use between Kyrgyz and Tajiks have also occurred in Batkin, between Khujand and Osh, where a small pocket of Tajikistan territory (as well as two larger areas of Uzbekistan territory) lies surrounded by Kyrgyzstan. As in many such cases, the initial conflict dated to an earlier Soviet decision, in this case to give Tajik land to a Kyrgyz collective farm; in the spirit of greater openness, in 1989, the Tajiks demanded it back. The mid-July violence left one person dead and nineteen injured, and the area has been the site of annual confrontations as the issues remain unresolved.

LESSONS FROM PAST CONFLICTS

Several important lessons emerged from the Osh and Ferghana riots and may apply to the other struggles as well. First, although the conflicts generally erupted along ethnic fault lines, ethnicity was not the underlying cause. As Rafik Saifulin, deputy director of Uzbekistan's Presidential Institute of Strategic Studies, noted, "The ethnic identity of the participants [in the 1989 Ferghana and the 1990 Osh riots] did not matter. What was important was the widespread social unhappiness and the need for reform."[45] Saifulin and others point out that all of the root causes of this unhappiness, in particular limited access to land and water, have only gotten worse in the transition period. The same grievances may well explain the outbreak of terrorism blamed on Islamic extremists, though the entire phenomenon of Muslim revival cannot be reduced to an expression of economic and social protest.

Second, when governments adopted policies such as limited affirmative action to help ethnic Uzbeks in Osh and Jalalabad, these tended to provoke resentment from others, namely ethnic Kyrgyz, many of whom saw the Uzbeks as economically better off. One observer in Bishkek remarked that many see democracy in Kyrgyzstan primarily as a way for the Kyrgyz to "take care of their own." Even apparently logical efforts to cool simmering tensions (efforts that are often supported by and identified with international organizations) can lead to new sources of strife and resentment.

Third, for all the appeals that many in the region have made for solidarity based on Islam or on a common Turkic or Persian-Tajik heritage, these conflicts broke out among groups with similar characteristics—Turkic Muslims against Turkic Muslims in Uzbekistan and Kyrgyzstan, and Tajik Muslims against Tajik Muslims and other groups in Tajikistan. Local disputes may or may not coincide with the most visible ethnic or cultural markers, but other concerns are clearly involved.

Finally, the origins of both the Osh and Ferghana crises and the specific roles in them of various organizations and authorities remain shrouded in mystery, as do more recent violent events, and most local and national leaders appear to want them to remain so. In Uzbekistan, the regime has stated that, as there is currently no unrest in the Ferghana Valley, except for externally based subversion, it is not useful to study past conflicts; in Kyrgyzstan, independent researchers have encountered political resistance to conducting an in-depth investigation of the Osh riots. The official line, repeated to our group by several people, is that these disturbances were the result of manipulations by unidentified "black hands" of the Soviet past. Suppressing discussion or projecting responsibility onto external enemies may promote stability, since scratching wounds that have not completely healed may only reopen them. Without a full understanding of the causes and triggers of these crises, however, societies and leaders in the region may be caught unprepared for further uprisings that might otherwise be avoided. People can sometimes learn from experience: while the horrible violence of the Osh and Ferghana killings remains an unforgettable tragedy for all in the region, the very memory of the scale of death and destruction may serve as a barrier to further incidents, and may remind both leaders and ordinary citizens in the region of the human cost of conflict.

— 4 —

SOCIAL AND ECONOMIC
TENSIONS AND REFORMS

All of the incidents described in the previous chapter were caused less by ethnic animosities than by a mix of elements—economic, social, political—embedded in complex political and ethnic strata that formed the fault lines along which these conflicts eventually exploded. Of these, increasing economic hardship and social strains top the list as sources of bloodshed and violence in the past and as threats to stability in the future. Demographic and economic pressures, regional schisms, corruption and organized crime, and a range of social challenges that affect the health and well-being of the population are all stresses that could set off future unrest. The price of strawberries in the bazaar, the allocation of a piece of land to the "wrong" collective farm, the perceived favoritism toward one district in the Ferghana Valley over another by government officials—all have been tiny sparks that ignited entire regions.

While conflict is not inevitable, these same forces have largely intensified throughout the Ferghana Valley over the past several years, regardless of the different paths the three constituent countries have taken. Indeed, while nongovernmental and governmental actions may be ameliorating problems in some areas, in others they may have only made them worse. We will first describe sources of tension and then present some of the measures taken to deal with these challenges since independence.

Sources of Tension

Population Pressure

With a young and rapidly growing population in a small region lacking the potential to expand its arable land, the Ferghana Valley faces tremendous demographic pressures. Current population density in the Valley reaches as high as 450 people per square kilometer, and almost half the people are under sixteen years of age. For example, from 1979 to 1993 the combined population of the three Uzbekistan *hakimiyats* in the Ferghana Valley increased by 44 percent, from 4.1 million to 5.9 million, an annual growth rate of 2.6 percent; at current growth rates, that number will rise to more than 7 million by the year 2000.[1] Central Asia is growing more populous more quickly than any other part of the former Soviet Union. The rapid increase in the number of young people seeking education and employment intensifies all the sources of tension to be described further here.

Economic Decline

Since the collapse of the Soviet Union, economic development has not kept pace with population growth. The past few years have seen poor, and declining, economic performance in all three parts of the Ferghana Valley: Kyrgyzstan's GDP, for example, fell to nearly half its 1989 level by 1996; it grew that year for the first time since independence, by 2 percent of its greatly reduced base of production and then by 10 percent the following year (see Table 4.1). The impact of this slump on southern Kyrgyzstan has been harsh, particularly in agriculture, which is heavily based in the southern Osh and Jalalabad regions.[2]

Uzbekistan's swath of the Ferghana Valley has likewise had continual economic problems. These are particularly pronounced in cotton production, a critical component of the economy. Repeated poor harvests, including a steep shortfall in the 1996 harvest and storms in May 1997 that reportedly damaged 60 percent of Uzbekistan's cotton crop, have brought significant hardship to farmers. Today many work on collective farms that are bankrupt and falling apart, and people live on what they can produce on the side, rather than the cotton and silk that are intended to be their mainstay. Many barely get by.

Unlike the Uzbekistan and Kyrgyzstan parts of the Ferghana Valley, Tajikistan's northern Leninabad province has long been that republic's most important area economically, and the war has made it still more so.

TABLE 4.1
ECONOMIC DECLINE AND GROWTH, 1989–97

Country	1997 Real GDP as percentage of 1989 GDP	Real GDP Growth 1997 (annual percentage change)
Kyrgyzstan	57	6.5
Tajikistan	40	1.7
Uzbekistan	87	2.4
Kazakstan	63	2.0
Turkmenistan	42	-26.0
Russia	58	0.8

Source: European Bank for Reconstruction and Development, Transition Report 1998: Financial Sector in Transition (London: European Bank for Reconstruction and Development, 1998), p. 50.

Before the civil war, the Leninabad oblast accounted for 65 percent of Tajikistan's GDP, and that figure is likely to have risen, as this was the only part of Tajikistan spared—until November 1998—the ravages of battle. But in a country that was already the poorest Soviet republic, and whose civil war plunged much of it (and its economy) into chaos and collapse, northern Tajikistan today receives little from the center. Leninabadis, who were always better off than their brethren in the south, are now much worse off than they were a few years ago. Having encountered greater difficulties in trading with their primary partner, Uzbekistan, Leninabadis today also have a growing sense of economic and political isolation and are developing seemingly independent local economic policies under often rival fiefdoms.

In all three nations, economic deprivation and decline have had two main repercussions. First, they have fostered significant resentment that the Ferghana Valley provinces are "losers" relative to the other parts of their countries. In southern Kyrgyzstan, this sentiment crosses ethnic lines, as expressions of resentment have grown among Kyrgyz and Uzbeks alike that the south is excluded from economic decision-making and that it does not benefit proportionately from government investment and foreign aid. Second, economic hardships have exacerbated tensions within the Valley among Uzbeks, Kyrgyz, and other ethnic groups, as competition for increasingly scarce resources and meager opportunities—land, water, jobs, and adequate living standards—intensifies throughout.

Bad times have also increased the gap between rich and poor. In Kyrgyzstan the low living standards characteristic of the country as a whole are particularly pronounced in the Ferghana Valley: the percentage of the population under the official poverty line is significantly higher in the two southern provinces than the average for all of Kyrgyzstan, and since independence this percentage has continued to grow. Similarly, wages in the south are significantly lower than the national mean, with the average monthly wage in the Osh district amounting to barely half the average wage in Bishkek, and average wages in agriculture around Osh (the lowest of all districts in Kyrgyzstan) amounting to barely one quarter of Bishkek wages.[3] 1996 survey data for Jalalabad province indicated that two-thirds of the population were below the poverty line.[4]

Economic decline has accentuated divisions, provoking deep resentment, which is partly directed at ethnic rivals. Many Kyrgyz, for instance, fear that they are losing out to Russians in the north of Kyrgyzstan and to Uzbeks in the south. They historically have not been engaged in trade or industry, and they believe that ethnic Uzbeks, especially traders, control a disproportionate amount of the south's wealth.

In the Tajikistan and Uzbekistan segments of the Ferghana Valley, the picture is similar. Tajikistan's Leninabad province, which had enjoyed the highest wages in Tajikistan throughout the Soviet period, has experienced a drastic drop in living standards since independence and the outbreak of war: as of September 1996, the average monthly wage in Leninabad oblast (2366 Tajik rubles, about $8) was not even half the average wage in Dushanbe (5065 Tajik rubles, about $18).[5] And in Uzbekistan's part of the Valley living standards have likewise been both lower than the national average and falling. According to one estimate, the average monthly income for rural families engaged in agricultural production in the Uzbekistan part of the valley is $10, versus $15 in the rest of the country. These amounts further contrast sharply with the $30 per month average income for Uzbekistan's urban dwellers.[6]

In all three countries, poverty is compounded by high inflation, corruption, and wage payment arrears. Some of the people we met in the Valley had not been paid for six months; some farmers have not received wages for more than two years. Increases in bribes demanded in exchange for basic services have likewise made day-to-day survival more difficult. While some basic food staples reportedly are rationed— for example, we were told that authorities in Namangan allow five kilograms of flour per family per month at state prices—the political aftereffects of scarcity may be growing. "People are wondering why there is no cotton oil, when we grow so much cotton, why there is no flour, when we grow wheat," a human rights activist in Namangan told us. He continued:

> Everyone is afraid to say anything. But you must understand that while people are not politicized here, they only think with their stomachs. People who are political understand their own worth; people here do not understand their own worth. But if they can't eat, they will react.

LAND

Competition for land may well be one of the most tension-ridden of these demographic and economic challenges, especially when it finds expression in terms of ethnicity or nationalism. While the Ferghana Valley contains much of the arable soil of these three countries, land is still limited in the Valley, especially in Kyrgyzstan, where more than half of the tillable acreage is concentrated in one narrow strip. According to UNDP, while in 1940 each individual in the Valley could claim about one-quarter of a hectare of irrigated arable land, by the early 1990s this share had declined to an average of about one-tenth and, in some areas, to only about .06 hectares.[7]

As land becomes more scarce, competition is widely perceived to take place along ethnic lines—especially between Uzbeks and Kyrgyz in southern Kyrgyzstan—although these groups differ in their assessments of winners and losers. With the highest population density in Kyrgyzstan, Osh's land available per capita has become more limited since the time of the riots, and high population growth rates mean it will become scarcer still. According to Uzbek groups in Kyrgyzstan, the Kyrgyz have been pushing the Uzbeks out of the best spots, areas that they consider their own. Several Kyrgyz we interviewed, in turn, believe that the Uzbeks have grabbed the best land. Each group feels its very survival is at stake as economic conditions deteriorate.

Access to land is also an important issue in the Uzbekistan part of the Valley. In areas where the population is overwhelmingly Uzbek, the fault lines may not be ethnic. But, increasingly, land distribution in Uzbekistan is displaying an important ethnic dimension as well. According to local experts, the best holdings in the Uzbekistan side of the Valley are already in the hands of Uzbeks, but as land is reallocated to accommodate a rapidly growing Uzbek population, many believe that the Kyrgyz and Tajiks have been disadvantaged even more, pushed increasingly toward the foothills of the mountains, where the soil is poor.

In northern Tajikistan, with a somewhat lower population density and a higher level of industrialization, access to land has not emerged as a vital issue. The growing number of refugees, increasing demographic pressures, and factory closures, however, may change that in the near future.

WATER

Together with land, water is the most precious resource in Central Asia. As in the Middle East, its scarcity makes it a constant source of low-level tension both between and within states. Periodic conflicts over water use between residents of northern Tajikistan and southern Kyrgyzstan, as elsewhere in Central Asia, illustrate how water can trigger a larger crisis.

Only two main rivers, the Syr Darya and the Amu Darya, feed the entire Central Asian region. Water originates in the sparsely populated, mountainous areas of Tajikistan, source of the Amu Darya, and Kyrgyzstan, from where the Syr Darya and its tributaries flow into the Ferghana Valley. While water is not abundant in Kyrgyzstan and Tajikistan, it is even scarcer in the other three countries of Central Asia. Both rivers once flowed steadily into the Aral Sea, which now receives only a trickle, causing enormous environmental and economic damage there.

The allocation of water among various users and uses is an issue in regions like the Ferghana Valley and among the states of Central Asia. Small-scale conflicts have already erupted over water within the Valley and continue to this day. While there is plenty of water flowing through the Valley itself, deciding who gets how much and when is a political question of the first order. In 1996, representatives of the U.S. embassy in Dushanbe, after visiting Isfara, a city in Leninabad near the town of Batkin, Kyrgyzstan, reported that "there is an undercurrent of suspicion that the Kyrgyz are scheming to tap more Tajik water resources to irrigate additional lands on the Kyrgyz side of the unmarked, indistinguishable border. Almost all available arable land is already being intensely cultivated."[8] These remarks could apply to many places along the borders within the Ferghana Valley. Like the Batkin conflict, these disputes tend to break out along the ethnic and other fault lines throughout the region.

This problem derives not just from scarcity of water but also from its inefficient use. Conflicts can arise over quantities of water made available for irrigation, scheduling of irrigation flows, and water quality. In southern Kyrgyzstan, neglect of irrigation systems at the farm level in recent years has resulted in enormous waste of water, leading to periodic flooding, rising water tables, and increased soil salinity.[9] The continued use of large amounts of pesticides and the increased salinity of water used for cotton irrigation is of growing concern to the local population.

Similar problems emerge on a wider scale in Central Asia. Both the amount of water retained by Kyrgyzstan for hydroelectric production and the amount used in the Valley for agriculture affect the ability of farms elsewhere in Uzbekistan and in southern Kazakstan to raise irrigated crops, especially cotton.

In other words, it is not simply water scarcity that is at issue but the power relations among the region's states. Water is the one resource that gives Kyrgyzstan and, to a lesser extent, Tajikistan some leverage over their larger, downstream neighbor, Uzbekistan. Hydrocarbon-poor Kyrgyzstan has huge hydroelectric potential, but tapping too much of it risks leaving much of Uzbekistan and Kazakstan without sufficient water supplies. This is especially controversial because peak demand for hydroelectricity is in winter, while Uzbekistan needs more water in the summer, when demand for electricity in Kyrgyzstan is low. Uzbekistan has repeatedly made clear that any unilateral acts on the part of Kyrgyzstan that would diminish water supplies to the Ferghana Valley and beyond would be of great concern.

EMPLOYMENT

Competition among ethnic groups for scarce jobs is high, and unemployment is growing, particularly among youth, in the Ferghana Valley. All of our interviewees mentioned this as a key cause of conflicts in the region.

Throughout Central Asia the employment problem stems from an economic legacy that manages to combine the worst aspects of the Soviet system and the third world. Owing to the collapse of the Soviet Union and its network of suppliers and distributors, many industries in Central Asia are now idle. These have proved unable to employ an increasingly large proportion of their countries' rapidly growing young population. Today, an estimated 35 percent of the work force in the Uzbekistan part of the Valley is unemployed, including the majority of those under the age of twenty-five.[10]

Aside from adversely affecting family incomes, youth joblessness has two additional consequences. Raised at the end of the Soviet period, many of these young people have expectations of the state, in particular for full employment, that simply can no longer be met. Beyond being disgruntled, young people also have the most time on their hands, especially now that Soviet-style youth organizations and the like have ceased to function.

The problem of dismal job prospects, many believe, lay at the heart of earlier conflicts, and it is still worrisome today. It is compounded by the reported inability of many of the unemployed to collect unemployment payments for the past several years, and further by the ethnic distribution of those unemployed.[11] In the Kyrgyzstan part of the Valley, in the words of one U.S. official, "while unemployment is high among everyone, it is higher among Uzbeks than among Kyrgyz. The Uzbeks get very frustrated, even if the Kyrgyz are not to blame." Many other local observers confirmed this observation, suggesting that even if Uzbeks in Kyrgyzstan were, in fact, not disproportionately affected by employment problems, the perception is widespread enough to be a source of trouble in its own right.

As life's hardships have become magnified, so, too, has competition for scarce jobs, especially among different ethnic groups—at the bazaar, in state bureaucracies, and in the newly privatized sectors of the economy. This is particularly true in southern Kyrgyzstan, where the ethnic mixing is most pronounced, and most of all at the bazaar, the site of earlier conflict and unrest. Uzbek parliamentarian Alisher Sabirov told us:

> Most of the economically active population is now in the bazaar. In 1992, the sellers were Uzbek and the buyers were Kyrgyz. Now it is hard for an Uzbek to sell goods. . . . Now, if any [conflict] occurs, it will be in the bazaar.

There seems to be little disagreement that while Uzbeks used to dominate trade in the bazaar (they are often characterized as more oriented toward trade than Kyrgyz), they may be losing this position as the market is gradually taken over by Kyrgyz.

Perceptions differ, however, on how this plays out. One member of our group discussed some of these differences with sellers at the Osh bazaar. Some Uzbeks claimed, "They take places from us on any pretext and give them to the Kyrgyz." Others disagreed. "That isn't exactly right. I don't know that they've ever actually taken a place from us. But if somebody leaves Osh, or dies, or the slot becomes vacant, . . . then it will go to a Kyrgyz, you can count on it. Like the places near the entrance. They are new, and they all went to Kyrgyz." Either way, even Kyrgyz we spoke with agreed that the bazaar has become "Kyrgyzified."

According to a U.S. official based in the region, "The Uzbeks losing their spots at the bazaar to a Kyrgyz, or losing land with water to a Kyrgyz and getting land without water—these are things that can trigger real conflict."

If the Kyrgyz lament that Uzbeks have had, at least until recently, an unfair advantage at the bazaar, the Uzbeks complain that they are increasingly underrepresented in the state sector. The shift to ethnic Kyrgyz in the bureaucracy described to us by Americans and locals alike has been a source of unrest and worries many about the future. As the deputy governor of Osh, Nuriyla Joldosheva, told us, "During the Osh events, there was much criticism of cadre policy by nationality: for example, the service sector is mostly Uzbek, while state structures are mostly Kyrgyz." There continues to be a great deal of dissatisfaction that there are not enough Uzbeks in the government bodies, including in law enforcement and the police. Opposition politician Ali Sabirov argued:

> We [Uzbeks] are losing access to state structures. There are 60 territorial administrative units in Kyrgyzstan, raions and cities. Of these 60 local units only one is headed by an Uzbek. . . . In these 60 there are only 2 Uzbek procurators [state's attorneys], even though we are 13 percent of the population of the republic. There are no Uzbek ministers. There are two Uzbek deputy governors, in Chu and Jalalabad. During the Soviet period 7–8 of the raion [subdivisions of oblasts] administrations were governed by Uzbeks. Now the percentage of Uzbek representation in the administrative organizations is not more than 2 percent. There are practically no Uzbeks in the monitoring organizations, such as the customs service and tax collection. When a person has to appeal to the state structures, he cannot find a fellow Uzbek to help him.

Some data bears out these charges. Of 128 people in the tax inspection department of Osh oblast in 1997, only eight were Uzbeks, and they were all inspectors, the lowest job in the hierarchy. The same situation is found in the customs ministries. And the proportion of Uzbeks in the police in Osh declined from 14 percent in 1990 to 5.5 percent in 1997. Uzbek representation has, however, grown in communications and small businesses. Large businesses, which depend much more on relations with state power, are still dominated by Kyrgyz.

A Kyrgyz high official in the Ferghana Valley explained it this way: "You must take into account the fact that by tradition, Uzbeks have been more inclined to work in the agricultural and commercial sectors, whereas the Kyrgyz look for public service positions and associate them with prestige. As we move to a free market economy, it is the Uzbeks who have been quickest to capitalize on the benefits and opportunities this affords." In other words, as another interviewee put it, for the time being, "Uzbeks have money, Kyrgyz have power. . . ."

CORRUPTION AND ORGANIZED CRIME

One of the most important obstacles to change in Central Asia is the *informal* economic mechanisms that have developed over many decades—despite their at times stabilizing effect filling gaps in the official economy—with the resulting corruption and organized crime. Corruption in Central Asia represents probably the single biggest impediment to carrying out reform policies effectively. It has the potential to destabilize the society. Corruption distributes opportunities unfairly, impedes openness and transparency, and blocks the creation of the rule of law and a sense of fairness among the population. Where hardship abounds, perceptions of such injustice may provoke or legitimate violent means of settling disputes.

One of the legacies of Soviet rule in Central Asia was the deeply systemic and entrenched corruption and organized criminality that became an integral part of the Central Asian economies. In a centralized regime where all basic goods and services were in short supply—and where there was little oversight and accountability—a parallel, criminal economic system emerged that was just as firmly ruled from the top as the official one, and often involved the same powerful people. By the end of the Soviet period, it was no longer considered a "second" economy; by all accounts, it *was* the economy.[12]

While the rules of the game have changed since the Soviet period, most estimates are that corruption and crime have grown extensively. A recent public opinion survey suggests that corruption has been widespread particularly among those with control over goods and services in short supply (service- and trade-oriented ministries, businesses) and those with power over economic activity (high government officials, law enforcement, the procuracy and courts).[13] The bribes that applicants must pay to be trained or employed in these influential fields reflect the value of such positions. In Uzbekistan, for example, the average bribe to enter the police academy or to join the procuracy is upward of three years' salary, although it costs little or nothing to get a job in a heavy industrial factory, where the ability to extort on the side is limited. With the collapse of the Soviet Union and emergence of greater opportunities for private gain, most observers believe that corruption has skyrocketed.

As in other parts of the world, some argue, corruption and the parallel economy have had a stabilizing impact. Supporters of this view believe that this unofficial economic activity redistributes income and fuels economic growth. At least some of those who enrich themselves will reinvest to help spur development and change, as did the robber barons in the United States.

But there is little evidence of such reinvestment in the economy of this region, whereas the potential for crime and corruption to destabilize Central Asia is enormous. Anecdotal information suggests that the poor are more often the targets than the beneficiaries of crooked practices. Corruption and organized crime have visibly widened the disparities between rich and poor in a population used to believing that egalitarianism is a key goal. Corruption has also intensified the anger and resentment commonly felt against government officials and bureaucrats and has eroded confidence that political leaders, law enforcement officers, economic ministers, and others can be guided by anything but self-interest.

Most fundamentally, corruption has so distorted the formal economy that it now represents one of the greatest, if not the single greatest, obstacle to the democratic and market reform so necessary before grappling with the economic and other challenges that have led to violent conflict in the past and persist to this day. The more widespread corruption and criminal economic activity become, the more the population becomes skeptical of the reform process itself and of legitimate private economic activity, including small business. Indeed, the vast majority of respondents to the survey mentioned above associate economic reform directly with the growth of dirty dealings and disorder. And because of deep and lucrative vested interests, few at the highest levels are seriously interested in revamping the system into something more transparent and fair. A market economy based on the rule of law cannot be established if a huge chunk of economic activity continues to operate underground.

Corruption also has a corrosive and destabilizing political effect on society at large. Throughout the Soviet period, impropriety was used as an excuse to crack down on individuals for purely political reasons. Throughout Central Asia, this practice continues to be used today, perhaps especially against journalists—and those journalists who investigate corruption seem to be persecuted particularly stridently. The court system is among the most crooked sectors of society, so few believe they can get a fair crack at justice at any level. Finally, as life becomes harder, the additional burden of bribes and payoffs has at least in some cases also become a destabilizing influence.

All of this is particularly true in the Ferghana Valley, where, according to some of our interviewees, corruption may be particularly pronounced. According to Emil Alymkulov of Goskominvest (a state investment bank) in Kyrgyzstan: "There is a different psychology in the south [of Kyrgyzstan] than in the north; there is more corruption in the south. The south also retains more of the psychology of old Soviet leaders, . . . and the role of family and connections is bigger there."

NARCOTICS TRAFFICKING

The informal economic system, corruption, and organized crime have nurtured the development of one of the biggest businesses in Central Asia, and certainly in the Ferghana Valley: the illegal production and trafficking of narcotics and other contraband. The smuggling of narcotics and other substances has long characterized the Central Asian area, but it reportedly exploded in the mid-1980s and early 1990s with the wars in Afghanistan and Tajikistan and the collapse of the Soviet Union. Today, while the geography of the Ferghana Valley may cut it off from ordinary trade and intercourse with other parts of Central Asia, it is perfectly situated for the production and, more importantly, trafficking of opium and other drugs, mainly from Afghanistan to Russia and the West.

With the disintegration of Soviet control, the borders of Central Asia with Afghanistan and Iran have become more porous and poorly controlled. The border with Russia is nearly as open as it was during Soviet times, when internal borders were hardly noticeable. The drug and arms trafficking routes that go through the Ferghana Valley originate in South Asia, especially Afghanistan, and move across the former Soviet Union into Eastern and Western Europe and sometimes on to the United States and Canada. Much of the traffic in drugs moves along the 750-kilometer highway from Khorog, the capital of Tajikistan's Gorno-Badakhshan province, on the Afghan border, across the mountains to Osh, Kyrgyzstan. According to the United Nations International Drug Control Program, this route is used to smuggle at least one-fourth of the total opium production of the Badakhshan province of Afghanistan (that is, about sixty metric tons of dry opium per year).[14] Not just raw opium but "clean" heroin has also been reported, suggesting that rudimentary heroin processing has begun in the region as well.

Some maintain that, as elsewhere in the world, the drug trade can mitigate the potential for instability by providing work and income for many and even furnishing start-up capital for legitimate business ventures. In the words of an observer, "Osh is a new Bogotá. When you see so many fancy houses and cars, there are only two ways to earn that: through drugs and arms. There is not as much trafficking in arms." Asserts one westerner living in Osh for several years, "Every successful business is tied to drug trafficking."

Many also argue that contraband benefits the poor and impoverished throughout the Ferghana Valley, who have few alternative sources of income. Simple "camels," as the human couriers are called, carry twenty-to-thirty-kilogram backpacks through mountain passes at altitudes up to 4800 meters, higher than any mountains in Europe. "Why is the drug trade here?" an Uzbek parliamentarian in Kyrgyzstan asked. "Why do our citizens resort to it? For economic reasons—there is no alternative. There is simply an absence of money."

But, as in other countries of the world, the net effect of drug trafficking is debilitating: it, too, exacerbates income disparities, distorts the formal economy, sharpens the rivalry among criminal groups, and impedes the development of a rule of law, especially when law enforcement itself is involved in the trade. Ultimately, it may represent another of the biggest obstacles to fundamental reform.

Domestically, some fear that drug cultivation, production, and transit in the Ferghana Valley will create problems of drug consumption that have a significant impact on cultural and family structures, the economy, crime, and the like, and will assist the proliferation of small weapons. As one western specialist has noted, strong criminal groups involved in the drug trade may also "deliberately and successfully seek to disrupt peace efforts, because weak institutions, unrest, and disarray better serve criminal agendas. This belief has a following in Central Asia as well."[15]

The drug trade could have mixed effects on interethnic relations. Trafficking and organized crime were always among the most "internationalizing" forces in the Soviet Union, and in some ways that, too, continues. According to a former police officer in Osh, "Where there is an issue of transport or sale of narcotics, our criminal groups cooperate. The Tajiks bring the opium. If they are smuggling it through Uzbekistan, they use Uzbek camels. If it is going via Almaty, they use Kyrgyz to take it through Bishkek. . . ." Professor Anara Tabyshalieva of the

Institute for Regional Studies (Kyrgyzstan) described the drug mafia as a "model of inter-ethnic cooperation." To date, the drug trade has not led to conflict among drug mafias of different ethnic groups. Nonetheless, this pattern has emerged elsewhere commonly enough to cause concern for the future.

Perhaps most detrimental from the perspective of our purposes is simply the effect that corruption, crime, and narcotics trafficking have on the ability of security and law enforcement agencies to do their job. Evidence suggests that some in the Russian military—especially the 201st Motorized Rifle Division in Tajikistan and the Russian border troops—are themselves involved in the drug trade. This allegation is buttressed by the reportedly frequent and astronomical disparity between what Russian border troops claim to confiscate from criminals and what they submit for inspection.

One observer reports that, "the main route of transit of Afghan opium is no longer the Khorog-Osh road, . . . but the military transport aviation of Russian troops based in Tajikistan."[16] Locals referred to one Russian general as "Narco Baron number one." A former Kyrgyzstan law enforcement officer pointed out to our project director at the Osh airport that the Russian helicopters we saw were flying in and out with no searches or inspections. That these crews report directly to Moscow rather than locally has done little to dampen widespread impressions of shady conduct.

The deep involvement of police and the military in the drug trade, arms trade, and crime makes law enforcement itself arbitrary. In the words of a Western specialist, Graham Turbiville, the profits from these activities "promote and sustain a particularly pernicious form of institutional corruption that has its worst effects on those military, law enforcement, and governmental bodies that are most essential to maintaining peace and order."[17]

DECLINE IN SOCIAL SERVICES

Sudden declines in social welfare, especially in comparison to other groups, can also spark conflict. The Soviet state created an extensive network of social services that the newly independent states of Central Asia have been unable to maintain. Causing greatest concern today are the severe budgetary cutbacks in all of these areas and the transfer of responsibility for most social services from the national government and formerly state-owned enterprises to local and regional administrations. In the long run, this decentralization should strengthen the regions politically, breaking the Soviet pattern of centralized rule. In the interim, however, local administrations are saddled with immense responsibilities in the areas of health care and education at a time when national subsidies are being reduced.

While the regional governments have been given some new powers of taxation, their administrative inexperience, coupled with an absence of enforcement and the inability of many enterprises to pay taxes, has resulted in a severe fraying of services. Ineffective decentralization has worsened regional and ethnic disparities in access to what social services remain intact.

EDUCATION. As public services are cut throughout Central Asia, access to education, especially education in one's own language, has become a source of tension. At the same time, some new projects are using educational institutions to mitigate conflicts by teaching tolerance and pluralism.

Cutbacks in education have become a problem throughout the Ferghana Valley. A government report on Osh province, for example, observes that decreases in the real levels of funding are putting the education system under increasing strain. Funding shortages have resulted in substantial arrears in teachers' salaries, which have undermined staff morale and performance.[18] Even as real salaries fall or go unpaid, the nonwage element of the education budget is estimated to have fallen by more than 70 percent in real terms since the late 1980s, resulting in shortages of textbooks and teaching materials and inadequate maintenance of school buildings. The report notes that it has been especially difficult to staff schools in rural areas, and consequently average class size has increased.

Cutbacks in education have meant a downturn in job placement, and many see this as disproportionately affecting some ethnic groups. Alisher Sabirov, an ethnic Uzbek member of the Legislative Assembly (in Kyrgyz, Jogorku Kenesh), explained that this is a particular problem in secondary schools: budgetary cuts by the Ministry of Education, he told us, have led authorities to reduce the number of classes offered and to encourage children to leave secondary school after the ninth grade. Sabirov believes this is occurring more in the Uzbek schools than in Kyrgyz schools. He does not think that this is a deliberate government policy as much as it is "just the result of economic difficulty which hits the minorities more." But, deliberate or not, the effect is one that disturbs Uzbeks in southern Kyrgyzstan greatly. In institutions of higher learning, Sabirov adds, minority representation is low. He claims that fewer than 2 to 3 percent of students in institutions of higher learning in Kyrgyzstan are Uzbek, versus roughly 13 percent of the population as a whole.

Access to education in one's own language is a sore spot among the nontitular nationalities in Kyrgyzstan, especially the Uzbeks. They face increasing difficulty owing to both cutbacks in educational outlays in Kyrgyzstan and the loss of ready access to their own titular states as a result of the Soviet breakup. Those states formerly supplied textbooks and trained teachers. Now both functions impose new burdens on Kyrgyzstan's shrinking education budget.

The cultural reforms adopted amid the construction of post-Soviet national states have imposed particular hardships on the Uzbeks of Kyrgyzstan. The Soviet-era Uzbek and Kyrgyz languages, like all the Soviet-designed languages of Central Asia, were written in modified versions of Russia's Cyrillic script. As part of the process of national differentiation, however, Uzbekistan has adopted a Latin script for Uzbek, in which it is now printing textbooks. In Kyrgyzstan, however, a country with a larger Russian population, the Cyrillic script has been kept for both Kyrgyz and Uzbek. For the first time, therefore, Uzbeks in Kyrgyzstan must produce their own Cyrillic Uzbek textbooks, for which there are few facilities and little funding.

Although Uzbekistan and Kyrgyzstan have engaged in some limited cooperation to assist the ethnic Uzbeks of Osh and Jalalabad by setting up a joint Uzbek-Kyrgyz college in Osh, the Uzbek minority remains a political football between the two states. As a result, 300,000 Uzbek children reportedly are without textbooks. "In ten years, we won't have any teachers," parliamentarian Sabirov told us, "because we cannot prepare new ones. Our children will be without education in our own language."

These issues present real challenges to authorities with limited budgets for education. Another approach, however, has been to attempt to blur these differences through programs to teach greater tolerance toward other groups and peoples as well as an appreciation of democracy and reform. This is part of the logic behind the Bradley program, one of the only programs to bring high school-age children from Kyrgyzstan to the United States. Our Council on Foreign Relations group was somewhat surprised to find that the majority of the passengers on our flight from Osh to Bishkek were high school students and teachers from Jackson, Mississippi, on the last leg of their exchange with the cotton-growing south of Kyrgyzstan. The Soros Foundation has likewise initiated various projects to teach values of openness and cultural awareness to students in Kyrgyzstan. Otherwise, few international or nongovernmental organizations concern themselves with the attitudes of the young. One of the only programs designed to inculcate values of tolerance and pluralism for elementary school students is a UN High Commissioner for Refugees program in Kyrgyzstan. It produces texts and popular books with stories about tolerance and respect for differences, based on materials collected from students in classrooms throughout Kyrgyzstan. It has been quite popular but will be ending shortly, as it is not part of mainstream UNHCR activities.

ENVIRONMENT AND HEALTH. Problems triggered by cutbacks in education have been matched only by the difficulties posed by the deteriorating health of the populations in the Ferghana Valley and the devastating environmental situation. As these problems intensify, so too, it seems, do perceived regional and ethnic inequalities.

Environmental pollution affects the potential for instability in the Ferghana Valley in two ways. First, the dramatic degradation of the water and soil has significant economic repercussions, altering the political climate for market-friendly reform. Second, as in Soviet times, environmental issues remain a relatively safe conduit for expressing discontent. Some observers believe that local environmental disasters are being used as symbols of protest against declining living standards generally.

The most famous case of environmental calamity in Central Asia is the Aral Sea, the fate of which is directly tied to water use in the Ferghana Valley. Because of the siphoning off of water from the Syr Darya and Amu Darya, the two main rivers that feed the Aral Sea in the westernmost regions of Uzbekistan and Kazakstan, what was once the world's fourth-largest inland sea has shrunk to only about one-third of the volume and half of the geographical size it had in 1960. For the past few years, the Syr Darya, the river that waters the Ferghana Valley, has barely reached the Aral Sea, and the situation worsened in 1995 and 1996. The environmental impact—sand and salt storms, water pollution, and disease and malnutrition in the population—has been enormous.

This manmade disaster has remained the focus of most internal and international environmental efforts in Uzbekistan, Kyrgyzstan, and Kazakstan. In 1992, shortly after independence, the five Central Asian states signed two international agreements to structure a viable water management and allocation system. The World Bank assisted the effort. The agreements, which established an interstate coordinating committee, were designed to decrease water consumption and waste and to defuse tensions over water among the Central Asian states. The Bank has devolved management of its Aral Sea Basin program from its Washington, D.C., headquarters to its Tashkent office.

One of the worst Soviet legacies was disregard for the environment, which resulted in devastating ecological problems affecting the air, soil, and water throughout Central Asia. And one of the most hazardous (potentially lethal) examples in the Ferghana Valley is Mayli-Suu (also spelled Mayli-Say), home to twenty-three uranium dumps with few environmental controls.[19] Located in a sensitive area in the Jalalabad province of Kyrgyzstan, adjacent to the Uzbekistan border, its drainage systems no longer work, and a series of natural disasters, especially flash floods and mudslides, have weakened the foundations surrounding the dumps. This could wreak ecological catastrophe on the entire Ferghana Valley region.

Efforts are reportedly under way in Kyrgyzstan to facilitate a cleanup of the Mayli-Suu uranium dumps. It is questionable, however, whether local authorities have the expertise or technology to clean up the dumps or design properly and build new ones. Both main options being considered (rebuilding and securing the dumps or transferring the waste to a site in Uzbekistan) are costly and controversial.

As with education, access to health and other social services has become increasingly difficult. Since independence, most health indicators in the Ferghana Valley region have worsened. In addition to elemental diseases, the incidence of AIDS and venereal diseases has become quite high. According to an official report on Osh, "increased poverty, coupled with deteriorating public health services, and behavioral and social changes have resulted in a rise in infant mortality and increased incidence of diseases such as cholera, hepatitis A, venereal diseases, and tuberculosis." In Osh oblast, infant mortality has continued to climb, and since 1992

> there has been an alarming rise in the number of cases of tuberculosis, syphilis and chronic drug addiction. Inadequate maintenance of water supply and sewerage systems threatens outbreaks of diseases such as typhoid and cholera. . . . Reductions in the real level of funding since 1991 have resulted in shortages of drugs and supplies, as well as a growing backlog in maintenance and equipment replacement. The number of vehicles supplied to the Health Department fell from around 40 per year to 3 in 1994. Low salaries and salary arrears often extending over several months have contributed to poor staff morale and increasing staff attrition. These factors now severely threaten the quality of health service provision. . . .[20]

Many services are now offered on a fee basis—which means, according to the report, that, with the high incidence of poverty in Osh oblast, many will not be able to pay.

People view the decline in health and rise in mortality through ethnic and regional lenses as well. The plunge in health standards has appeared far more serious in southern Kyrgyzstan than in the country as a whole, exacerbating north-south tensions. Rates of disease and infant and maternal mortality in Osh oblast have remained the highest in the country and have grown disproportionately since 1990; the incidence of communicable disease has also grown rapidly. And, against this background, Uzbeks also lament the severe underrepresentation of Uzbek doctors in the Osh and Jalalabad health services—a ratio far below what their numbers in the population of southern Kyrgyzstan would indicate. As families deal with more illness than before, their tendency to view their hardships in ethnic terms grows only stronger.

ECONOMIC INTEGRATION

Ironically enough, the people of the Ferghana Valley are making the transition to a market economy even as their access to the most immediate markets is blocked by the maintenance of new international borders, separate currencies, and different paths to economic reform. While trade is still possible—and almost everyone we spoke to knew of ways to get around some of the restrictions—the new obstacles are aggravating other problems and pose a serious challenge to reforms in all three countries.

While the problem exists throughout the Valley, it is felt most acutely in southern Kyrgyzstan and northern Tajikistan, where many people depend on trade with neighboring Uzbekistan, which has implemented the most restrictive border and currency regimes. As discussed previously, the Tajikistan-Uzbekistan border was the site of attacks on Uzbekistan border guards during the first visit to the region on behalf of this project in February 1997. U.S. embassy officials and others have confirmed that the Uzbek customs authorities are charging irregular customs fees (that is, bribes) from people crossing the border, even if only in transit between parts of northern Tajikistan. Reportedly, the customs officials are more vigilant and demand higher payments from Tajikistan-registered vehicles than from Uzbekistan-registered ones.[21] Given the extent to which the Tajik and Kyrgyz populations depend on trade with Uzbekistan, those states have so far been too fearful to react.

Analysts from northern Tajikistan do, however, argue that an apparent policy on the part of Uzbekistan officials to favor ethnic Uzbek over Tajik traders from the Leninabad region is changing the balance of power within that region and leading to considerable resentment.[22]

Uzbekistan also introduced measures in April 1995 intended to reduce barter, a prevalent method of trade in the Valley, which has apparently increased in prevalence with the introduction of different national currencies. The government of Uzbekistan declared barter trade "an exception to be carried out with the permission of the cabinet of ministers and the heads of regional administrations." A total of thirty-five groups of goods, mainly raw materials, can now be exported only with the permission of the cabinet of ministers, while cotton and several other items require convertible-currency contracts.[23] Indeed, the measures succeeded in cutting officially acknowledged barter trade by more than half between 1994 and 1995 (from 17.1 percent to 8.1 percent of total trade turnover). While these statistics probably reflect only a fraction of the cross-border barter commerce in the Valley, the regulations may already be having a dampening effect on trade. At the very least, they are providing more opportunities for bribe seeking on the part of those officials whose permission is required.

REFORM PROGRAMS

ECONOMIC REFORM

To address the challenges of nation building, all three states have emphasized the need for significant economic reform, including privatization, support for new small business, attracting foreign investment, land reform, and revision of water policies. Yet, despite their similar starting points, the three have moved in radically different directions, from early, rapid reform in Kyrgyzstan to more gradual or purely cosmetic reform in Uzbekistan to a general breakdown of the national economy in war-torn Tajikistan. While there have been some successes in Kyrgyzstan and Uzbekistan, many of the underlying causes of instability remain. In some cases, reforms have actually aggravated the socioeconomic and political problems and could become threats to stability in their own right.

For the Ferghana Valley's highly integrated regional economy, the policies implemented by the three national governments have had a detrimental impact. Customs controls, the establishment of separate currencies, and differences in rates and means of economic liberalization are all policy decisions that tear at the fabric that has woven the Valley together over the course of centuries. Uzbekistan's policy of strict border controls, instituted for both security and economic reasons, is causing particular hardship. We found that while cross-border trade in the region continues, it has become much more difficult, and the complications are resulting in serious grievances, especially in southern Kyrgyzstan and northern Tajikistan. In addition, efforts are under way in Kyrgyzstan and Uzbekistan to integrate their respective parts of the Valley more tightly with the center, by extension weakening ties within the region. Nevertheless, there are important, if limited, efforts at economic cooperation within the Valley on various levels, which could greatly benefit from international support.

Since Western donors and corporations have been instrumental in advising on economic affairs, they are closely identified with the perceived successes and failures of the reform process in those countries. The following briefly outlines the most important macroeconomic policies each country has instituted before turning to policies on specific issues—shortages of land and water, unemployment, corruption and the drug trade, and environmental decline—that lie at the heart of the quest to maintain stability in the Valley.

MACROECONOMIC POLICIES

KYRGYZSTAN. Serving as a model of economic transition in Central Asia, Kyrgyzstan embarked early on a serious, far-reaching program of market reforms, and it is being greatly assisted by the West in that effort. As U.S. ambassador Eileen Malloy told us, "We have made a real commitment to reform in Kyrgyzstan; if it fails here, it will fail everywhere." Privatization has moved rapidly, and Kyrgyzstan is making concerted efforts to attract Western investment. With the help of Western organizations, the main privatization agency has even created web pages with detailed information on firms to be privatized. The country has been a pioneer within the former Soviet Union in the areas of tax reform, currency deregulation, and protection of foreign investment. In October 1998 Kyrgyzstan became the first post-Soviet state to enact measures for comprehensive privatization of land, passed overwhelmingly in a referendum.

In the last few years, however, signs have emerged that the program of economic reforms is in some trouble, even as many macroeconomic indicators are finally showing some improvement. We found almost universal agreement that the reforms have resulted in a rapidly widening gap between rich and poor and greater distress for many. While this may be a cost of transition, it may well be too high a cost in regions where economic distress is already so deep. The privatization process is perceived as permeated with corruption. Many believe that state enterprises have been sold for far less than their true value.[24] Kyrgyzstan's tight fiscal policy, which has reduced the deficit and helped bring down inflation, has also resulted in months-long arrears in the payment of salaries to government employees, including teachers and doctors. And the banking system remains embryonic: the 1996 collapse of Kyrgyzstan's largest savings bank, Kyrgyzelbank, affected nearly half of the country's population. Such a collapse, which could be repeated, led to civil war in Albania.

In southern Kyrgyzstan, privatization has moved more slowly, and locals there tend to be more skeptical about the concept.[25] This has kept unemployment numbers artificially low, but it perpetuates a drain on economic resources as the state subsidizes money-losing enterprises. The south has also received comparatively little foreign investment and remains poor relative to Bishkek and the north. Regional differences may only be exacerbated by President Askar Akaev's decision to end agricultural subsidies in 1998. This has had a severe impact on the south, confirming suspicions among Kyrgyz and Uzbeks alike that their interests are secondary to those of the north. Given the already low income levels in southern Kyrgyzstan and the ethnic splits there between Uzbeks and Kyrgyz, the government's policy of decentralizing service delivery—shifting responsibility for the social safety net, education, and health care from the national to the local and regional levels—is causing considerable friction.

Notwithstanding, Kyrgyzstan has embarked on a policy of promoting the economic integration of the country. This is likely to have profound, if ambiguous, effects on the Osh and Jalalabad regions, which have long traded far more with nearby Uzbekistan than with the northern parts of their own republic. The Asian Development Bank is providing support to improve north-south infrastructure, particularly the road link from Bishkek to Osh. Weaning the south away from dependence on the Uzbek part of the Ferghana Valley and increasing central control appear to be unstated goals of these policies. At the same time, however, Kyrgyzstan has favored a regional approach to Ferghana Valley development, which has been blocked by Uzbekistan.

UZBEKISTAN. Uzbekistan's macroeconomic reforms rest on three sometimes contradictory pillars: the need for social stability, closely identified with maintaining the power of the regime; the drive for self-sufficiency in critical areas such as energy and food; and the desire to diversify trade away from Russia. Reforms in Uzbekistan began slow-ly and have been characterized by abrupt changes in policy. The coun-try retreated from reform after a promising start in 1995 and 1996. The government had made steps toward significant economic revamp-ing by, for instance, easing restrictions on currency conversion. In late 1996, however, new regulations largely reversed this progress. The reimposition of strict currency controls in the fall of 1996 had a par-ticularly deleterious effect on the reform process at home and on investment from abroad.[26] An announced liberalization of currency conversion rules in July 1998 turned out to be another occasion to enact new restrictions.

Uzbekistan is still characterized by a top-down structure of eco-nomic management, with the central government retaining almost full control over even nominally privatized economic entities. For instance, "privatized" farms are still told by the government how much land they must devote to wheat and cotton, a fixed proportion of which must be sold to the government at below-market prices. And even more so than Kyrgyzstan, the government of Uzbekistan seems still to be suffering a large gap between the adoption of policies and laws and their actual enforcement. This means that many reforms exist only on paper or are implemented selectively.

Assessments of the effectiveness of Uzbekistan's gradual course of reform vary considerably.[27] Certain experts argue that Uzbekistan is well on the way to renewal, avoiding some of the pain experienced in other former Soviet republics. These analysts stress that Uzbekistan's GDP has fallen much less since independence than that of any other ex-Soviet state (the Baltic states excluded) and that it has managed to maintain economic and social stability (see Table 4.1). But most observers believe the reform process has been significantly hedged, in a kind of shell game, leaving the economy still largely in government hands and perhaps putting off the pain of real economic restructuring. In the case of land reform, privatization means little when almost all agricultural yields (and much of industrial production as well) are ded-icated to state orders, with officials determining the choice of product, price, and output levels. In the words of an Uzbek businessman we met in Namangan:

> The economy has stopped. Our country is like a car that is just sitting and rusting. The more it sits, the harder it will be to get it moving again. As I see it, there are two paths Uzbekistan can take: towards a centralized economy or a market one. If [President Islam] Karimov

wants a centralized monarchy, then let him feed us; we will be quiet. But Karimov is somewhere in between, wavering back and forth, and getting lost. . . .

The results of Tashkent-devised policies in the Ferghana Valley have been mixed. On the one hand, self-sufficiency and the desire to break free from Russia have produced several changes important for the Valley. The agricultural sector has been directed to turn over significant areas of cultivation to grain and food production rather than cotton. At the same time, through improvements in the way cotton is grown, such as greenhouses that we saw in the Ferghana oblast, the government is still hoping to keep up output of its main export earner.

But as the Council on Foreign Relations group saw in Andijan and Ferghana, productivity is kept down by the maintenance of the old collective farm system under a new name. Furthermore, the imposition of highly restrictive currency controls has had a ruinous impact on the business climate. Many new entrepreneurs have closed down shop because the exchange regime makes it impossible for them to survive. The combination of the currency controls and new tax regulations, which seek to promote larger-scale manufacturing investments in Uzbekistan, are severely hurting small- and medium-sized enterprises, the very companies that were struggling the most already. The result in the Ferghana Valley, according to a local businessman we interviewed, is that of the seven thousand small businesses that existed in Namangan alone, most are closing as unprofitable; of the five our interviewee had started, only one is still functioning. As he commented:

> Everything is done the opposite of the American experience. When the US was in crisis, you lowered taxes; according to my textbook from America, "lowering taxes raises investment and productivity." But here we do the opposite: when we are in crisis, we raise taxes. It makes no sense.

Despite the obstacles, a number of large companies are investing in the Ferghana Valley. In addition to the well-known Daewoo facility in Andijan, Coca-Cola has renovated a bottling plant in Namangan, and Turkish companies have formed joint ventures for silk production, cotton processing, sewing machines and textiles. Oil exploration in Mingbulak has attracted U.S. companies' interests, while the Japanese firm Mitsui is investing more than $100 million to improve Uzbekistan's largest oil refinery in Ferghana. But members of the Western business community told us in Tashkent that almost all foreign investors in Uzbekistan are seriously affected by the country's policy changes since late 1996 and have been unable to exert enough pressure to change the situation, even though potential large-scale new investment is already being held up.

Official Western pressure and assistance have been unable to prompt a change in course. In July 1998 the government announced new, seemingly more liberal regulations for currency conversion, but in fact further restrictions were enacted, with dire consequences for investment in and trade with Uzbekistan. U.S. assistance has made economic reform a primary focus for its efforts. Some projects have been extremely effective: making economic training available to a wide range of would-be entrepreneurs; providing loans, such as through the Central Asian American Enterprise Fund; and offering women the opportunity to become real players in the business world, however nascent that world. But Western agencies have not met the same level of success in influencing economic policy. Despite two years of working with Uzbekistan officials on a new tax code, for example, the new rules were seen as counterproductive and acknowledged even by USAID to have "significant deficiencies." The U.S. and other Western ambassadors, for their part, have continued to urge the government in Tashkent to liberalize currency conversion. In spring 1997, the IMF suspended the half of its $185 million structural adjustment loan that it had not yet disbursed. While all understand that Uzbekistan's backsliding is hurting economic reform at home and investment from abroad, political concerns—primarily, retaining administrative control of the economy and, through that, of the population—remain paramount for Uzbekistan's leaders.

TAJIKISTAN. While significant economic reforms exist on paper in Tajikistan, the government's ineffectual and overriding concern for its own security has assured that little state-sponsored transformation has taken place. At the same time, however, warlords in southern Tajikistan, as well as local government structures and businessmen in northern Tajikistan, have taken matters into their own hands, creating significant de facto privatization, though without any effective legal framework. In such a context, the line between enterprise and crime is not always easy to draw. Several members of our group noted on a May 1998 visit that the number of Mercedes and BMWs jumped as we crossed from Uzbekistan to Khujand, despite a generally poorer economy.

While official data suggest that most enterprises are still under state control, businesses are in fact quite independent and determine their markets and prices freely. Still, formal privatization is occurring slowly. According to the chairman of Tajikistan's State Committee for Management of State Property, Matlubkhon Davlatov, the slow pace is attributable to the "introduction of the national currency, lack of money among the population and work collectives, and also lack of motivation of a number of ministries and institutions, regional and district *Hukumat* [administration] in reforming of the economy of the republic."[28] While the government is beginning to reform tax structures and is working with the World Bank and other international institutions to deepen economic reform, the commitment of many officials, at all levels, must be questioned.

The often-cited entrepreneurial spirit in northern Tajikistan's Leninabad region, the country's economic powerhouse and the most industrialized part of the Ferghana Valley, appears to be alive and well, but it is encountering new obstacles. In April 1996, after an extensive trip through northern Tajikistan, several officials of the U.S. embassy in Dushanbe reported that "much grassroots privatization of land and state enterprises is occurring, with or without government acquiescence."[29] The report confirmed accounts by others, though, that the regional economy was suffering from major power cuts because of a dispute between Tajikistan and Uzbekistan over payment for electricity. This affects not only industrial facilities and homes but also farms, many of which irrigate their fields using electric-powered pumps.

What remains unclear is the extent to which the government in Dushanbe is trying to control this "grassroots privatization," and what levers it is using to do so. The May 1996 demonstrations and their aftermath focused attention on grievances by northerners, who claim that the southern-dominated government or organized crime groups are trying to muscle their way into the regional economy and exact ever higher extortion and bribes from the north's profitable trading companies and industries.[30] These pressures are clearly causing increased resentment among the business community, as well as political frustration, in northern Tajikistan.

In the realm of foreign investment, northern Tajikistan has always played the lead role in its country, and it is not surprising that the Central Asian-American Enterprise Fund's (CAAEF) first project in Tajikistan was a Pepsi-Cola plant in the north. American, Israeli, French, Indian, and other companies are active in the Leninabad region, and the range of joint ventures runs the gamut from animal fodder and textiles to gold and antimony extraction and processing. The largest single foreign investment was by the Canadian firm Nelson Gold Corporation, Ltd., which has poured approximately $54 million so far into the development of the Zarafshon gold mine. While the mine is not directly in the Ferghana Valley, it is located under the jurisdiction of the Leninabad oblast.[31] Dealings with the Dushanbe government, essential in almost all joint ventures, frustrate Leninabadi businesspeople, who believe they could attract far more foreign investment were it not for the civil war and for the Kulabi-dominated government's interference.

LAND REFORM

Uzbekistan, Kyrgyzstan, and Tajikistan have all passed land reform legislation designed to privatize most land while retaining ultimate state control of its use. All three have transformed collective and state-owned farms (*kolkhozes* and *sovkhozes*) into private and cooperative farms, with private farmers given long leases and inheritance rights to their holdings. At the same time, none has allowed outright land ownership; in practice, for various reasons analyzed below, land reform has not moved along nearly as far as it may initially appear. The large farming collectives are the main institutions of state control and the only social safety net in the rural areas, where most of the population lives. Land reform means breaking up these institutions, for which no substitutes are available. Recognizing the particular sensitivity of this issue, the Uzbekistan and Kyrgyzstan parts of the Ferghana Valley have moved especially slowly into real agricultural privatization; Tajikistan's Leninabad region has moved much faster toward private ownership of land than the rest of the country or the neighboring areas of the Valley, though more as a result of lack of state control than of policy.

On paper, Uzbekistan and Kyrgyzstan have succeeded in transforming most state farms into private collective and individual farms. Official Uzbekistan reports, for example, claim that in the Ferghana and Andijan *hakimiyats* 65 percent of land is now being cultivated by "private" farmers. Similar figures for Kyrgyzstan show that only 46 percent of the arable land in Jalalabad and 39 percent of such land in Osh is owned by private (individual or family) farms; much of the rest, however, is owned by cooperatives that would be considered "private" under Uzbekistan's definition. Reliable figures for Tajikistan are unavailable, but anecdotal reports suggest that much grassroots land reform has taken place in the north.[32] This much faster transition to genuine land privatization in northern Tajikistan probably results from a mix of desire and necessity, fostered by the relative absence of central control over events in the region and the need to find alternative sources of supplies and markets.

In Uzbekistan political control by the center and its fear of losing leverage over the rural population seem to be the main obstacles to true land reform; not surprisingly, most locals still refer to their farms as *kolkhozes*. Most agricultural production, and all grain and cotton, are still in practice sold to the state, which also remains the main supplier of agricultural inputs (seeds and fertilizers), even though producers are theoretically only required to sell 30 percent of their cotton and 50 percent of their wheat to the state (at prices far below world levels). Additionally, with the state controlling those companies allowed to engage in international trade and the supply of currency for foreign exchange, it would be difficult for producers to sell independently. Through these mechanisms, the state extracts significant resources from the impoverished agricultural sector.

The Council on Foreign Relations working group visited a farm associated with the Private Farm Association in Kuvai, Uzbekistan, in the Ferghana *hakimiyat*. The owner, a former brigadier of the collective farm before it was "privatized," explained that she had rented the land for a ten-year period and employs eighty-three people on sixty-seven hectares. It is considered a "private farm" in which the farmers own stock. The owner saw little contradiction between her private ownership and the reality that all production from the farm goes to the state, the state and state-owned cotton pressing plant set the prices, and farmers have no alternative but to accept the low prices offered.

Discussions of some members of the working group with the workers indicated that they did not understand the difference between what is private and what is not; they recognized that the farm was private, but they also said they belonged to the collective. They were visibly upset when one member of our group told them that the owner of the farm has the right to buy and sell agricultural production without their agreement. In short, a collective consciousness still permeates the new private farms. The woman who was their boss before remains their boss today. And she remains under the same obligations: she must hire a certain number of workers and sell cotton to the state at its prices. To keep her under control, the state grants her no rights to water, and she has the right to the land for only ten years. By law, she must sell much of her harvest to the government; in practice, she sells it all to the government.[33]

An early policy initiative of President Karimov's, and apparently one of the initial sources of his popularity, was to grant every farm family a small plot of land for private use. Although the amount offered was very small, it relieved at least a bit of the pressure from the rural population for increased access to private land. At the same time, as various analysts have pointed out, these private plots are not sufficient for subsistence, let alone commercial use. A total of 800,000 hectares was distributed, with the average family receiving just 0.33 hectares, or 0.81 acres, of land. Given the large size of Uzbek families, this is, as a Russian newspaper put it, "a drop in the bucket." [34] Furthermore, with a rapidly growing population, these plots will be further subdivided among family members in the future. Despite the scarcity of arable land, the presidential initiative shows Karimov's adroit handling of the land reform issue at a critical juncture. It also shows how the government of Uzbekistan is committed to keeping tight central control over land privatization, in order both to ensure social stability and to enforce national priorities (such as moving from cotton to grain production) in the agricultural sector.

The main obstacles to Kyrgyzstan's land reform process are quite different, more a reflection of the Soviet legacy and fears of ethnic problems than of a desire to retain direct state control of agricultural production. Ever since the 1990 Osh riots, how to parcel out land has been of prime concern to the government of Kyrgyzstan, and it is thus not surprising that land reform has moved more slowly in the south than in other parts of the country. Since most of the collective farms were either overwhelmingly Uzbek or Kyrgyz, and since much of the land privatization effort so far has turned on transforming some collective land into family farms, the reform has not provoked direct ethnic confrontations over land distribution.

As land registries are established and land becomes a marketable asset, however, significant concerns remain among both Uzbeks and Kyrgyz over what reform will mean for them as ethnic groups. Many Kyrgyz, who already believe that Uzbeks control much of the best land, fear that the Uzbeks will use their allegedly greater wealth to buy out Kyrgyz land. Uzbeks, on the other hand, worry that the local and national governments, dominated by Kyrgyz, will force them off their land and redistribute it to Kyrgyz; exactly that kind of action triggered the 1990 Osh events. So far, no policies have addressed the ethnic aspects of this issue directly, and the economic strategy reports for Osh and Jalalabad aided by UNDP do not even mention competition among nationalities in their discussion of land reform. [35] Finally, some Kyrgyz appear to be opposed to the very principle of privatizing land, as they believe that privatization will make it easier for the Uzbeks, whose birthrates are higher, to push them further into the mountains over time.

Since Western aid agencies and NGOs are assisting these efforts at land reform, the West is firmly associated in the region with both the benefits and costs of the reform process. Western assistance has come mostly in the form of legal advice on how to draft laws on land reform, especially in Kyrgyzstan, but some has gone beyond that. For example, in October 1996 the World Bank (through its International Development Agency) helped set up the Kyrgyz Agricultural Finance Corporation to facilitate lending to farmers. This effort was complemented by a Caritas pilot project in Jalalabad to provide technical and business advice to farmers, backed with a $200,000 revolving fund for rural credit.[36] USAID's "farmer-to-farmer" programs in the Valley—in the oblasts of Osh in Kyrgyzstan (connecting local farmers with the Oregon Farm Bureau) and Ferghana in Uzbekistan (with the Kentucky Farm Board)—have initiated projects to assist private farmers in the Ferghana Valley and Syr Darya regions. The European Union's TACIS agency has a similar project.

Given the constraints on true privatization, however, these and other projects are themselves controversial. While some may have helped prepare the soil for fundamental restructuring to take shape in the future, according to several area commentators some of these aid programs suggest that Westerners have accepted land reform half measures as real privatization, even though farms are not private in practice. With Westerners providing loans and expertise, one Uzbek observer in the Ferghana Valley asked whether "Americans are simply helping to create new collective farms." On the other hand, he cautioned, to the extent that the West has begun to support true privatization, this must be pursued carefully, as it could spark instability. Particularly in southern Kyrgyzstan, where the issue of land distribution has already led to hundreds of deaths in an outburst of interethnic violence, few things could be more dangerous than to push for rapid, complete privatization of land without taking other considerations into account. This is a sensitive subject that requires that every program have a full understanding of the ethnic and political realities as well as the economics of land privatization.

WATER REFORM

Against the backdrop of the Aral Sea disaster, the independent states of Central Asia have made great strides toward better water management. Given the importance of irrigation in an area that receives little rain, and the absence of rational water allocation in the Soviet era, water policy reform is a likely source of friction among various local groups, as well as between these groups and the government. In practice, most of the effective power for implementation of rules regarding water use remains with the ministries and collective farm administrations, which are responsible for carrying out government directives.

Pricing water, a policy often recommended by foreign advisers, remains controversial. Water has been allocated without charge through administrative decisions, a system that encourages waste. Some form of pricing will ultimately be necessary to give consumers an incentive to use this scarce resource wisely and to pay for the maintenance and improvement of the vast system used for its distribution. As with land reform, however, sudden and drastic implementation of new water pricing laws could have a destabilizing effect because enterprises and individuals may not have the financial resources to pay water charges. Fair and comprehensive water pricing may be impossible in the short run in any case, since many areas lack equipment for measuring water consumption.

In Uzbekistan in particular, the lack of a market, even a controlled or regulated one, in water supplies is one of the primary obstacles to independent farming. Even if farmers assert their right to private land (difficult in itself), they still face great difficulties getting the local water officials, usually tied to the larger collective farms, to provide them with the water they need. Reports indicate that the enforcement of water pricing laws is used more as a carrot or stick to ensure political loyalty or elicit bribes than as a real means to distribute water efficiently or increase state revenues.

For the Kyrgyzstan part of the Ferghana Valley, a principal problem is decentralization of the water supply system, which has given nominal control over water to local and regional authorities, who often have little or no technical expertise or funding. The Ministry of Agriculture and Water Resources, which is responsible for the operation and maintenance of the main systems, is now funded through a system of water charges.[37] Those charges, however, have produced only 20 percent of the revenues needed to cover basic maintenance requirements; no money has become available for improving or expanding the irrigation and water use system. A UNDP-aided strategy report for southern Kyrgyzstan comments: "Funding from the Republican budget is provided to meet the costs of capital works and also to cover the operating costs of large-scale pumps, although such provision has fallen to a fraction of former levels."[38]

As in other parts of the world, these matters are complex, and all three countries, with the help of the international community, are seeking to manage water resources better and reduce waste. Caritas, TACIS, and other organizations have brought to the region Western water specialists who have dealt with similar problems in the Middle East and the American Southwest. The World Bank has examined water-sharing arrangements in the Ferghana Valley, and NGOs such as ISAR have worked on local management issues. Some advocate organizing water users' associations and tying water rights to land tenure. In southern Kyrgyzstan, TACIS and Caritas are working to set up such associations, and UNDP is assisting in efforts to compile land and water registries.[39] The challenge is to shape these disparate approaches so that they fit the economic, political, and social realities of the Valley, where water concerns are so potentially volatile.

UNEMPLOYMENT

In all three countries the combination of a rapidly growing population and a sharply declining economy has meant that employment, especially of youth, is one of the most explosive social issues. In Kyrgyzstan's Osh province, officials have attempted to implement policies dealing with the critical unemployment situation. In 1991 the national government created an Employment Service to monitor the level of unemployment, provide job training and information, and administer special job creation initiatives. Programs such as these, however, currently help only a fraction of the unemployed: fewer than 10 percent of all unemployed received benefits during the six months preceding one survey, and fewer than 5 percent had participated in any retraining courses or job creation schemes between January 1995 and mid-1996.[40]

Uzbekistan's employment program is off to a slower start. Labor exchanges have been set up, but they appear to be overwhelmed by the demand for their services. Many unemployed persons are not receiving benefits or are only getting them months late. Benefits themselves, moreover, are meager. In Andijan, we were told by the head of the employment agency there that benefits would purchase two eggs per day—"two eggs alone—with no tea, no bread." Job placement schemes often do not exist, "and where they have been drawn up, they are gathering dust in the recesses of office cabinets."[41] At the same time, some of the pressure is apparently relieved by the informal *mardikor* labor markets, where people are hired for occasional jobs without official documentation and paid directly by the private contractor for their services.

President Karimov has recognized the potential for political trouble that the unemployed represent, especially in the Ferghana Valley. In Central Asia, however, unlike in other developing regions, people have tended not to migrate en masse to large cities, and the problem of unemployment and underemployment is most intense in largely rural zones like the Ferghana Valley. The inefficiency of the collective farms (including those that have been formally privatized) in part disguises their function as the only social safety net for the unemployed. As early as 1994 the president publicly stated his desire to locate labor-intensive manufacturing industries in the Valley to absorb the surplus workforce. Creating jobs has been one of the main purposes in guiding foreign investors, such as the Daewoo corporation, to build their plants there. Yet, considering the scope of the problem in the Uzbekistan part of the Valley, that area still is not receiving enough foreign investment in manufacturing and processing industries to make a large difference, and economic policies are inhibiting their expansion.

EFFORTS AGAINST CORRUPTION AND THE DRUG TRADE

The growth of narcotics trafficking, corruption, and organized crime in this region has led to a number of domestic and international efforts to bring them under control. All the presidents in the region have denounced smuggling and the drug trade, and some corrupt officials have been removed. In addition, a small army of Western law enforcement officials have been training local police officers in drug interdiction, organized crime investigations, and fighting corruption, while others have focused on helping to institute a workable rule of law.

New Western campaigns promise to address problems of narcotics trafficking more aggressively than before. Until recently, drug control assistance had been limited mainly to training courses for customs officers and police personnel, financed by the United States and United Kingdom. But this area has become an increasing priority for the United States, as demonstrated by the channeling of Freedom Support Act and other funds to expand such training courses. Perhaps the most ambitious program on the international front is the two-year UN International Drug Control Program project initiated in 1996. The roughly $2 million project is designed to help strengthen interdiction capacities in the border areas of Kyrgyzstan, Tajikistan, and Uzbekistan. It is directed toward supporting regional law enforcement cooperation in the three neighboring areas of Osh, Murghab (Tajikistan), and Andijan and "the construction of a new border post, improving cross border telecommunication facilities and mobility of border control forces."[42]

These programs may have little effect, however, if they do not commit the individual countries to concrete, verifiable steps. All of the programs to train and equip law enforcement will be useless or worse if law enforcement itself is corrupt. Past efforts have failed because they were not blessed with a full understanding of the situation, lacked an effective on-the-ground presence for monitoring and oversight, and, of course, were not backed up by local political will. For example, one westerner who has been living in Kyrgyzstan for several years noted that the European Union had provided the country with highly trained drug-sniffing dogs, all of whom died within five months. The Kyrgyz said the death of the dogs was due to the climate, but this observer is sure that "the dogs were poisoned or killed" because local officials do not want this capability.

The westerner's comments were underscored by the former governor of Osh, Janysh Rustambekov, who noted that the main target of these efforts is only one road (from Murghab to Osh) where traffic, two thousand trucks per month, is relatively light. "We talk so much about *one road!*" he told us. "It would be so easy to close it; the rest would be insignificant. But no one *wants* to shut it. A lot of military forces are involved in all of this, including Russian border guards and the Russian military." These observers argue that by turning training into "how-to" courses (in the words of one UN official) on illicit activities, and by providing equipment, these efforts could well make things worse.

ENVIRONMENTAL ACTIVISM

Nongovernmental organizations in Uzbekistan and Kyrgyzstan have undertaken some small-scale efforts to deal with soil, air, and water pollution. These projects both conduct environmental cleanups and try to increase awareness among the local populations about the extent of problems in order to encourage local initiative. One of the most successful has been the ongoing endeavor by ISAR, an American-based NGO, to fund small projects and work with colleagues in the field to confront the vast environmental distress facing the population throughout Central Asia, including the Ferghana Valley. Indeed, ISAR is one of the few NGOs to have had a permanent presence in the Valley. Jointly with its Central Asian counterparts, the group provided small grants (sometimes as small as $50) to local environmental activists for a range of activities and provided larger partnership grants so that local and Western groups and individuals could tackle these problems jointly. The program was frequently named by USAID as a model, but because of USAID cutbacks for environmental work, ISAR's office in the Ferghana Valley was closed, and future funding for the program in Central Asia is uncertain.

REGIONAL ECONOMIC COOPERATION

Some initiatives have begun to address economic and social issues on a regional basis. For example, Uzbekistan and Kyrgyzstan, together with Kazakstan, established the Central Asian Union aimed at promoting greater economic integration in 1994. Russia and Tajikistan became observers in August 1996, and in January 1998 Tajikistan indicated its intention to join. Uzbekistan and Kyrgyzstan have also cosponsored a binational technical college in Osh. Another venture involves improving the road that connects Andijan to Kashgar, China, via Osh and building a railroad along the same route. Uzbekistan is attaching high hopes to this project, which will provide an alternative to export routes via Russia and Iran. Some Kyrgyz expressed concern to us about a possible Uzbekistan-China alliance at Kyrgyzstan's expense, and they favor a different route from that proposed by the Uzbeks. Nonetheless, the planned road and rail links could provide a major economic boost to the Valley as a whole.

But proposals for broader economic and political cooperation specifically in the Valley have met with resistance, mainly from Uzbekistan. Tashkent rejected the UNDP's Ferghana Valley Development Program, which is intended to coordinate policy across international borders as well as to establish ongoing forums for dispute resolution in the Valley. In an interview with our project director, the Uzbekistan minister of foreign affairs expressed fears that the program might create or exacerbate problems where few currently exist. While the UNDP project might require development and modification, we describe in Chapter 3 why we believe that this concept or something similar should be developed.

On the commercial side, discussions to construct a plant in Osh to manufacture parts for the Daewoo plant in Andijan, just across the border, have been on hold for some time. Some Kyrgyzstan local officials were enthusiastic about the project; others cautioned that much depended on Uzbekistan president Karimov's personal decision, and that he seemed unlikely to support the idea. These examples illustrate how difficult cooperation has become for those in the area.

On energy and water, the record of cooperation has been mixed. On the one hand, the Tajikistan and Kyrgyzstan parts of the Valley have experienced disruptions in energy supplies, as the government of Uzbekistan began to demand full, immediate payment for its gas at world prices. The inability of those governments to pay led to widespread gas shutoffs in the winters of 1994 and 1995. In 1995, the Tajikistan government responded to the gas cutoffs by demanding high transit payments for electricity traveling from central Uzbekistan through northern Tajikistan on its way to the Uzbekistan part of the Valley. Thanks to the disagreement, electricity was cut off to Tajikistan's Leninabad region with great frequency during an unusually cold winter, resulting in orders to heat public buildings to only 5 degrees Celsius (41 degrees Fahrenheit) and often closing down the area's industrial enterprises. Subsequent efforts to resolve these kinds of disputes look promising: in May 1996, the three states agreed on the purchase of electricity from Kyrgyzstan and, for the first time, on the distribution of sufficient amounts of water.

Likewise, an agreement on water was negotiated as part of the Central Asian Union. The Union's ambitious program—harmonizing tariffs, reducing obstacles to labor and capital flows, and the creation, in 1998, of a single economic area—was slow to get off the ground but has gained momentum. Since 1996, under the leadership of its Almaty-based Interstate Council, the Union has become far more active and may have helped to significantly increase trade among these three states.[43] It has also taken on political and military issues, and its frequent summit meetings are one of the more important forums for discussing peace in Central Asia. While, except for the above-mentioned water agreement, the Union does not directly affect the Ferghana Valley at the moment, it has the potential to increase trade and reduce border restrictions there. Its institutions could contribute meaningfully to any regional development plan.

Foreigners have played a mixed role in the area of regional cooperation, as we found during several visits to the region. On the one hand, a limited number of international organizations are mobilizing efforts for action across the Ferghana Valley. These include UNDP, which has established the Ferghana Valley Development Program, in which Uzbekistan thus far declines to participate; the UN Drug Control Program; the office of the High Commissioner on National Minorities of the OSCE, which has mounted some initiatives on interethnic relations in Kyrgyzstan; and the UNHCR, which has established a post in Osh. Most other programs, foreign and local NGOs, and foreign investors, however, tend to work in and on only one state; if they do have representatives in more than one, the coordination is vertical—to the national capital—rather than lateral, to other offices in the Valley. While this is understandable, it is also an obstacle to increased coordination and better awareness of how problems in one area of the Ferghana Valley affect other areas.

— 5 —

POLITICAL FACTORS

While all of the economic and social issues detailed in the previous chapter have political consequences and causes, other, more overtly political questions also affect the prospects for stability in the Ferghana Valley. Leaders invoke identities like regionalism, Islam, and ethnicity to mobilize people to deal with problems through either cooperation or conflict. How grievances are expressed is shaped in turn by the general political environment, which in Central Asia includes increasingly powerful presidencies and trends of diminishing human rights and freedom of the press. Restrictions on liberty are partly a response to the implicit threat of strife, which has also helped define the task of creating national security forces for these newly independent states. Military organization and doctrine will affect the prospect for stability and, in particular, the potential for spread of localized conflicts to other parts of the region.

OVERVIEW OF POLITICAL SYSTEMS

Their shared Soviet history and geographic location have left Uzbekistan, Kyrgyzstan, and Tajikistan with certain common political conditions and challenges. All three regimes are trying to stabilize their rule in the midst of socioeconomic crises, regional instability, and potential (or actual) ethnic and religious quarrels. In all of these states, the increasingly impoverished population stares across a growing chasm separating the haves from the have-nots, and, more often than not, wealth is inextricably related to corruption and access to political power. As in economic policy, however, since independence Uzbekistan, Kyrgyzstan, and Tajikistan have pursued three very different political paths, with the result that the ways in which pressures are manifested and the fault lines along which they could potentially ignite are distinct in each state.

Politics and policy are personality-driven and closely centered on the person of the president in all three of these countries (as well as the other states of Central Asia, Kazakstan and Turkmenistan). In Uzbekistan President Islam Karimov's authoritarian rule seemed for a time to be remarkably stable, but the outbreak of violence in the Ferghana Valley in 1997 and the bombings of February 1999 have shaken that record. President Karimov has not created a personality cult on the scale of his Turkmenistan counterpart, but he enjoys personal control over domestic political developments and major economic contracts. Simultaneously, however, the president has succeeded in creating a veneer of decentralization, insulating himself from criticism, which is instead directed at local and regional officials. The result is that President Karimov has conveyed an image that he sincerely desires democratic reforms and a free press, but that officials in charge of implementing the policies are subverting his goals. In fact, it is illegal to defame the honor of the president in Uzbekistan. Such a law exists in each Central Asian state, though Kyrgyzstan's President Askar Akaev rarely makes use of it.

The concentration on the person of the president in any of these countries has direct repercussions for stability, as it tends to make policy implementation more arbitrary. The personality-driven political climate of Uzbekistan (and most other former Soviet republics) impedes institution building and establishment of the rule of law. If one-man rule creates short-term stability, does this imply that the sudden death or incapacitation of the ruler will lead to crisis? The experience of many third world countries is ambiguous, but securing effective political processes and practices and implementing laws fairly is likely to be a better long-term guarantor of stability.

As in the economic sphere, Kyrgyzstan's political system has been, by contrast with Uzbekistan, the West's role model for Central Asia, with genuine political pluralism, a free press, guarantees of human rights, and a president unburdened with a Communist apparatchik mind-set. In the past few years, however, the Akaev regime appears to have backtracked. The President had his term extended, albeit semidemocratically; some newspapers have been closed; and some journalists and opposition figures have been arrested and tried on criminal charges, including criminal libel. There are also persistent reports of corruption, reaching up to the highest levels of government.

The Tajikistan civil war has left much of that country in ruins, not just economically but also politically. So far-reaching has been the disintegration that in certain ways an independent, post-Soviet state has still not been established there. With a government largely dependent on Russia and on armed groups that were involved in the most brutal fighting of the civil war, the current peace agreement is only a first, small step toward building Tajikistan's statehood. The peace agreement at best marks a transition from the authoritarian, arbitrary rule of the southern Kulabi group, headed by President Imomali Rakhmonov, toward greater pluralism.

While religious and ethnic differences are likely to continue to play important political roles in Tajikistan, the more salient concern for the country as a whole is regionalism. As will be explored in greater detail below, regional divides are both an issue in themselves and a way of expressing mounting discontent with the social and economic problems that the civil war has exacerbated. The Leninabad region, with its long history of dominating Tajikistan's governing structures and economy, has experienced a precipitous industrial decline exceeded only by its obliteration as a player on the national political scene. The exclusion from the peace agreement of parties claiming to represent the north reinforces the impression that Tajikistan's most important schism is not religious or ethnic but regional.

QUESTIONS OF IDENTITY: FISSURES AND FAULT LINES

Discussions of stability and the fault lines along which grievances may find expression often focus on identities. But the divisions among religious, ethnic, and regional groups are not always clear-cut. Instead, multiple and crosscutting identities complicate the ability to sort out where the most serious schisms in fact may lie. Indeed, we are all a compilation of different identities—defined by our region, country, religion, gender, and a host of other markers whose relevance is often contextual. Ethnic Kyrgyz in southern Kyrgyzstan, for example, may view themselves as Kyrgyz vis-à-vis Uzbeks, as southerners vis-à-vis people from northern Kyrgyzstan, as Muslims or Central Asians vis-à-vis Russians, and even as of a particular clan or tribe as distinct from other Kyrgyz. Serious differences have divided even small communities among themselves.

These competing or complementary identities affect all relationships and the prospects for instability or peace. Nevertheless, the predominant fault lines in various parts of the Ferghana Valley differ markedly. Political Islam has been involved in past and recent conflicts in Andijan and Namangan and remains important generally in the Uzbekistan part of the Valley. In southern Kyrgyzstan, by contrast, people spoke of ethnicity as the main dividing line, and some Kyrgyz depicted Islamic activism as part of an Uzbek threat. Ethnic questions involve not only politics (for example, representation in the government and administration) but many other aspects of life, from the bazaar to religion. And in Tajikistan, the concern seems to be more the relationship of Leninabad to other regions of the country. For the people of the Ferghana Valley, however, split among three sovereign states for the first time, all of these polarizing forces are fluid and all present new political challenges.

ISLAM

No area of Central Asia has a higher concentration of practicing Muslims than the Ferghana Valley. The reported rates of Islamic observance are highest in the Andijan and Namangan *hakimiyats* of Uzbekistan.[1] What part in politics Islam and Muslim believers will play in the years ahead is one of the most controversial debates in the Ferghana Valley and among those analyzing events there. Some observers have rushed to see a "fundamentalist" threat to the region, as in other parts of the world, and the rulers of all three states have also expressed concern over that danger. At the same time, Islam is also acting as a critical *stabilizer* in a region wracked by social, economic, and political change. It is once again resuming its traditional role as a way of life and anchor of local communities.

As leaders throughout the region have turned away from the official atheism of the Soviet period, they have tried to promote forms of Islam that legitimate their power and policies while suppressing what they perceive as antiregime political Islam. The line between the two is not always clear, however. The current government of Tajikistan fought a civil war against Islamists; they are now supposed to share power under the peace agreement. President Akaev has allowed Muslim activists more freedom than any other ruler in Central Asia, but consequently Uzbekistan has expressed concern that Osh may serve as a center of subversion for its own portion of the Ferghana Valley. President Karimov has chosen to draw a distinction between legitimate and political Islam by considering popular, independent Muslim leaders, even if they are not overtly political figures, as threats. But this could cause a backlash among Muslims who otherwise might be more quiescent in the face of political power.

In Kyrgyzstan and northern Tajikistan, Islamic divisions among the titular nationalities are not as strong as in Uzbekistan. In Tajikistan as a whole, of course, political Islam has been more important than in any other post-Soviet state. Political Islam in Tajikistan has found most of its supporters not in the Ferghana Valley but among those tracing their origin to the mountainous areas of Qarategin or Gharm in southern Tajikistan. The separations in southern Kyrgyzstan fall more along ethnic lines, though a number of Kyrgyz sounded the alarm to our group about the growth of Islamic movements among Uzbek youth in the south.

In Uzbekistan, however, there are not only splits between some Islamic leaders and the state but also deep divisions within the Muslim community, usually centered around the poles of "official" and "parallel" Islam in the Uzbekistan part of the Valley. Indeed, one does not have to look far to find open hostility between the official mullahs and "Wahhabis." This term, a derogatory reference to the puritanical version of Islam enforced in Saudi Arabia, is used rather indiscriminately to refer to Islamic activists, implying both that their views are extreme and opposed to Central Asian traditions and that they may receive foreign support.

In all of these countries, policy responses to the perceived threat of political Islam have been a balancing act between claims to support Islam as a faith and attempts to co-opt and control it in order to limit the potential for any emergence of an antigovernment, political Islam. In Uzbekistan, President Karimov has been actively promoting religion and religious activities through the construction of mosques, support of the hajj (pilgrimage) to Mecca (though the number of plane tickets is limited), and the granting of considerable financial and political clout to the official Islamic clergy, who in return remain under tight control. Funds from Muslim sources abroad, especially Turkey and Saudi Arabia, are funneled through the state bureaucracy to the official clergy, creating a dependency on the part of the official mullahs and an obvious lever of control for the government.

The president has also "Islamicized" himself, transforming himself from a Communist Party leader committed to a policy of atheism to a devout Muslim who took his oath of office on the Qur'an and has gone to Mecca. On a visit to a newly built neighborhood mosque in Andijan, members of the Council on Foreign Relations group heard local Muslim leaders boast that President Karimov was the only world leader taken into the inner sanctum of the Kaaba in Mecca by King Fahd of Saudi Arabia.

At the same time, in a way reminiscent of the Soviet era, the Karimov government is trying to rework the message of Islam to suit its needs. Some on the scene have commented that the message in community mosques has been watered down to focus on family relations and physical rituals without truly exploring the content of Islamic teachings. Local mullahs say that they are occasionally requested by government officials to ask the faithful to support President Karimov's policies or to oppose "extremism."[2] Despite this association with the government, at least some of the official mullahs seem to have a considerable following, perhaps reflecting many believers' unwillingness to back more demanding religious leaders. Besides, the official mullahs offer access to much-valued services (official weddings, the pilgrimage to Mecca). Others, however, dismiss the official mullahs as stooges of the government and accuse them of concentrating on nonreligious themes, ignoring the Qur'an.

If the widespread presence of official mullahs represents the Uzbekistan government's "carrot" with respect to Islam, Tashkent has also shown that it carries a large "stick," which it has often been willing to use, especially in the Ferghana Valley. Uzbekistan has banned political parties based on religion, like all of the countries of the region, though this provision is supposed to be lifted in Tajikistan.[3] As part of its declared policy to prevent political Islam from organizing, the government has used various methods of intimidation. Hundreds of Islamic activists have been jailed, and at least six have disappeared.[4]

The first to disappear, Abdullo Utaev, led the Uzbekistan branch of what was originally the all-Soviet Islamic Renaissance Party. He was abducted in 1992, the first year of independence, and his whereabouts remain a mystery. Additionally, many belonging to Namangan's Adolat ("Justice") movement, members of which were among those who briefly seized control of the former oblast party committee building in a November 1991 demonstration, remain in detention, where they reportedly are singled out for worse treatment than other prisoners.[5] We were told by some in Namangan of the activists' popularity, in particular because the period when Adolat was active was marked by a relative absence of crime, and many of the more corrupt officials were pushed aside.

One of the most revered independent religious leaders in the entire Valley, Andijan's Sheikh Abduvoli Qori Mirzoev, and his assistant, Ramazon Matkarimov, disappeared at Tashkent's airport in August 1995 while on their way to a conference in Moscow. Neither have been heard from since. In September 1997, another assistant of Mirzoev, Nematjon Parpiev, also disappeared.[6] The CFR working group spoke to the son of Abduvoli Mirzoev, who talked about the kidnapping of his father two years before, which he claimed was followed by the arrest of more than one hundred Mirzoev supporters. Soon after the disappearance, his father's popular Jom'i mosque was closed. It has since been used as a dumping ground for construction materials—a decision recapitulating Soviet times, when mosques were converted to secular use or destroyed.

Most recently, perhaps as part of the crackdown after the December 1997 killings in Namangan, an important religious leader in Tashkent also disappeared, as did his thirteen-year-old son. Obidkhon Nazarov was the imam (prayer leader) of the Tukhtaboi mosque, which was closed by the authorities. In early 1995 his residence was reportedly under constant surveillance by vehicles with no registration. He and his son, Khusnutdin, have not been seen in public since March 5, 1998. Neither his associates nor human rights groups have been able to verify if he is in detention or in hiding. The government of Uzbekistan denies knowledge of his whereabouts.[7]

These policies of Uzbekistan's government have led some Muslim activists to move to the Kyrgyzstan part of the Valley. Especially around Jalalabad, they have established their own mosques and religious schools (madrasahs), with an overwhelmingly ethnic Uzbek following.[8] Their activities have prompted Uzbekistani pressure on Kyrgyz authorities in Osh and Jalalabad to clamp down on the exiles. Over the long run, the presence of militant Islamic proselytizers may also increase Uzbek-Kyrgyz friction. Already, as we heard in Osh and from the head of the Kyrgyz Peace Research Center, Uzbeks often claim to be "better" Muslims than the Kyrgyz, whose nomadic past has given them a different (and less lengthy) Islamic experience; mosques and madrasahs are apparently increasingly segregated by ethnicity.

Tajikistan and Afghanistan may also be a temporary home to exiled Uzbek Islamic leaders. There are frequent, if unconfirmed, reports that several hundred Islamic activists from Namangan joined Tajik fighters in Afghanistan. We were told that Tohirjon Yuldashev, one of the leaders of the Adolat movement, fled the country but continues to have a considerable following in Namangan. The government of Uzbekistan has claimed that he was one of the leaders of the "Wahhabi" group that carried out the 1997 assassinations, though Yuldashev has denied this.[9] The creation of a coalition government in Tajikistan that included the Islamic party could be a catalyst for greater activism on the part of

Islamic groups throughout the region, notably in the Uzbekistan part of the Valley.[10]

With the exception of Afghanistan, the foreign influence on political Islam has, to date, been limited. Contrary to widespread stereotypes, Iran has been one of the least important players. The theological differences between Iran's official Shi'a and Central Asia's Sunni Islam largely account for why Iran does not seem to have made significant efforts to support Islamic groups in the region. Additionally, Tehran appears more interested at present in pursuing commercial and trade ties with these states, which could be endangered by support for fundamentalist groups. Even before the high-profile government campaign that followed the December 1997 assassinations, we found that there were frequent accusations on the part of official religious figures in the Uzbekistan parts of the Valley that "Wahhabi" groups were receiving large amounts of money from Saudi Arabia and Pakistan. The government itself is sending students to religious schools abroad, mostly in Turkey, Egypt, and Saudi Arabia, where they may absorb ideas other than those the government intended.

In the aftermath of the 1997 assassinations, the government has become more repressive toward unofficial or parallel Islam. During the mass arrests in the Ferghana Valley, men were forced to shave off or cut their beards, and women were harassed for wearing full veils. At least a dozen women students were also expelled from the university in Tashkent for refusing to remove their veils.[11] In May 1998 the government enacted a law barring the use of unregistered places of worship, requiring that all clergy be registered with and approved by the government and prohibiting the wearing of "clerical garb" by anyone other than registered clergy. While the law is written without reference to any particular religion, its enforcement is directed at Muslims outside the official Islamic bodies. In the wake of the February 1999 bombings, President Karimov warned against erroneous teachings in mosques and ordered local officials to pay close attention to what is preached there.

These repressive dictates are directed not only against the violent activities of a small group but against the much broader revival of interest in and practice of Islam that has taken place since independence, mainly in the Ferghana Valley. Thousands of new unofficial mosques were constructed; preachers have been invited to weddings; life cycle rituals are increasingly celebrated in a more genuine Islamic fashion (with Islamic preaching rather than drinking); and Ramadan, the month of fasting, is beginning to be observed. In the market in Namangan our group saw many books for sale explaining basic elements of Islam, such as how to pray. We also visited one of the newly built mosques in Andijan. At least in our presence, all discussion on politics was strongly in favor of the government and against "Wahhabis," but the young men in particular were clearly seeking meaning and direction in their ancestral faith. This revival evidently has deep roots in society. Repression is likely to politicize rather than neutralize it.

ETHNICITY

Ethnic conflict has generally been taken in the West to be the prime risk factor for conflict in the entire former Soviet Union, including Central Asia. Yet considering the potential for trouble in the region and violent incidents in the late Soviet period, there has been relatively little interethnic strife since the collapse of the old regime. In part, this may be because Uzbeks, Tajiks, and Kyrgyz have a centuries-old history of relative ethnic harmony. In northern Tajikistan, for example, there has been so much intermarriage between Uzbeks and Tajiks that many inhabitants are hard-pressed to state to which nationality they belong. The violence that did take place, in the Tajik civil war, for instance, was primarily among different parties from the same ethnic group.

At the same time, the creation of independent states, based, in principle at least, on the concept of nationality, has seriously complicated ethnic relations. Although all of the states have responded by papering over some of the differences, such as differentiating between "Uzbek" (an ethnic term) and "Uzbekistani" (referring to the country and its citizens), the fundamental challenge of building a national identity not based on the ethnicity of the titular group remains. Uzbekistan, with its relatively homogeneous population, has been the most direct in promoting its national destiny as the state of the Uzbeks. Despite fears by some of his neighbors, though, President Karimov has not sought a "Greater Uzbekistan." Ethnic Uzbek politicians in Kyrgyzstan told us that President Karimov had told them clearly that they were citizens of Kyrgyzstan and should look to Bishkek, not Tashkent, to solve their problems. With the departure of the Meskhetian Turks, the likelihood of ethnicity being a source of future conflict in the Uzbekistan part of the Valley seems remote. Similarly, in northern Tajikistan, ethnic divisions between Uzbeks and Tajiks appear to be less important than other schisms, especially regional ones.

By contrast, while Kyrgyzstan's public policy has been oriented toward diminishing the importance of nationality, the potential for ethnic conflict in its sector of the Ferghana Valley appears to be more salient than in the sectors of the other two countries. Efforts to reduce the salience of ethnicity are displayed in the decision of the Kyrgyzstan government to make "nationality" (that is, ethnicity) an optional item in the internal passport. Representing a significant break from the Soviet past, this practice might make it easier to establish a system whereby ethnicity becomes less relevant to hiring and other public decisions. Ethnic minorities, however, worry that omission of "nationality" on the passport will simply make it easier for the government to ignore them, since statistics indicating the ethnic origins of people in different occupations may no longer be available. Yet, despite these efforts, greater openness, and a more complex ethnic mix in the population as a whole, the ethnic divides may be becoming wider in Kyrgyzstan than in its more authoritarian neighbors.

In southern Kyrgyzstan, most economic, social, and political grievances are expressed along ethnic lines, and we found a more palpable sense of interethnic tension there than in the rest of the Ferghana Valley. While the memory of the Osh riots makes all parties aware of the dangers of communal conflict, Uzbeks and Kyrgyz continue to mistrust each other. While individual views differ, as elsewhere, Uzbeks often express fear of the (growing) political power of the Kyrgyz, and Kyrgyz resent the Uzbeks' perceived relative wealth. In interviews with ethnic Kyrgyz and Uzbeks in Osh, as well as with international officials there, we found numerous indications that, despite official efforts to bridge the gaps in understanding, interethnic relations are deteriorating. One foreign officer estimated that marriages between Uzbeks and Kyrgyz, which had accounted for 15 percent of all marriages before 1990, now almost never occur.

In addition to economic and social policies, one of the most sensitive and problematic areas is the allocation of official positions among ethnic groups in Kyrgyzstan. Kyrgyz officials told us that, while some improvements are still needed, there is now significant Uzbek representation in the local and regional administrations. By contrast, Uzbek politicians and activists claimed that their community continues to be severely underrepresented there, as well as in the police, courts, and other official bodies.

Kyrgyzstan has, however, instituted a number of mechanisms to address these complaints. Chief among these has been the establishment after the 1990 Osh events of "cultural centers" for the ethnic communities in southern Kyrgyzstan. The purposes of the centers are to perpetuate cultures of individual ethnic groups ("to raise the culture of Uzbeks and revive historical values," according to Dovron Sabirov, deputy head of the Uzbek center) and to reinforce the official doctrine of friendship among peoples. According to the deputy governor of Osh, Nuriyla Joldosheva: "We live by a policy that Kyrgyzstan is our common home. . . . We have ten various cultural centers where people can get together under the umbrella of various cultural aspirations."

But while these cultural centers do provide an outlet for airing grievances, there is no means provided for resolving them, as the centers themselves are barred from political activity. Because there is no other resource, ethnic Uzbek parliamentarian Alisher Sabirov told us, "many citizens come to the cultural center for help with their economic, political or daily problems. But we have no power to resolve these problems. We are forced just to listen to them." The centers cannot act as intermediaries, bringing grievances of minorities to the government like an ombudsman, although, in the words of Dovron Sabirov, "it would be good if the government recognized us as a channel of communication." These centers are also poor conduits for dialogue among the different ethnic groups. Dovron Sabirov says that the centers do not organize any programs among different ethnic groups to promote conflict resolution. According to the head of the Kyrgyz center in Osh, "We do not divide each other by having such programs. We all support President Akaev."

Frustration with the limitations of the cultural centers has led several of their members to consider creating a political party based on the centers to channel dissent into the political system. Unlike Uzbekistan, which bans ethnic-based parties, Kyrgyzstan's constitution permits them while forbidding political parties based on religion. Were an ethnic Uzbek political party established, it could be a vehicle for the Uzbeks to exercise greater political influence. For the same reason, however, it could also result in a severe backlash from Kyrgyz nationalists. In another example of how efforts to placate one minority can upset another, current efforts by the Kyrgyz government and parliament to make Russian an official language alongside Kyrgyz have been criticized by ethnic Uzbeks, who are far more numerous in southern Kyrgyzstan than Russians (see Table 3.2).

A final ethnic issue that is particularly important in southern Kyrgyzstan but also affects other parts of the Valley in a more limited way is the departure of mainly European ethnic minorities, notably Russians, Germans, and Ashkenazi Jews. Their departure risks exacerbating other tensions. For example, when these people leave their jobs, they open up economic opportunities for those indigenous to Central Asia, who nonetheless may lack the needed expertise. In southern

Kyrgyzstan, there is a widespread perception among Uzbeks that the Kyrgyz have taken most of these positions and are using other tools, especially privatization and political reform, to consolidate their hold on formerly Russian-run enterprises and the country's levers of power.

REGIONALISM

Regional identity, in the context of the Ferghana Valley, encompasses two distinct issues. The first is that of schisms *within* each part of the Valley, say, between Osh and Jalalabad within Kyrgyzstan. Only in the vast northern Tajik region of Leninabad do these rise to the level of potential conflict, given the historical struggle between the capital of the region, Khujand, and Ura-Teppe (to the south) and Penjkent (to the southwest, closer to Samarkand). Even in northern Tajikistan, however, this friction pales in comparison to the other aspect of regionalism: the conflict between the parts of the Ferghana Valley in each newly independent state and their respective national capitals.

While regional political elites from the Valley do not dominate any of their respective states, this relative exclusion from power has been felt most acutely in northern Tajikistan. In that state not only has the process of shutting out been more complete, but the now excluded northern groups are accustomed to holding central power, having done so for nearly fifty years before the collapse of the Soviet Union and the resulting civil war. The removal from power of these once-dominant elites is the root cause of the current strife in the Leninabad region and a much stronger source of conflict than either ethnicity or religion there. Regional identity, as much as if not more than ideology, has been a key force driving Tajikistan's civil war.

Regional exclusion exacerbates the other tensions in Kyrgyzstan and Uzbekistan, since long-term economic prosperity in the Ferghana Valley depends on political decisions made in the national capitals. Like Tajikistan, Kyrgyzstan faces the challenge of strong, competing regional interests. While not as dramatic, the status of southern Kyrgyzstan as a "loser" in national politics was strongly conveyed to us during our stay in Osh. This is the result of competition between the more industrialized north, around Bishkek and Lake Issyk-Kul, with its large Russian minority, and the predominantly agricultural southern regions comprised of the Ferghana Valley regions of Osh and Jalalabad, with their large Uzbek minorities. Even though southerners account for slightly more than half of the population of Kyrgyzstan, they remain relatively rare in central government positions of power.

While Kyrgyzstan does seem to be making efforts to assist the south, many southerners (Kyrgyz and Uzbeks alike) feel that the Akaev government has a strong northern bias. Taking one example, the most recent three governors of the Osh region have been northerners appointed by President Akaev (himself a northerner). Many southerners also feel that much of the investment and aid from abroad is directed to the north, and to Bishkek in particular.

In Uzbekistan, the importance of regionalism remains somewhat less clear, as President Karimov has succeeded in personalizing his authority so extensively. Nonetheless, many interpreters of Uzbek politics have emphasized the importance of regional alliances in determining who controls the affairs of state. According to their analyses, the Ferghana Valley is not part of President Karimov's power base. While he himself does not come from a regional clan, he balances the Tashkent and Ferghana clans to maintain his personal power. In the fall of 1998 a round of personnel changes appeared aimed at weakening the Samarkandi clan, led by Deputy Prime Minister Ismail Jurabekov.[12] As in southern Kyrgyzstan, Ferghana Valley denizens feel that, despite the joint ventures with Coca-Cola and Daewoo, the region is not receiving its share of foreign investment. This is compounded by the fact that farms are still obliged to sell cotton to the government at well below the world market price. The perception of being an excluded region does exist in the Valley, and the discontent may help explain why President Karimov has so frequently dismissed local and regional heads of administration.[13] (Between November 1996 and March 1997, all regional *hakims*, or governors, in the Valley were relieved of their duties.)

President Karimov has practiced a carrot and stick approach to the region—attracting some investment and pushing for a restructuring of the agricultural sector while frequently criticizing the political and economic performance of the three *hakimiyats*, and, since 1998, indiscriminately arresting suspected Islamic activists.

HUMAN RIGHTS/FREEDOM OF THE PRESS

How the issue of human rights, including media freedom, may affect stability in the Ferghana Valley is one of the most controversial topics in Central Asia and among those in the West and Russia evaluating the potential for conflict there. Some argue that limits on public freedoms are necessary to maintain stability while governments focus on consolidating independence and making the transition to a market economy.

Others argue that heavy censorship, a lack of any truly independent media, and bans on rallies and independent political thought may be destabilizing in their own right by preventing citizens from airing their grievances in a peaceful way. By stifling discussion, repression can prevent both locals and outsiders from seeing the warning signs of impending danger.

The three states have followed different and often changing trajectories on human rights. As the Center for Preventive Action study group found, greater openness in southern Kyrgyzstan may lead to the impression of greater instability there, which some have blamed precisely on that openness; this may account for the government's recent backtracking on human rights, especially in the area of freedom of the press. In the Uzbekistan parts of the Valley, which during our 1997 visit seemed calmer, the repression of human rights, particularly the arrests and disappearances of popular Islamic figures, could ignite, indeed, may have ignited, a violent backlash against the government. In Tajikistan's case, the current crisis in the north is directly linked, in part, to the suppression of human rights by the central authorities, in particular the squelching of the May 1996 Khujand demonstrations and the subsequent killing of leading demonstrators in the Khujand prison.

KYRGYZSTAN

As in the economic sphere, the Kyrgyzstan government long led the way in Central Asia in respecting human rights. It has allowed opposition political parties, nongovernmental human rights organizations, and independent media to act freely. Kyrgyz authorities even stood up to pressure from Uzbekistan when a leading human rights activist from that country, Abdumannob Pulat, was kidnapped by Uzbek secret police in downtown Bishkek while attending an international human rights conference. Kyrgyzstan has become the frequent meeting ground for regional conferences and groups for discussions that would not be permitted in Uzbekistan.

But this openness has brought its own set of challenges to Kyrgyzstan.[14] In the past few years the situation in Kyrgyzstan has deteriorated considerably, particularly in the area of freedom of the press. A number of journalists have been arrested or beaten, and they are sometimes charged with political crimes such as slandering public officials. Libel is a criminal offense, not merely a cause for civil action, in all the Central Asian states. Journalists say they are ready to be held accountable for the accuracy of their reporting but see no reason why they should be tried under the criminal code, with long prison sentences, even if they are guilty of libel. In the meantime, government pressure, a large number of legal cases to contend with, lack of money (even to hire defense attorneys), and ideological splits within the journalistic community make it difficult for the press to operate effectively. While there is no indication that the Bishkek regime will become as repressive as Tashkent's, the intimidation of those reporting on controversial topics is already having a stifling effect on the media. If stability is related to good government, which in turn benefits from the scrutiny of public officials by an independent press, then the current trend toward repression is clearly having a negative impact and may reinforce the belief of some officials that they are above the law.

The ramifications of Kyrgyzstan's fairly open, democratic system are especially controversial in the Osh and Jalalabad provinces. Democracy has led to the public airing of problems. It has attracted some Uzbek dissidents and religious figures who cannot operate freely in Uzbekistan. It has led to greater discussion regarding the political inclusion of ethnic Uzbeks in the region's administration and allowed a fairly full accounting of the array of socioeconomic and political problems plaguing the area. On the one hand, this may lead to open, healthy debate about a range of regional issues that can only be helpful in resolving them. On the other hand, some argue that full discussion of problems without the resources to address them may only exacerbate difficult situations. Several interviewees, such as Dr. Bakyt Beshimov, rector of Osh State University, expressed a nervousness—evidently widespread—about the consequences of the influx of political exiles: "This has led to a growing presence of Uzbek dissidents in southern Kyrgyzstan that is a real, destabilizing threat for us."

While critically important in opening up the region and encouraging public participation in addressing the problems of everyday life, then, free expression in Kyrgyzstan had also resulted in a more palpable sense of tension than in neighboring Uzbekistan, with ethnic Uzbeks and Kyrgyz overtly blaming each other for various problems. There are still certain subjects that remain taboo, precisely because of the likelihood that they could cause interethnic strife such as that which occurred in Osh and Uzgen in 1990. Among the forbidden areas are in-depth investigations of the Osh conflict itself and Uzbek demands for autonomy or secession. Nonetheless, the violence and mass arrests in the Uzbekistan part of the Valley since then confirm our sense that repression was masking rather than solving problems.

UZBEKISTAN

Of the three countries in the Ferghana Valley, Uzbekistan has had the most systematically repressive record on human rights in Central Asia; Kyrgyzstan has been more liberal and Tajikistan more chaotic and, at times, brutal. While the Uzbekistan government's policy on human rights has fluctuated somewhat since late 1994, the stifling of certain groups and individuals remains common, and, particularly in the Ferghana Valley, the repression has actually worsened. The May 1996 Human Rights Watch/Helsinki report on Uzbekistan included a litany of human rights violations:

> All media are rigorously censored and some newspapers are banned outright. . . . Individuals are punished for even the slightest attempts to express peaceful opposition to the government, or even for a lack of perceived loyalty to the government, through arbitrary arrest, detentions, "disappearances," discriminatory dismissals from work, and intimidation . . .; opposition associations are arbitrarily stripped of their legal status; public rallies are banned; law enforcement and the judiciary carry out the will of the authoritarian regime or of corrupt officials, including planting narcotics and weapons on a suspect during arrest. . . .[15]

A recent update found that little had changed, despite the brief hopes of a few years ago.[16] Mid-1996 marked what many believed would be a turning point in the attitude of the Uzbekistan government toward human rights. In September of that year, it allowed an international conference on human rights to be held in Tashkent. Several well-known victims of repression spoke freely and openly there, and their remarks were reported in the press. President Karimov's speeches during the year consistently called for an independent press and criticized journalists for being "toothless." On August 30, 1996, he told parliament:

> The press and television carry no profound analysis or serious political, economic or international reviews; there is no debate. . . . Many journalists are still bound up in the old ways of thinking. . . . We must fundamentally alter our attitude to criticism in the press. . . . We must do everything to encourage those who help us rid ourselves of our shortcomings. . . . *You [officials] should know that if there is criticism in the press and you come down on it the next day, then you won't keep your job for long* [emphasis added].[17]

In January 1997, the government authorized the publication of a new journal, without censorship. Within five weeks of its launch date, however, that new journal was closed, and crackdowns began again on human rights activists. Despite the continuing favorable rhetoric, the regime seems to have returned to the policy it had before: that human rights, freedom of religion, and freedom of the press may be desired aims of society but cannot be instituted until the economy is righted and the stability of Uzbekistan is ensured. Press freedom is encouraged as long as the right messages are sent to the population; religious rights are accepted as long as they do not incite the population to "extremism." Rafik Saifulin, deputy director of the President's Institute for Strategic Studies in Tashkent, in an interview with our group, declared, "We need guarantees for journalists—of course we need laws to protect them in courts. But we must also guarantee that journalists cannot manipulate the population." Thus, today, religious activity is closely monitored, the press (including Russian newspapers brought into Uzbekistan) remains heavily censored and controlled, and independent organizations and opposition parties remain banned.

Suppression of independent media, opposition parties, and demonstrations, while unlikely to be the direct cause of unrest, could contribute to instability in more ways than one. It makes it more difficult for an increasingly frustrated local population to find legitimate vehicles for expressing discontent and for holding local and national officials accountable for their actions. As stabilizing as this may seem in the short run, and as successful as it is in giving the appearance of normality in the region, it can also create a pressure cooker effect that may result in an unexpected explosion of tensions. Suppressing these outlets of expression also makes it more difficult for all parties, including the Uzbekistan government and outside organizations, to gauge the prospects for violence. As the government is taking the position that a lack of protest and violence in the Ferghana Valley implies all is well, the likelihood decreases that Uzbekistan authorities might deem it useful to cooperate in multilateral efforts to reduce the potential for conflict in all parts of the Valley.

TAJIKISTAN

Although initially spared the worst violence and human rights violations of southern Tajikistan, in the past few years the northern Leninabad region has become the target of concerted efforts by the Tajikistan government to limit political freedoms. Dushanbe banned most opposition political parties in the wake of the civil war and has only recently agreed to reinstate them as part of the peace agreement. In southern Tajikistan human rights and the press have been severely curtailed, less through systematic control (as in Uzbekistan) than through arbitrary disappearances and murders of hundreds of people, many of them not even politically active. Many such killings appeared to be based on the victim's region of origin. Dozens of journalists, including Russians and a correspondent for the BBC, were murdered, though it is not clear if this was done on direct orders of someone in the government or simply tolerated by it. Few if any of the murders or disappearances have been solved.

An additional problem is that the proliferation of arms and armed groups has eroded central authority. Hostage taking for ransom has increased and has even spread to victimize workers of international humanitarian organizations. Several multilateral agency or foreign representatives have been murdered there, including a French aid worker in early 1998 and four UN employees (Japanese, Uruguayan, Jordanian, and Tajik) in July 1998. These killings all occurred in southern Tajikistan, mainly in the lawless mountainous region east of Dushanbe.

Until 1996 the problems of the south were not shared by the residents of northern Tajikistan, where a moderate level of openness remained during and after the civil war. Owing to the limits of central control there, political groups banned in the south, such as the Democratic Party of Tajikistan, continued to operate quietly in Leninabad. At the same time, the local administration did exert efforts to bar other groups, in particular the Tajik nationalist movement Rastokhez and the Islamic Renaissance Party. In response to the May 1996 demonstrations in Khujand and Ura-Teppe, however, the central government has stepped up efforts to crack down on opposition in the north. During the bloody suppression of the April 1997 Khujand prison riot, the government reportedly targeted and killed many of the organizers of the May 1996 demonstrations. In a sign of how human rights violations can lead to further conflict, it appears that those later arrested for attempting to assassinate President Rakhmonov were brothers and friends of those killed in the attack on the prison. Since the end of April 1997 the regime has arrested dozens of people, including the younger brother of northern Tajikistan's important exiled leader, Abdumalik Abdullajanov. Some who were said to have resisted arrest were killed, while others have been taken for interrogation, and for an uncertain future, to Dushanbe. Further arrests took place in the wake of the failed uprising of November 1998.

REGIONAL POLITICO-MILITARY CONCERNS:
CONTAGION AND CONTAINMENT OF CONFLICTS

At the intersection of three states with different political and military capabilities, the Ferghana Valley finds itself the subject of regional struggles. First, some in Kyrgyzstan, Tajikistan, and elsewhere fear domination by Uzbekistan, the largest and most powerful state in the region. Second, the important yet unclear role that the national militaries, as well as Russia's remaining troops in Central Asia, might play in local conflicts deserves greater attention. Finally, any conflict that erupts in one part of the Valley may spread through the region, but the kind of risk, and the likely response to it, will differ according to the circumstances.

Uzbekistan government officials and many ordinary Uzbeks are proud that their state is, in their view, the least dependent of the Central Asian states on Russia in all spheres, from economics to the military. As shown by its military intervention in Tajikistan in 1992 and its support for Uzbek factions in Afghanistan, Uzbekistan believes it has strong regional responsibilities. But while Uzbekistan's officials emphasize their concern for stability, some of their neighbors fear hegemonic designs. As the most powerful country in the neighborhood, Uzbekistan is viewed as rivaling only Russia in its designs for regional control. The government's selection of Amir Timur—a great but vicious conqueror—as the historical founder of Uzbekistan has exacerbated these fears. Timur is perceived very differently among various groups in the region. In the words of one Kyrgyz we talked with in southern Kyrgyzstan, "Why are the Uzbeks celebrating Timur? The Germans don't celebrate Hitler!"

Many Uzbeks, and particularly the decisionmaking elite, argue that Uzbekistan aims only to assert its newfound sovereignty to secure its rightful place among nations. Successful measures aimed at conflict prevention and regional cooperation must take into account Uzbeks' and others' sensitivities concerning any possible erosion of national sovereignty. But they also must not be seen in Kyrgyzstan or Tajikistan as tools that Uzbekistan could use to press a hegemonic agenda on them. Offering constructive suggestions for regional cooperation against a backdrop of perceived Uzbek designs is thus a difficult balancing act.

The security forces of Uzbekistan, Tajikistan, and Kyrgyzstan are vastly different. Only Uzbekistan has a sizable military presence of its own in the Ferghana Valley (excluding Security and Interior Ministry troops and police forces), and it is the only state in the area whose regular army can avail itself of extensive training and equipment. In the aftermath of the Tajikistan civil war, Uzbekistan Interior Ministry troops constituted the main security force in Leninabad.[18] More recently, Uzbekistan security forces have put pressure on Kyrgyzstan to allow them to arrest Uzbek Islamic dissidents in Osh without prior arrangement.

By contrast, Kyrgyzstan made a conscious choice soon after independence not to develop a large military, instead forming a National Guard. Some members of the National Guard serve together with the Russian border forces on the Tajikistan-Afghanistan border, and others participated in the joint exercises of Centrasbat (the joint Central Asian Battalion, described below), but on the whole it has been given a very restricted scope of action. Guarding Kyrgyzstan's borders with China and Tajikistan has been left to Russian border guard units. Clearly, were major conflict to break out in any part of the Valley, even in Kyrgyzstan, Kyrgyz forces would not be sufficient to restore order. At best, they would be able to participate in a larger Centrasbat force.

With the signing of the peace agreement in June 1997, Tajikistan's limited, factionalized armed forces are due for a significant overhaul as opposition combatants are integrated into the nation's military and irregular units disbanded. However, quarrels over the size and nature of these forces and continued disputes among rival warlords within the ostensibly progovernment ranks mean that the military remains both ineffective and heavily dependent on Russian military and financial support. To our knowledge, before the November 1998 uprising there were no regular armed forces stationed in Tajikistan's part of the Ferghana Valley. There were, though, significant numbers of heavily armed Interior Ministry, National Security Ministry (the former KGB), and Presidential Guard troops in the north. While we do not know the number of these troops, who originated from the southern Kulab region, they reportedly extorted tribute from businesspeople and intimidated antigovernment activists. Given the part these forces played in the civil war, it seems likely that they would act as combatants (and perhaps even instigators) in any conflict rather than as peacekeepers. They, along with regular army troops and some units of the opposition, suppressed the November 1998 uprising.

Given concerns about Uzbekistan hegemony and the continued security and economic dependence of Kyrgyzstan and Tajikistan on Moscow, Russian troops are also significant, especially in Tajikistan. While this subject is discussed further in the next chapter, it is important to note here Russia's vital role in the current military (im)balance in the region.

Uzbekistan, Kazakstan, and Kyrgyzstan have established a joint Central Asian peacekeeping battalion (Centrasbat), which is receiving significant backing from the United States and NATO. Centrasbat exercises held in the Kazakstan desert near Uzbekistan in September 1997 included U.S., Turkish, and Russian troops. Those exercises received some media attention in the United States, particularly as the airdrop into Kazakstan marked the longest nonstop flight to an airdrop in American military history. Additionally, the U.S. military held joint exercises with Uzbekistan troops in the Ferghana Valley, eighty kilometers from the Tajikistan border, in June 1997.[19]

While the goal of supporting and training peacekeeping forces is clearly laudable, there are several inherent risks. First, statements from some American officials during the exercises may have led Central Asian leaders to believe that the United States would be willing to use military force to protect them against outside aggression. Secondly, despite cautionary measures, such as keeping the exercises under Kazakstan's command, the sheer size of Uzbekistan's military has led to increased fears of Uzbek hegemony in the region. Finally, and perhaps most important in the context of conflict prevention in the Ferghana Valley, it is not clear at this stage whether the Centrasbat forces the West is assisting would end up as peacekeepers or combatants in any conflict in the Valley involving one or more of the states, or different ethnic, religious, or regional groups.

The risk that conflict in one part of the Ferghana Valley could spread to other adjoining areas is real, but the dangers of contagion vary in different parts of the area. This is the case because history has determined that the fault lines along which conflict is likely to break out are distinct in each of the discrete zones of the Valley, and because the military capabilities of each country to deal with an outbreak of violence are also so unequal.

Interethnic conflict, particularly between Kyrgyz and Uzbeks in southern Kyrgyzstan, is the scenario that carries the greatest threat of contagion, as was demonstrated in the 1990 Osh riots. It is also the situation for which foreign military intervention, especially by Uzbekistan or the Russian border troops stationed in Osh province, is most likely. In the northern Tajikistan and Uzbekistan parts of the Valley, by contrast, interethnic violence seems less likely, as does the risk of contagion. It should be recognized, however, that the possibility of conflict between ethnic Tajiks and Kyrgyz, either directly along their common border (where it has already erupted occasionally) or between Kyrgyz residents and Tajik refugees in the Osh locale is also genuine. Neither Kyrgyzstan nor Tajikistan has any domestic force that could quell such an outbreak.

A clash between the government of Uzbekistan and Islamic activists, the most significant peril in the Uzbekistan part of the Valley, is difficult to analyze in terms of potential contagion for adjoining regions. There is less widespread risk if this represented purely a revolt against the Karimov regime. Two developments, however, make clear that adjoining areas could readily become conduits (which helps explain why Uzbekistan is trying to control its borders so closely). First, Islamic forces now participate in Tajikistan's government of national reconciliation, while several hundred fighters from Namangan may have joined the Tajik Islamic battalions in Tajikistan or Afghanistan. Second, exiled Uzbek Islamic leaders have established independent mosques, madrasahs, and other centers of activity in more permissive Kyrgyzstan.

Regionalism, while important to politics in southern Kyrgyzstan and eastern Uzbekistan, threatens to unleash violence primarily in northern Tajikistan, where it could lead as far as demands for secession from the rest of the country. Such conflict, however, is unlikely to provoke any kind of mass unrest in adjoining areas of the Ferghana Valley. The presence of armed rebels in Leninabad, however, a genuine possibility since the November 1998 uprising, could destabilize neighboring regions. In 1992 Uzbekistan sent Interior Ministry troops to Tajikistan, and they were still the main security force in and around Khujand when one member of our group visited in June 1993.[20] Uzbekistan will not support secession. President Karimov and the government of Uzbekistan have clearly stated their opposition to changes in borders, and the Leninabad-based factions depend on them for support.

Conflicts, once they erupt, are rarely so clearly delineated according to regional, religious, or ethnic loyalties. The lines are often obscured, and other catalysts, including external forces, play major roles. The messiness of such conflicts has already been illustrated with deadly results in the Tajik and Afghan civil wars, both of which continue to affect the Ferghana Valley deeply.

— 6 —

EXTERNAL SOURCES OF
CONFLICT AND STABILITY

The wars in neighboring southern Tajikistan and Afghanistan have
profoundly influenced the Ferghana Valley, in both direct and indi-
rect ways, while continuing to serve as stark reminders of the high cost of
conflict among ethnic and regional groups in lost or shattered lives. Some
participants in these wars have developed ties to groups in the Ferghana
Valley. The drug trade these wars have spawned is penetrating north-
ward. Refugees have fled both conflicts, most of them in other directions, but some have ventured into the Ferghana Valley and nearby areas.

Though these two wars dominate the regional security picture,
this part of the world is also affected by broader international issues.
Russia remains the predominant military power, while China is a rising
economic power just to the east. Other Muslim nations seek access to
Central Asia, largely for economic reasons. And the United States and
other developed countries have also become involved in an area with
which they had little contact for decades.

REGIONAL CONFLICTS: AFGHANISTAN AND
TAJIKISTAN

AFGHANISTAN: FRAGMENTATION, ANARCHY, AND EXTREMISM

For almost twenty years, Afghanistan has been wracked by
violence—by a Communist coup d'état, the Soviet invasion, and
since 1989, after the Soviet withdrawal, fighting among a great
variety of groups. Since April 1992, when the ex-Communist government of Najibullah fell, all the contesting factions have claimed

to be Islamic. Each is based in a different region or ethnic group of the country, and for several years the war essentially became a struggle for power and security in an anarchic environment. With the rise of the Islamic Movement of the Taliban (Islamic students), the war again took on the contours of a two-sided civil war, with battle lines drawn on mainly ethnic lines. By the end of 1996 the Taliban controlled the predominantly Pashtun south, as well as the major cities of Kabul and Herat and an enclave in the north centered on Kunduz, where there is also a significant Pashtun population. The groups opposing them were based in areas where the population is predominantly Tajik, Uzbek, or Hazara (the only major Shia ethnic group). In the summer of 1998, the Taliban captured nearly all of the rest of the country. By mid-1999, only an area in the northeast, dominated by the Tajik troops of General Ahmad Shah Massoud, held out, though Hazara fighters in Central Afghanistan also kept up some resistance.

The surrounding countries, especially Pakistan and Iran, have been deeply involved, to the point where the struggle has become a new proxy war. Pakistan actively supports the Taliban, both politically and militarily. In reaction, Iran, Russia, and to a lesser extent, Uzbekistan and Tajikistan stepped up their aid to groups holding out against the Taliban.[1] The Tajikistan government and the Russian military have allowed Massoud to use airstrips in southern Tajikistan to resupply and repair his aircraft.[2] In short, virtually all of Afghanistan's neighbors are involved in its internal conflict over control of the country.

At stake in Afghanistan is more than the balance of power among ethnic groups. This war has continued to attract foreign support to various factions largely because it is linked to the battle for control of the hydrocarbon resources of the Caspian basin. Oil and gas pipelines from Turkmenistan to Pakistan via western Afghanistan constitute the only southern outlet for these resources other than through Iran. Pakistan sees its ability to construct such pipeline routes as key to its future, in which it hopes to ally its destiny with that of Central Asia. Iran, on the other hand, sees an advantage in blocking such pipelines, at least for as long as they are not just economic assets but part of a strategy to isolate Tehran and keep it subject to U.S. sanctions. Many in the Pakistani establishment see the Taliban as the sole force capable of establishing the security and control needed to finance and construct the pipelines. Others argue that only a broad-based government would be able to do so. The main consortium competing for the pipeline contracts has been led by the U.S.-based firm Unocal, creating an additional American interest in the area. Unocal announced its withdrawal from the project, however, after the August 12, 1998, U.S. missile attacks on camps in Afghanistan linked to exiled Saudi dissident Usama Bin Ladin. Bin Ladin, who received refuge from the Taliban, is charged by Washington with being the mastermind of the August 7, 1998, bombings of U.S. embassies in Kenya and Tanzania and of other terrorist acts. Despite suspicions in the region to the contrary, the United States has not supported the Taliban and claims to see a broad-based settlement as the country's only chance for investment-based economic development. The slow warming of U.S.-Iran relations could remove much of the incentive to build transit routes through volatile Afghanistan.

The war has also increased local reliance on narcotics growing and smuggling, both for the mere survival of impoverished farmers and for financing the war itself. This has had a severe impact on the Central Asian states in general and on the Ferghana Valley in particular. Refugee flows into neighboring Uzbekistan and Tajikistan, on the other hand, have so far been quite limited, despite escalation of the violence during the Taliban capture of the north in August 1998. We consider refugees separately later in this chapter.

One danger for Central Asia and the Ferghana Valley emanating from the war in Afghanistan lies in its interaction with the Tajikistan civil war. Since about 1996 Massoud has had use of an air base in southern Tajikistan to transfer supplies and repair aircraft. His forces move back and forth between Afghanistan and Tajikistan. The ethnic Uzbek troops of Afghan general Abdul Rashid Dostum, however, have turned up fighting directly in the Tajikistan war: several were reported found among the dead and captured soldiers of the ethnic Uzbek Tajikistan rebel Colonel Makhmud Khudoiberdiyev, who briefly captured parts of Leninabad in November 1998. Taken together with the Taliban's extensive networks of support and recruitment in Pakistan, these events point to the formation of cross-border, militarized ethnic coalitions, a phenomenon with potentially threatening consequences for the region.

TAJIKISTAN: THE FRAGILE, NONCOMPREHENSIVE PEACE

Together with the civil war in Afghanistan, the conflict in Tajikistan has been the most serious disruption of stability in Central Asia. The most militarily active phase of the Tajik civil war in 1992 and 1993 cost the lives of an estimated 50,000 people and was the bloodiest conflict in the former Soviet Union until the war in

Chechnya. As many as one million refugees fled the fighting, primarily to other parts of Tajikistan and to Afghanistan, but also to Kyrgyzstan, Uzbekistan, and Russia. While open battles largely ended after 1993, when most of the opposition forces were driven into Afghanistan, guerrilla raids and other violent incidents continued and have even persisted despite a peace agreement.

While a peace treaty was signed in June 1997 by the Tajikistan government and the Islamist-dominated United Tajik Opposition (UTO), real settlement has so far remained elusive, in part because the signatories were pressured into a quick settlement by their foreign benefactors, Russia, Iran, and the anti-Taliban Tajik forces in northern Afghanistan, against the backdrop of Taliban successes.[3] Especially after the Taliban occupied Kabul, Russia and Iran wanted a unified rearguard through which to aid the anti-Taliban legions. Massoud, too, found it awkward to depend on the Kulabi regime in Dushanbe for access to aid at the same time he was harboring guerrillas fighting against it.

Since the peace treaty was signed, however, problems of implementation (especially protecting UTO leaders returning to Dushanbe) have been compounded by the actions of heavily armed, independent warlords who control various areas of southern Tajikistan, some in immediate proximity to the capital. These warlords and their militias, including Khudoiberdiyev, while ostensibly progovernment, have fought official forces or their allies whenever the government tried to impose its control on the south or threatened the warlords' mastery over economic or political resources. Some of them opposed the peace agreement, which would force them to share the booty of war with their opponents, and one of them—Khudoiberdiyev—led repeated revolts, including one that took over parts of northern Tajikistan for a few days in November 1998.[4]

There continue to be disparate accounts of the origins of the war. The Uzbekistani and Russian governments, as well as the Russian and Western media, have tended to portray the conflict as ideologically based, that is, as between the secular, pro-Communist forces that emerged victorious and an alliance of democrats and Islamic "fundamentalists" in which the Islamists pushed the democrats to the fringes. In this view, events were connected to the fighting in Afghanistan and to a more general "fundamentalist" threat to all of Central Asia. To contain the violence in Tajikistan and support the government of President Imomali Rakhmonov, according to Russian foreign policymakers, is to stop Islamic extremism's assault on Central Asia.

Other analysts have noted that while the conflict may have begun as an ideological one, it became a struggle among forces based in different regions of the country. The current government is dominated by Kulabis, the Islamic opposition by Gharmis, and the ex-Communist leaders from Leninabad have now formed their own explicitly regionalist party. Ideological questions have been marginalized, though they could reemerge.[5]

The signatories to the agreement have hardly begun the most difficult tasks in establishing a lasting peace in Tajikistan: disarming combatants and integrating opposition fighters into the government-controlled armed forces; appointing members of the opposition to posts in a new coalition government; fully enabling the final group of returning refugees to move back into or rebuild their former homes in safety; drafting a new constitution; and holding free and fair, competitive elections. Just as the government is having great difficulty asserting control over groups supposedly loyal to it, it is also far from clear that the UTO will remain united. Allegedly renegade groups have been involved in kidnappings and even killings of international staff.

As discussed in previous chapters, one of the most glaring problems with the peace treaty is its failure to include a role for representatives of a "third force," the northern-based National Revival Movement (NRM). The chief signatories of the pact came only from southern groups. While all of the fighting did take place in the south, the treaty not only ends the fighting but establishes a new political order for Tajikistan—and, in its current form, that order has no explicit place for groups from northern Tajikistan. An attempt to establish a lasting peace in Tajikistan without the inclusion of such economically and politically vital players as the former elites of the Leninabad region is likely to fail. Adding to the sense of fragility is that Uzbekistan, alone among the guarantors of the peace negotiations, initially refused to sign on. Only intense U.S. diplomatic pressure, including a personal visit to Tashkent by Ambassador Bill Richardson, the U.S. permanent representative to the UN, persuaded President Islam Karimov to assent. Uzbekistan's continuing ambivalence about the new arrangement in Tajikistan could ultimately undermine it.

IMPACT ON THE FERGHANA VALLEY

As discussed in Chapter 2, the domination of the Kulabi regime over northern Tajikistan has already resulted in repeated violence.

Escalation of such violence could affect neighboring areas of the Ferghana Valley, especially if it drove refugees into adjacent areas of Uzbekistan. Under such circumstances, Uzbekistan might intervene militarily, as it did in 1992–93.

If fighting in Tajikistan resumes, especially in Leninabad, or if the Taliban engage in more violence in northern Afghanistan, Central Asia faces a possible influx of refugees as well as seeing more displaced within Tajikistan, adding to the considerable number already in the region. In Kyrgyzstan, this is likely to put even greater pressure on the resources of UNHCR, which are already stretched very thin. In northern Tajikistan, where demonstrations have already protested the lack of humanitarian aid given to that part of the country to assist the internally displaced persons who fled the fighting in the south, another influx will only make those demands more urgent.

For the Tajikistan part of the Valley, economic development and investment are closely tied to peace. Private firms and multilateral agencies were reluctant to invest in the north even before the recent outbreaks of violence, thanks to the lack of an effective national government in Dushanbe. On the other hand, an effective Tajik government that deliberately ignores northern Tajik interests or even works against them is also likely to be a significant impediment to investment in the Leninabad region. Official statistics indicating that as little as 7 percent of state investment is going to the north point up the magnitude of the north's exclusion. In these circumstances, economic problems are likely to be doubly destabilizing. In addition to being a direct cause of increased tension (through falling living standards, rising unemployment), they are very likely to provoke more resentment against the central government of the type that has already resulted in demonstrations and violence.

The ongoing fighting in Afghanistan, especially if coupled with continued disorder or weak authority in Tajikistan, is likely to continue to foster ideal conditions for drug trafficking throughout the Ferghana Valley. If the Taliban's record is any guide, its control of most of northern Afghanistan will lead to a rise in drug production and smuggling. In Tajikistan and Kyrgyzstan, this is bound to corrupt officials further. It is also probable that the drug trade will continue to distort the local economy of the eastern Ferghana Valley and to touch off a proliferation of weapons and drugs. Even an effective peace in southern Tajikistan is not likely to produce any immediate crackdown on the narcotics trafficking. Too many Tajik officials are themselves profiting from the smuggling, while others lack the technical and financial resources to mount an effective antitrafficking operation. Any crackdown would have to rely also on the cooperation of the Russian border guards stationed on the Tajik-Afghan frontier and along the Khorog-Osh road; such cooperation is far from assured.

It has been against the backdrop of the conflicts in Afghanistan and Tajikistan that Uzbekistan's President Karimov has cracked down on any manifestations of Islam taken to be political or antiregime. As described in Chapter 2, he explicitly referred to these two civil wars in his televised denunciation of the February 1999 Tashkent bombings. Since much of the Islamic revival is based in the Ferghana Valley, this has been the locus of the Karimov regime's most concerted efforts to avoid a "Tajik scenario" in Uzbekistan. In addition, there have been frequent reports of Islamic activists from Namangan, mainly, joining Tajikistan's Islamic opposition fighters in northern Afghanistan (before the latter repatriated).

In the geostrategic contest over Central Asia in general, and Tajikistan in particular, Uzbekistan appears to be using its economic and political influence in northern Tajikistan as a check on Russian interests and as a lever to challenge the Russian-backed peace agreement. The war in Tajikistan brought Russia back into the region; Moscow guards both the Tajik-Afghan and Tajik-Kyrgyz borders, the latter along the Osh-Khorog road. Taliban successes and the threat of an Islamic insurgency in the Ferghana Valley have also pushed President Karimov into greater reliance on Russia for Uzbekistan's security. In May 1998, at the height of the crackdown in Namangan, Karimov paid a state visit to Moscow to seek support in his battle against Islamic fundamentalism. He and Russian President Boris Yeltsin joined President Rakhmonov (who participated by telephone) in announcing a joint effort.[6] This meeting suddenly reversed Uzbekistan's policy of distancing itself from Russia.

REFUGEES

Conflicts animated by regionalism, ethnicity, and Islam (or fears of Islam) are only compounded by the growing refugee emergency throughout the Ferghana Valley. Large numbers of refugees who fled the civil war in southern Tajikistan pose one of the most pressing problems in the Tajikistan and Kyrgyzstan parts of the Ferghana Valley. Our interviews in Osh and reports from the region indicate that the refugees' presence has put even greater strains on already scarce resources. As in the Democratic Republic of Congo and elsewhere, the impoverished local population has at times also reacted with resentment when refugees are perceived as receiving preferential access to those resources, often with the help of international humanitarian organizations. In northern Tajikistan, the refugee issue has also been a focal point of northerners' anger at the Dushanbe regime; although it is home to many of the internally displaced Tajiks, the Leninabad region has received relatively little of the extensive humanitarian assistance provided to the south.

Uzbekistan, for its part, does not appear to have a significant refugee problem in the Ferghana Valley; most of the ethnic Uzbeks and Tajiks who fled Tajikistan have gone to other parts of Uzbekistan. The problem is that the Uzbek government, for political reasons, refuses to acknowledge that it is home to refugees from Tajikistan at all. Outside observers believe that tens of thousands of people, especially those with extended families in Uzbekistan, fled southern Tajikistan and are living on the margins of Uzbek society, never knowing when they might be expelled. The issue of future refugee flows from either Afghanistan or northern Tajikistan into various parts of the Ferghana Valley is a delicate but pressing question, as large-scale population transfers would only intensify all of the ethnic, religious, and other societal tensions already troubling the region. After the first Taliban successes in northern Afghanistan at the end of May 1997, humanitarian organizations and Russian border troops went on full alert in Osh, preparing for a possible exodus from Afghanistan into the Valley via eastern Tajikistan. Such preparations are still in effect.

SOUTHERN KYRGYZSTAN. Because of its relatively open borders and its geographic position at the end of the road connecting Afghanistan and Tajikistan's impoverished Pamir region to the Ferghana Valley, Osh oblast has received a large number of refugees from southern Tajikistan and Afghanistan. Many there fear that further violence in northern Afghanistan could lead to a far more massive influx in the future. A May 1997 visit by the UN high commissioner for refugees, Sadako Ogata, to various countries of Central Asia highlighted the urgency of the refugee issue in southern Kyrgyzstan. As of 1997, 16,000 people had been granted official refugee status. But, according to interviews with UNHCR in Osh, the true number was believed to be between 40,000 and 45,000. More than half of the refugees are ethnic Kyrgyz, creating fears of a change in the ethnic balance where Uzbeks dominate the urban areas of Osh. About 20 percent, largely Tajik, fled from Afghanistan. In the winter of 1996, the Russian news agency Interfax reported that many of the recent arrivals were in dire need of humanitarian aid and that "most of the families arriving in Kyrgyzstan have neither clothes, nor food, nor fuel for the upcoming winter. The children cannot go to school because they have no shoes, clothes or textbooks."[7]

The Office of the UN High Commissioner for Refugees is the key international agency tackling refugee problems in this region. Although its program in Kyrgyzstan is small—on the order of $300,000 in 1996 and $500,000 in 1997—UNHCR is the only UN agency with an office in Osh; this provides it a way to understand more effectively what is going on in the Valley and to provide direct support to refugees arriving from Tajikistan. Beyond offering humanitarian and medical assistance, according to Helmut Buss, UNHCR's representative in Bishkek, the organization's more important focus is on the bigger picture: capacity building to cope with the large numbers, linking the refugee issue to the overall economic and narcotics trafficking situation, and creating an environment that minimizes the prospects for conflict. UNHCR works in conjunction with local and international NGOs that are also active in this area.

While assistance from UNHCR has been important in meeting the needs of the refugees already in Kyrgyzstan, two problems remain. First, we found that, as in so many other refugee situations, some local people were unhappy that aid organizations were often providing the refugees with more than they had themselves. Second, although humanitarian organizations and the Kyrgyzstan government have been stepping up efforts to prepare for a possible influx of refugees from Afghanistan, it is unclear whether the measures will be sufficient. A related problem is that, while many of the past arrivals from Tajikistan have been ethnic Kyrgyz, the vast majority of those fleeing northern Afghanistan (or possibly northern Tajikistan, were conflict to erupt there) would be ethnic Tajiks. This could put strains on interethnic relations, especially in the western part of Osh oblast abutting Tajikistan, where there have already been conflicts between Tajiks and Kyrgyz over land and water.

NORTHERN TAJIKISTAN. Tajikistan's civil war caused a refugee crisis of staggering proportions in neighboring countries, especially Afghanistan and Kyrgyzstan, and also led to the displacement within Tajikistan of up to 700,000 people.[8] The situation of internally displaced persons who fled from southern to northern Tajikistan is complex. The difficulty of understanding it is compounded by a lack of hard data on the actual numbers of those who came to the Leninabad district during and after the civil war. One analyst put the number at tens of thousands.[9]

Two highly charged political issues do, however, indicate how important the refugee issue has become in northern Tajikistan. First, one of the main demands during the May 1996 demonstrations in Khujand and Ura-Teppe was for fairer distribution of humanitarian aid in the north, taking into account the large number of displaced persons who took shelter there. The widespread perception in the north is that international organizations, in cooperation with the Tajik government, have focused exclusively on southern Tajikistan, where the fighting took place, and on the refugees who fled into northern Afghanistan. Some take this to be another sign of the Dushanbe regime's efforts to exclude the north politically and economically.

The second issue concerns the ethnic makeup of the displaced persons, many of whom are apparently ethnic Uzbeks. Since Uzbeks already account for as much as 40 to 50 percent of the population in some areas of northern Tajikistan, the arrival of large numbers of Uzbeks could exacerbate interethnic tension in the area, particularly given the fragile state of relations between northern Tajikistan and the central government.[10] Up until now, despite the volatility of the situation in the Tajikistan part of the Valley, there have been no significant outflows of its residents into adjoining areas of Uzbekistan and Kyrgyzstan. This is mainly because, even after a period of dramatic economic decline, Leninabad province continues to be better off, in general, than the other parts of the Valley. If, however, a more violent conflict does emerge in the north, refugees might flee north toward Tashkent, west toward Samarkand (from Ura-Teppe), or east into neighboring areas of the Ferghana Valley since they would not have to cross natural boundaries such as mountains or rivers.

UZBEKISTAN. While the Uzbekistan part of the Ferghana Valley does not appear to be experiencing a major problem with refugees at this time, the Uzbekistan government policy regarding spillovers from the Tajik civil war makes it difficult to ascertain the impact those fleeing fighting have had on the country. That policy, which amounts to a denial of a refugee problem within Uzbekistan's borders, complicates efforts, such as those of UNDP, to address issues of stability comprehensively in the Ferghana Valley.

The Karimov regime seems to be worried that according official refugee status to those who fled to Uzbekistan would create two interrelated problems. First, if the number acknowledged were high, a public admission of the scope of the problem could lead to open tension between residents and refugees. Second, the refugees currently in Uzbekistan are in legal limbo, which affords the government great flexibility in how it deals with them; were they to be officially registered, they would become wards of UNHCR, making it more difficult for the Karimov regime to deal with them as it deems expedient. This attitude was reflected in Uzbekistan television's strangely ambivalent coverage of Sadako Ogata's May 1997 visit to Central Asia: "[Ogata] expressed gratitude for our country's consent to render assistance to repatriate Tajik refugees to Tajikistan *if necessary* and expressed the desire to cooperate on matters arising from this." [emphasis added][11] While the Karimov regime's refugee policy may be politically expedient, it does make it far more difficult for everyone, including the government itself, to understand the scope of the problem in Uzbekistan.

ROLE OF RUSSIA AND CENTRAL ASIA'S OTHER NEIGHBORS

Continued stability in the Ferghana Valley is likely to depend, to a significant extent, on the role that Russia, the United States, China, Iran, Pakistan, Turkey, and others play in the affairs of Central Asia in the years to come. Especially against the backdrop of the conflicts in Tajikistan and Afghanistan, and in view of the larger geostrategic prospects for bringing Central Asian oil and natural gas to the world market, most outside players have a stake in promoting a stable, peaceful Central Asia. Their competition, however, could provoke or aggravate conflicts.

Five years after the Central Asian states were thrown into unexpected statehood, several surprises have emerged. First, while many had envisaged a smaller-scale replay of the old colonial powers' "Great Game," this time between Iran and Turkey, those two countries' influence in the region pales in comparison to that of Russia and the United States. Despite the undisputed yearning of the Central Asian states to break free of Russian dominance, they continue to be inextricably tied to Moscow (to different degrees) politically, militarily, and economically. While the countries of the region have joined various Islamic organizations and regional associations of Muslim countries, those so far have been much less effective vehicles of cooperation than the Russian-dominated Commonwealth of Independent States (CIS), even if the CIS itself is hardly a model of unity. Finally, in these first five years, all Central Asian leaders (with the possible exception of

Tajikistan's) have adapted well and with considerable savvy, in their own distinct ways, to the international system within which they operate. Given instability to the south and the presence of powerful neighbors in all other directions, this is perhaps one of the most important guarantors of stability in the region.

RUSSIA

As the Central Asian countries have joined the international system, all have sought to diversify their international links away from Russia without excluding Moscow. They are seeking other trade partners, and they look to join political and economic alliances with the West and with Asia. English has become the second language of choice over Russian. Despite these efforts, Russia remains the most important external player in Central Asia and the only one with significant military assets in the region.

The Russian government, both bilaterally and through the CIS structures, has consistently maintained that it favors stability throughout the former Soviet Union. But the examples of military intervention in Tajikistan, Abkhazia, Transdniestria, and Chechnya have made some Central Asians fear that Russia may provoke conflict in order to put pressure on the newly independent states. These concerns were intensified when leading foreign policy analysts in Moscow (reportedly with the approval of Russian foreign minister Yevgeny Primakov) wrote an article suggesting that certain influential Russians believe that destabilizing Central Asia and fomenting claims by one state on the territory of another is in Russia's interest. Nonetheless, since Primakov became foreign minister and subsequently prime minister, Russia has supported moves aimed at resolving or de-escalating a number of these conflicts, including the war in Tajikistan. It appears that Russia has now concluded it should expand its influence by playing a stabilizing role.

There are several reasons why Russia will remain a key player in Central Asian affairs for some time to come. The primary routes for many of Central Asia's exports and imports, including pipelines for its energy resources, still pass largely through Russia. The continued presence of significant ethnic Russian communities, at least in Kazakstan and Kyrgyzstan, also maintains Russian interest.

Despite U.S. participation in the Central Asian peacekeeping battalion's exercises, Russia remains the only external power willing to commit its own military resources. It has sent both "peacekeeping" and border troops to Tajikistan and stationed troops along most of Central Asia's new international frontiers. The government of Tajikistan might have fallen long ago (or become dependent on Uzbekistan instead) were it not for the Russian military presence along the Tajik-Afghan border and within the republic itself. Of no less importance, the incipient national militaries of the region are still equipped with Soviet-made weaponry, leaving them dependent on Russia for spare parts and training.

The structures and agreements of the CIS have served to cement Russian influence in the region. While it is doubtful that the CIS will ever be a powerful structure for economic cooperation, it provides a basis for Russia's politico-military involvement in the Central Asian states. Russian border troops guard the CIS's external borders with China, Afghanistan, and Iran under the CIS collective security agreement. In the economic realm, while the breakup of the Soviet Union and the collapse of the command economy network have reduced the region's trade with Russia, that commercial traffic is still large. Russian Foreign Ministry officials claimed in a discussion in Moscow with members of the working group that trade links weakened during the first years of independence are being reestablished and intensified.

Russia has significant troops stationed near the Ferghana Valley. In 1997, following the Taliban advance into northern Afghanistan, it moved some of its soldiers guarding the Kyrgyz-China border into the southern and western parts of Osh, bordering Tajikistan. While this was ostensibly to block any Taliban advances through the Badakhshan autonomous province of Tajikistan into Kyrgyzstan, the troop movements also put Russian forces within easy reach of the Ferghana Valley.[12]

The Kyrgyzstan and Tajikistan parts of the Ferghana Valley still depend on the Russian market for the sale of their cotton and other agricultural exports and for the import of energy, other inputs to local industries, and consumer goods. Any further disruption of trade relations could result in a dramatic worsening of the economic situation in those areas.

Russia and its role in Central Asia are perceived differently by the various states of the region. Uzbekistan, given its own ambitions, has sought to diminish Russian influence both domestically (by reducing trade and military links) and regionally (by opposing a Russian-dominated settlement in Tajikistan). As noted earlier, this may be changing under the impact of the government's perception of the need to close ranks against an Islamic threat from the south.

Fears of Uzbekistan's hegemonic intentions, on the other hand, have made Kyrgyzstan more willing to continue political and economic ties with Russia; this is also a function of the large Russian-speaking community in northern Kyrgyzstan. At the same time, Kyrgyzstan is trying to foster economic relations with the distant West and with its neighbor, China, and it remains eager to reduce its trade dependency on both Russia and Uzbekistan. Tajikistan's case is rather straightforward: the Rakhmonov regime depends on Russia, militarily and economically, for its very survival.

China

As in the Central Asian-Russian relationship, there are both stabilizing and destabilizing elements in relations with China, and these have implications either way for the Ferghana Valley. Although its role in the Ferghana Valley is limited, China's presence is likely to become increasingly important in the years to come. Given China's burgeoning prosperity, vast market, geographic proximity, and ostensible lack of a political agenda in trade, the Central Asian states have been quick to expand their trade with the area's fastest-growing and largest economy, especially as a means of reducing dependence on Russia.

China is also the only non-CIS country that borders a Ferghana Valley region, namely, Kyrgyzstan's Osh province.[13] In this regard, the most direct impact on the Valley is likely to come from the improvement of the Andijan-Osh-Kashgar (China) road and the establishment of a parallel rail link, which are likely to improve trade with China greatly and to reestablish the Ferghana Valley's historical setting as a transit route from the Orient to the West. China might, however, be ambivalent about improving transport and communications that would link its own restive Muslim Turkic minorities in the area to Central Asia.

Kyrgyzstan and Uzbekistan have somewhat different views of China. The government of Uzbekistan clearly sees China as a counterweight to Russia in the region, while Kyrgyzstan, which has been the fastest to develop economic ties with China, fears that an Uzbek-Chinese alliance could be very detrimental to its own interests.

Of all of these issues, the most sensitive in relations between China and the Central Asian states is the status of the Xinjiang Autonomous Region, with its large Muslim Uyghur (Turkic) population and a three thousand-kilometer border with Kazakstan, Kyrgyzstan, and Tajikistan. The Uyghurs' quest for independence was highlighted in early 1997, when pro-autonomy demonstrations were violently repressed, and

Uyghur militants responded with a bombing campaign in Beijing and the regional capital, Urumqi, on the day of Deng Xiaoping's funeral. While the Central Asian states have made good relations with China a priority, they are also sympathetic to the fate of a people that has a history of repression in many ways like their own. In addition, Uyghurs living in Kazakstan and Kyrgyzstan have set up their own organizations, some of which aim at liberating "East Turkistan" (the traditional name for Xinjiang) from Chinese rule.

The Beijing regime wants to ensure, as its primary interest in relations with the Central Asian states, that the "independence bug" that the Central Asians caught in 1991–92 does not spread to Xinjiang. At the same time, in a sign of the continued relaxation of tensions between China on the one hand and Russia and Central Asia on the other, these states signed an agreement to reduce and limit the military forces stationed in a two-hundred-kilometer-wide strip along the China-CIS border in April 1997.[14]

MUSLIM STATES

In the years after independence, some argued that other Muslim states would be dueling for influence in Central Asia, and that the Islamic nature of this rivalry would be most strongly expressed in the Ferghana Valley, given that area's level of religious activity and history of rebellion. However, the ties that have emerged have been very different from those initially imagined in the West and perhaps even locally. Notably, Iran has not become a significant religious player. Instead it has emerged as a vital economic partner of Central Asia in general and (through markets and infrastructure links) of the Ferghana Valley specifically. Iran was planning to open its first consulate in Osh in late 1997, but by mid-1999 this had still not been established.[15]

By contrast, predominantly Sunni Muslim states, or private groups based in them, have helped fund mosque building, the training of religious leaders, as well as the printing and distribution of Qur'ans and other religious literature throughout Central Asia. Pro-Western Turkey and Saudi Arabia rather than Iran thus became the main sources of the propagation of Islamic texts and ideologies in Central Asia.

In general, however, the Central Asian states have attached greater importance to their Muslim neighbors for trade and transit routes than for religious or political tutelage. Iran, with its long border with Turkmenistan and its Caspian coastline, is a key player in the competition for Central Asia's oil and gas, and its geographic location makes it the most logical route for pipelines linking Turkmenistan (and Kazakstan) to the Persian Gulf or Turkey. Similarly, Turkey and Pakistan are seen primarily as economic partners who can help develop the economies of Central Asia, especially through trade, pipeline routes, and (in the case of Turkey) education. The current view of Afghanistan is almost unrelievedly negative, as it is considered a source of Islamic radicalism, drugs, guns, and instability.

The Economic Cooperation Organization (ECO), which was founded twenty years ago by Turkey, Pakistan, and Iran, now also includes the five Central Asian states, plus Azerbaijan and Afghanistan. While potentially a useful mechanism for regional economic integration, it has only recently been able to overcome some of the many political schisms among its member states. Additionally, even the ambitious projects (pipelines, roads, and technological infrastructure improvements) that were approved at its May 1997 Ashkabad summit will have to be financed by others, as the member states do not have the capacity to do so themselves.[16] Despite the obstacles, however, Central Asia's predominantly Muslim neighbors represent a vital, growing link to the outside world. The improvement of road and rail links between Central Asia and the Middle East could facilitate the region's position as a crossroads, as the Andijan-Osh-Kashgar connection would reach on to China.[17] There is also a tie between cooperation and stability in the Ferghana Valley: economic development, fostered by enhanced trade within the ECO, would have a positive effect on many of the underlying socioeconomic causes of conflict.

All of the states in the region tend to see their political relations with the Muslim world through the prism of the ongoing Afghan crisis. Shared opposition to a possible Taliban victory throughout Afghanistan has served to improve relations between Uzbekistan and Iran, which had been frosty since Iran tried to use the ECO mechanism against Israel (a state with which all Central Asian nations maintain excellent relations). On the other hand, Pakistani support for the Taliban has soured its ties with both Uzbekistan and Tajikistan. Of prime concern to the Central Asian states is the specter of a fundamentalist, ethnic Pashtun regime governing all of Afghanistan, driving an exodus of hundreds of thousands of ethnic Uzbeks and Tajiks from northern Afghanistan and encouraging religious extremism regionwide.

While there has been a significant deepening of relations among all of the Central Asian states and their Muslim neighbors since independence, both bilaterally and through the ECO, the ties are different in character and less important than most analysts and policymakers expected at independence. Based on the historic, linguistic, religious, ethnic, and economic links between Central Asia and its southern neighbors, it is likely that relations will continue to expand, even if they will also always be fraught with tensions, especially in the case of Afghanistan.

THE UNITED STATES

While U.S. policy toward the former Soviet Union was originally focused on Russia, policymakers have increasingly come to realize the importance of other regions, including Central Asia. Energy resources provide the most obvious reason for external interest, but the need for a broad regional approach promoting an environment that supports profitable and productive economic activity is increasingly recognized in Washington.

The Organization for Security and Cooperation in Europe and other international organizations have echoed the necessity of a comprehensive approach. These bodies have stated their commitment to pursuing the kinds of objectives outlined by U.S. deputy secretary of state Strobe Talbott: "the promotion of democracy; the creation of free market economies; the sponsorship of peace and cooperation within and among the countries of the region; and their integration with the larger international community."[18]

We present our recommendations for U.S. policy in the Executive Summary and Chapter 2. Here we would like to signal our concern that unresolved tensions among multiple goals put forth by the foreign policy community may weaken American policy toward Central Asia. Among the tensions are those between maintaining stability on the one hand and, on the other, encouraging democratic reform; between supporting human rights and pursuing other U.S. political and commercial interests in the region; and between allaying fears about Uzbekistan's dominance in Central Asia and treating Uzbekistan as the "anchor of stability" in the region, in one diplomat's words.

The challenge for U.S. policymakers is to ensure that there is a broad framework or strategy in which these competing interests can be balanced consistently and predictably. Secretary Talbott's remarks notwithstanding, a narrow vision has all too frequently defined Central Asian policy: while policymakers and the president have recently granted Central Asia more attention than before, their focus has been primarily through the prisms of Caspian Sea energy reserves and relations with Iran. The notion of "stability" in Central Asia has often been associated with the status quo, particularly in those countries with strong authoritarian leaders. But this kind of stability is tenuous and may well prove threatening to U.S. interests in the long run, as well as remaining one of the biggest obstacles to reform. Likewise, despite American displeasure with the serious backtracking from reform and human rights in Uzbekistan, senior Uzbek officials told us they still believe they enjoy a special relationship with the United States. This perception may complicate efforts to prevent conflict, as it is seen by other states as further cementing that country's hegemony in Central Asia. It may also make Uzbekistan feel less compelled to cooperate with international efforts that have a regional orientation or suggest some measure of devolution, which may be precisely the measures needed to reduce tension in the long run.

The Central Asian governments and peoples see their futures as engaged with Western economic powers. In one public opinion survey conducted in Uzbekistan, about 90 percent of those respondents who believed Uzbekistan should look to other countries for help in solving its environmental and economic problems preferred turning to the United States, Western Europe, or Japan for that aid.[19] The challenge for the West is to take advantage of these opportunities so that not only wealth but stability and reform are compounded.

— APPENDIXES —

— Appendix A —

United Nations Development Programme (UNDP) Proposal for a Ferghana Valley Development Programme Draft Programme Outline[1]

Background

The Ferghana Valley, though shared by three newly independent states of the region, is a single region, historically, economically, and socially, endowed with certain distinctive features. For centuries it formed the core of a large cultural zone along the Silk Road which extended well beyond the Valley itself to large portions of Central Asia. Surrounded by the Tien-Shan mountains in the North and the Pamir mountains in the South, the Valley covers three regions of Uzbekistan (Andijan, Namangan, Ferghana), the Osh region of Kyrgyzstan and part of the Leninabad region in Tajikistan, an approximate territory of 20,000 sq. km. About 8 million people live in the Valley which represent 24 percent of the population of the three countries. The Valley produces 22 percent of the industrial production and 26 percent of the agricultural production of the three states.

Well developed traditions of agriculture, of trade, of diverse culture reflecting its rich multi-ethnic mix, have all shaped the special features of the Valley. Seen as a bridge between the Turkic and Iranian worlds, knowledge of several languages has been the norm for many centuries. Consequently, the ideologies and cultures of the respective societies in the Valley were formed on a multilingual basis. This interaction was reinforced by the facts of shared geography. For a long time, from the 10th to the 17th century, the Valley was part of larger central Asian kingdoms governed from Samarkand or Bokhara (which allied Turkic suzerainty with Iranian/Tadjik cultural norms). In the late 18th and 19th centuries, the Valley became the center of an important Timurid khanate with the city of Kokand as the capital. The khanate in its hey-day extended from western China to Tashkent.

During the Soviet period, the economy of the Ferghana Valley performed better than the overall performance of the three republics sharing the Valley. This can be attributed both to the high agricultur-al output of the area mainly in the form of cotton production—and to rapid industrialization. However, despite this performance, unemploy-ment (as well as underemployment) was relatively high in the Ferghana Valley throughout the Soviet period and remains so today. For example, in the Uzbek parts of the Valley where roughly one-third of Uzbekistan's 22 million people live, more than 35 percent of the work force remain unemployed, with the majority of those being below the age of 25. The three Uzbek provinces of the Valley—Andijan, Ferghana and Namangan—have traditionally been considered as "surplus labor" areas and have a high population density.

Demographically, the Valley was on the verge of social collapse at the beginning of the 1990s. In some parts, the population growth rate was double that of agricultural production. In 1940, each individual could claim about one quarter of a hectare (ha) of irrigated arable land. By the early 1990s, this share had dwindled to an average of 0.11 ha and to less than 0.06 in some areas.

The Soviet authorities in the early 20th century undertook delib-erate measures to change centuries-old traditions of mixed communities and attempted to force the formation of states along ethnic principles. By 1924, Uzbekistan and Turkmenistan had been formed, with Tajikistan, Kyrgyzstan and Kazakstan appearing later. One underlying reason behind the new definition of Central Asia's borders was the desire to prevent the formation of a unified front against Soviet rule by the predominantly Muslim people of the region. Although the Soviet plan worked to a large extent in suppressing national/religious resis-tance of the people of Central Asia, the Ferghana Valley remained the main theater of what little resistance there was to foreign rule. Indeed as events have shown, the epicenter of many of the recent security and peace problems can be traced to the Ferghana Valley.

As the UNDP/ILO Social Policy Review (1995/96) noted, "These new borders divided the people into separate ethnic groups which they themselves were reluctant to recognize as such. That is, the borders, being artificial, created ethnic groups and nationalities, not the other way around, and these divisions were perpetuated when the five Central Asian republics became independent. Where once there was unity, today there is national division and rivalry, at least potentially."

Independence, Transition, and Development

All three countries began their lives as independent states in 1991 with a huge shock: they lost transfers from the Soviet Union equivalent to one fifth of their gross domestic products. These transfers had financed a large part of government expenditures and enabled these governments to support a wide range of public services and outlays on human capital. The results over the years are impressive. Adult literacy reached 92.2 percent in 1989—roughly equal for men and women. Life expectancy is about 69 years and average incomes, whilst low by the standards of the USSR, are relatively high compared to that of neighboring Asian countries.

The transition from a centrally planned to a more market-oriented economy has been accompanied by:

♦ rapid inflation, which in fact accelerated between 1989 (when prices were stable) and 1993 (when retail prices increased by 851 percent in one year), and

♦ falling output levels, and as a consequence, a sharp decline in the real incomes of the population as a whole. The situation has been even worse in Tajikistan where armed conflict has added to the terms-of-trade loss and economic disruption.

The Governments of all three countries have expressed a commitment to economic reform, whilst seeking to maintain political stability. The countries of the region share common problems, though in the case of Tajikistan continuing civil unrest has made such reform difficult to initiate or manage. However, differences in economic, social and political contexts have led to different approaches and attitudes toward reform. By the end of 1993, with the adoption of national currencies, the states were clearly differentiated in terms of their progress during transition and in their development strategies.

It needs to be underlined that the transition which is taking place in the countries of the region is much more than just a shift from a planned economy to a market economy. It is also a social transformation, covering all aspects of human life. While a main concern of the countries remains economic, that is, to improve incomes and standards of living, there is also a fundamental desire to develop links with the outside world and to maintain peace and stability in the region.

Some of the principal regional concerns and challenges can be summarized as follows:

1. MAINTAINING INTER-ETHNIC PEACE AND GOOD COMMUNITY RELATIONS

The Ferghana Valley is home to many ethnic groups, with the Uzbeks constituting the majority, followed by Tajiks and Kyrgyz, and then by minorities such as Russians, Kazaks, Tatars, Koreans, Germans and others. Ethnic problems during the Soviet period were either suppressed or were not very prominent since everyone was technically a citizen of one state, the USSR. When the *glasnost* policies of Mikhail Gorbachev granted people more freedom to express themselves, one unfortunate outcome was a rise in ethnic tension between the many nationalities of the USSR. The transition has put renewed pressure on the maintenance of inter-ethnic peace and normal dialogue among regions and communities.

The Ferghana Valley reemerged on the international scene as the site of two particularly unfortunate ethnic clashes which are still vivid in the memories of the people of the region today and drive national policies. In 1989 there was a major clash between Uzbeks and Meskhetian Turks in Ferghana (and around Tashkent) and in 1990 there were gun battles between Uzbek and Kyrgyz in the Kyrgyz city of Osh.

Minority rights and an understanding of what these entail are likely to influence future peace and stability in the region. As such they deserve priority.

2. PROMOTING REGIONAL DIALOGUE AND COOPERATION

Inter-country relations in the Valley are complex and tend to escalate very quickly. For instance, Uzbek concern regarding security and drug trafficking from Tajik and Kyrgyz territory leads it to periodically clamp down on traffic into Uzbekistan, thus reducing trade—but also mutual trust—and increasing suspicion of respective motives. For the latter this is especially pressing given the events in Tajikistan and Afghanistan. Regional cooperation and dialogue are essential ingredients in keeping the potentially explosive Ferghana region calm and secure. Thus far there have been no formal meetings among the three countries on the issues relating to the Ferghana Valley save the June 1996 agreement on border drug control (signed in Tashkent).

Regional cooperation among the three countries that share the Ferghana Valley is essential. Actions and measures which do not limit national decision-making (as new states, these countries remain somewhat wary of any dependence) are especially important. Nonetheless, as nation-building processes develop and mature, there is a corresponding need to pursue the issue of regional cooperation and, given the realities on the ground of normal economic and social existence, some degree of regional integration.

At the Issyk-Kul Conference and the Tashkent Seminar on Peace and Stability—both in 1994—the five Central Asian republics acknowledged a shared responsibility for their common problems and undertook to work together on economic and social development, demographic issues and environmental concerns. The issues of illicit drugs, environmental protection and cooperation in trade and transit matters are some of the areas which the three countries undertook to focus on. Strengthening such cooperation in these and other areas will require the active involvement of local authorities and institution building.

3. REGIONAL INSTITUTIONAL BUILDING WHICH SHOULD COVER BOTH GOVERNMENTAL AND NON-GOVERNMENTAL ENTITIES

New institutions and new mechanisms are critical to the affirmation of a regional identity and to confidence building between the countries and their peoples.

Some UN agencies are attempting to deal with some facets of the existing problems. UNDCP has just approved a drug control project to help the Kyrgyz reduce the flow of drugs through Osh, though there is a fear that unless alternative income opportunities are created this control effort is unlikely to be sustainable. UNHCR is planning activities in the Valley to help in the resettlement of Tajik returnees from Afghanistan. A UNHCR office has been operating in Osh since 1995 to help guard against any re-occurrence of incidents like that which occurred in 1990. The Kyrgyz and Tajik governments have requested UN agencies to help them publish teaching materials for school children designed to promote ethnic tolerance. UNHCR is in the process of producing such teaching materials. UNICEF also has provided aid to the Kyrgyz and Tajik governments with the publication of reading materials on Peace Education.

FERGHANA VALLEY DEVELOPMENT PROGRAMMME

Despite both government and UN agency attempts, as outlined above, there has not been a serious effort to build a comprehensive program. There is a need to bring together these many strands and design a

Ferghana Valley Development Programme which will pay equal attention to income generation and job creation, peace education, inter-ethnic and inter-country confidence building, promotion of trade (and related dialogue on the maintenance of open boundaries) and the improvement of security conditions.

Rather than addressing a number of separate problems of the region, the thrust of the program is on securing the conditions for growth and development (i.e. issues of "preventive" development) *pari passu* with the promotion of sustainable development. Such a program would need to be formally owned by the three countries, with UNDP taking the lead in a UN system-supported process which may include the possible creation of a UN technical support office located in the Valley. It may also prove to be an attractive proposal for donors. And the very presence of the UN in the Valley will help promote transparency and reinforce mutual dialogue.

More specifically, the program's focus could be directed at the following areas:

1. GROWTH AND EQUITY CONCERNS

The resumption of economic growth, especially that based on labor intensive development, is one of the major tasks facing the countries of the region. But, as mentioned earlier, all the countries concerned are at different stages of economic reform and have differing expectations for the near future. Apart from the growing inequalities arising as the result of the transition, there is also some concern that the growing differences in living standards between the different parts of the Ferghana Valley may undermine future dialogue and peace.

The Valley has to be seen as an integral geographical area with unified strategies to develop and upgrade living conditions. Job creation would be the primary objective addressed by the FVDP. Programs and projects have to be defined to promote the accelerated creation of both jobs and incomes.

2. INTER-ETHNIC PEACE AND TOLERANCE

It is clear that for the newly independent states of the region, nation-building is one of the main political priorities. The strengthening of national identity is, at the same time, related to the appearance of new minorities—Uzbeks in Tajikistan and Kyrgyzstan, Tajiks in Uzbekistan and Kyrgyzstan, and Kyrgyz in Tajikistan and Uzbekistan.

Of particular importance is the status and well-being of the Russian population in the Central Asian region which numbers around 12 million—a large chunk of the total 50 million population of Central Asia—as well as other minorities (Tatars, Koreans, Uigurs and others).

In this context, the FVDP could be concentrated on establishing joint inter-ethnic confidence-building measures. Experience gained by UN agencies such as UNHCR and UNICEF and by non-UN agencies such as the OSCE could be utilized as a point of departure in encouraging all three republics to initiate regular and systematic dialogue among communities.

The work of NGOs like the Assembly of the Peoples of Central Asia could be encouraged by the FVDP and perhaps by doing so, similar NGOs could come into existence.

A special role in this part of the program could be played by local communities—mahallas—which play an important role both in influencing people's opinions and sympathies.

3. Transparent boundaries

The FVDP could start its cooperation with the three governments with questions dealing with the regulation of cross-border trade and "people" contact. At present, it appears that there is no agreed framework for such interaction; in particular there is a need for some guidelines for trade among the three states that share the Ferghana Valley. Lack of such guidelines generates much agitation and frustration among the local people who, prior to 1991, had no special regulations for cross-republic trade and now are faced instead with uncertainty and mistrust. This tends to create a breeding ground for demagoguery and extreme expressions of nationalism. The FVDP could help the three governments agree on immediate measures to regularize trade and people intercourse. In the medium-term, the formation of an economic zone in the Ferghana Valley could be discussed. The notion of such a zone has a special resonance for all the countries concerned since they are all land-locked.

4. Languages and education

Cooperation in the fields of language and education among the three countries is a very important step in promoting better understanding among their peoples, maintaining inter-ethnic peace, and ensuring future sustainable human development.

The FVDP could help the governments involved in producing textbooks in languages other than the national language and also in promoting minority language radio and television program broadcasts in the Ferghana Valley. Another area that could help ease inter-ethnic tension is the development of an understanding and appreciation of each others' respective histories.

5. REVIVAL OF CULTURAL HERITAGE AND COOPERATION

Cultural cooperation between Kyrgyzstan, Tajikistan and Uzbekistan in the issues that relate to their common heritage in the Ferghana Valley will not only produce closer relations between the three communities and promote the revival of a "common" cultural heritage, it will also lead to job creation with renewed crafts development and tourism.

Culture and its expression serve as important vehicles to cement emerging identities and incorporate positive values of cultural openness and dialogue. Interaction and dialogue are seen as assets in themselves. They directly enhance human capabilities. And the sharing of values and ideas regionally or nationally can serve to strengthen social harmony. Living in society harmoniously requires individual and collective skills which need to be nurtured and developed.

Nations are in essence "imagined communities." The Valley has for long perceived itself as a community. For new regional identities to emerge, with a positive image and role of culture and cultural self-expression in strengthening human capabilities, the conditions for the sustainability of human development are substantially enhanced. Social peace is necessary for human development to occur and social peace in turn requires that cultural diversity is seen as a positive force in keeping societies innovative and dynamic over the long run.

PROPOSED TIMETABLE AND PLAN OF ACTION

1. PREPARATORY MISSION

As a first step the concepts and program elements of the "Ferghana Valley Development Programme" need to be discussed in depth at the regional level itself to ensure there is full ownership. This would help determine the strategic areas of intervention and an outline of what to do next. For this purpose, there is clearly a need of a solid background note which outlines the issues involved and possible program elements. This note should be the subject of a preparatory mission which would visit all three countries (and the Valley) to identify, in close consultation with governments, NGOs and donors, potential areas of program intervention as well as to identify UNDP and other UN agencies' roles and comparative advantage in facilitating and supporting inter-country cooperation. This inter-agency mission (UNDP, UNHCR, UNDCP, UNICEF) could start its work by end of this year. Of the proposed 2–3 week duration, the mission would spend considerable time with official and unofficial groups in the Valley.

2. REVIEW AND "OWNERSHIP BUILDING"

The background note will be discussed at a review meeting convened in the Valley, possibly in Leninabad or Osh. It would bring together officials, especially those from the district level, NGOs, and UN Agencies to verify and develop those program elements of interest.

The program, as mentioned, should be formally owned by the three countries with UNDP taking the lead in a UN system-supported process. It is expected that other UN agencies, such as UNDCP, UNICEF, UNHCR, UNIDO and ILO would participate in the program, and/or closely coordinate program activities with UN agencies represented in the region. Coordination with other international agencies and organizations active in the area will be an essential part of the program.

3. FIELD STUDY

Following the above, a series of field studies and assessments related to different development issues in the region and in people's lives will need to be undertaken: poverty, employment, gender issues, access to basic human needs, the role of local communities and NGOs, and so forth. These can be locally organized, that is, led by national and regional experts.

4. JOINT PROGRAMME PREPARATION MISSION AND RESOURCES MOBILIZATION

Toward early next year, a joint team of national and international experts could be organized (preferably also including representatives of potential donor countries) to draft a program document. This program document would be finalized in consultation with respective national officials, NGOs and UN agencies. It could then be presented by the three governments to an informal donors/program launching meeting to raise resources and to initiate the implementation of the program.

TABLE A.1
MAIN ECONOMIC INDICATORS OF UZBEKISTAN, KYRGYZSTAN, TAJIKISTAN

	UZBEKISTAN	KYRGYZSTAN	TAJIKISTAN
Population (million) (1994)	22.4	4.5	5.8
Area (thousand sq. km.)	447	199	143
GNP per capita ($) (1994)	960	630	360
GNP per capita average annual growth (%) (1985–94)	-2.3	-5.0	-11.4
PPP estimated GNP per capita (1994)	2370	1730	970
Life expectancy at birth (1994)	70	68	67
Average annual inflation (1984–94)	109.1	100.9	104.3
Net present value of external debt as % of GNP (1994)	5	13	25
Labor force/annual growth rate (1990–1994)	2.9	2.0	3.3

— Appendix B —

Soros Foundation–Kyrgyzstan
FERGHANA PROJECT
Bishkek 1998

Executive Summary

The disintegration of the former Soviet Union resulted in a dramatic shift in the social, economic, and cultural relations of Central Asia. States in the region are now faced with reconciling differences in economic development, levels of integration into the interstate system, and traditions of administration. The Republic of Kyrgyzstan has suffered not only from low economic development, poor integration into the other states of the region, and an underdeveloped administrative system, but also from its immediate proximity to hotbeds of interethnic tension and military conflicts, particularly in Tajikistan.

The problems confronting the region as a whole are concentrated in the Ferghana Valley, a single territorial unit which is now spread over three states: Uzbekistan, Tajikistan, and Kyrgyzstan. The Ferghana Project is a pilot project addressing a number of urgent issues in need of attention within Kyrgyzstan's southern oblasts. Given the fact that about 48 percent of the entire population of Kyrgyzstan lives in the southern oblasts of the country, the situation in the southern region presents not just a local threat—instability there poses a threat to the entire country and to the stability of Central Asia as a whole. Based on results of this pilot project, further activity both within Kyrgyzstan and regionally is contemplated. Cooperation with other non-governmental organizations, international organizations, and the government is essential to the long-term viability of the project.

The Ferghana Project sets the major goal to promote cooperation, understanding, and stability in the Ferghana valley between the state and society, differing regions and ethnic groups. It aims to facilitate cooperation and determine which areas of civil leadership most need financial assistance and will help develop contacts between the local administration and representatives of community leadership. The Project pursues these goals through a four-program block focusing on public administration, NGOs, medicine, and education. The Project's outcomes will be improvements in the basic areas of water supply, heating development, and medical services, in addition to providing support for the development of NGOs, independent media, civil society, local business initiatives, cultural initiatives, and educational reform in the southern region.

The initial phase of the Ferghana Project will be implemented over the course of one year. This time frame will make it possible to achieve some short-term goals while providing a framework for later long-term achievements. Priority will be given to financial and material support for areas most in need; however, the effect of this support will depend on the level of connection with the economic and social activity of the local population and cooperation with local government as well as cooperation and coordination with international donors. Special attention will be focused on programs which have long-term sustainability and those which provide for cooperation and coordination with other donors, the government, and international organizations. The Project will be evaluated upon completion of the initial phase.

BACKGROUND

The disintegration of the former Soviet Union, which resulted in a dramatic shift in the social, economic, and cultural relations of the region, has affected all of the communities belonging to the sphere of interest of the former superpower. Having gained independence, the states in the region are now faced with reconciling differences in economic development, levels of integration into the interstate system, and traditions of administration. The Central Asian region, particularly the Republic of Kyrgyzstan, has suffered not only from low economic development, poor integration into the other states of the region, and an underdeveloped administrative system, but also from its immediate proximity to hotbeds of interethnic tension, particularly in Tajikistan.

Analyzing Kyrgyzstan in the context of internal and intergovernmental relations, one can't help seeing its increasing vulnerability. The basis for this vulnerability is partly geographic—mountain ranges tra-verse the border between the southern oblasts of Osh and Jalal-Abad and the rest of the country, hindering both transportation and com-munication, and isolating the southern region from the rest of the Republic. In addition, the exterior border of the southern region is almost twice as long as its interior border, and the lack of adequate pro-tection along this external border adds to a sense of vulnerability there.

The isolation and vulnerability of the southern oblasts is a possibly destabilizing force with the potential to intensify separatist pressure, and to jeopardize the development of a stable democratic system in Kyrgyzstan.

The external factor aggravating the situation in the Osh and Jalal-Abad oblasts is the civil war in Tajikistan. Ongoing military actions dur-ing the past few years have created a feeling of constant threat in the region. Lack of security at the external borders, a constant flow of refugees, and caravans of drug-traffickers going through the southern oblasts from Tajikistan to the European part of the CIS further add to the insecurity in the region and the desire of the majority for tighter governmental control. The situation in bordering Uzbekistan is also worrisome.

Such external pressures are exacerbated by the general social and economic situation in Kyrgyzstan. The collapse of the Soviet system has led to a difficult period of economic transition. The unemployment and drop in production caused by the reorientation of the economy, coupled with a drastic reduction of social benefits provided by the state, have left the population vulnerable to propaganda from outside, particularly to the militant strains of Islam that have threatened other areas in the region.

The problems of the southern region of Kyrgyzstan require imme-diate attention. The internal problems common to the entire country are exacerbated in the southern region because of its geographic sepa-ration from the rest of the country. Given the fact that about 48 percent of the entire population of Kyrgyzstan lives in the southern oblasts of the country, the situation in the southern region presents not just a local threat—instability there poses a threat to the entire country and to the stability of Central Asia as a whole.

PROJECT GOALS AND OBJECTIVES

The goal of this project is to alleviate the escalation of crisis in the southern region of Kyrgyzstan. By working within the framework of the Soros Foundation–Kyrgyzstan (SF–Kyrgyzstan), this project will help support improvements in such basic areas as water supply, heating development, and medical services, in addition to providing support for the development of non-governmental organizations (NGOs), independent media, civil society, local business initiatives, cultural initiatives, and educational reform in the southern region. As financial resources are limited, this project focuses particularly on those areas which are most in need of immediate assistance and which would make it possible to effect the most substantial improvement.

1. The first and most essential effort of the Ferghana Project will be to provide training to the Ferghana Project staff to ensure effective collaboration between local and regional administration and a strong connection to the communities for which they work.

2. Another important aspect of the Ferghana Project is the support of the nascent NGO sector, independent print media sources, civil rights organizations, and self-governance groups to encourage democratic tendencies through the structures whose very existence contradicts the authoritarian system and creates a counterbalance to antidemocratic methods of governance.

3. Support for local community initiatives to solve problems of water supply, heating, and provision of medical services is an area which requires special attention. Aid for such basic developmental concerns would have an enormous impact on easing tensions in the area and helping to stimulate community involvement.

4. Tuberculosis poses a very real threat to public health in Kyrgyzstan. Unfortunately, state financing for TB prevention is insufficient to control the ever-increasing problem. As such, immediate attention from international organizations is the only step which may be able to curtail the threat.

5. The last element of the Ferghana Project focuses on the strengthening of secular education, free from dogmas and strict totalitarian rules. This includes support for theaters, libraries, rural schools, and secular cultural organizations.

All of these program objectives fall within the framework of programs already under implementation by SF–Kyrgyzstan. The main difference of this particular project is its focus on the southern oblasts as a region which requires specific attention.

FORMS, METHODS, AND TERMS OF IMPLEMENTATION

A four-program block focusing on public administration, NGOs, medicine, and education will make up the basis of the Ferghana Project. All efforts will emphasize the development of independent local initiatives and activities, as well as provide training and professional development for employees of local administrations, representatives of local government, and NGO leaders.

An important aspect of the Ferghana Project's work will be establishing lines of communication with local government representatives in order to facilitate cooperation and determine which areas of civil leadership most need financial assistance. This aspect of the Ferghana Project's work will also help establish additional contacts between the local administration and representatives of community leadership.

The initial phase of the Ferghana Project will be implemented over the course of one year. This time frame will make it possible to achieve some short-term goals while providing a framework for later long-term achievements. Priority will be given to financial and material support for areas most in need; however, the effect of this support will depend on the level of connection with the economic and social activity of the local population and cooperation with local government, as well as cooperation and coordination with international donors. Special attention will be focused on programs which will have long-term effectiveness.

In all areas of project focus, we are planning to work closely with representatives of organizations of the Uzbek and Tajik communities in order to ensure their active participation in project implementation. Our goal is not to serve as a substitute for the state, but to attract attention to the issues of highest concern to the region and to guide the local government to creative collaboration with ethnic minorities in securing more lasting stability.

PROJECT COMPONENTS

SUPPORT FOR PHYSICAL INFRASTRUCTURE DEVELOPMENT

Financial crisis and a dramatic economic decline in Kyrgyzstan have been especially harsh on the low-income elements of the population. Residents of smaller communities have found themselves in a particularly vulnerable situation, having to face the liquidation and temporary shut-down of state-run enterprises coupled with the broken economic ties within and outside of the republic with almost complete abandonment by a government which insists on the principle of self-sustainability as the answer to its economic woes.

Because of the inability of the state to provide economic support to the region, the only guarantee of survival is the extent to which people can solve problems using their own resources. Raising money for common needs and collective work projects have helped somewhat, but in the majority of cases, the local population simply does not have the resources to combat this far-reaching economic crisis on its own.

Problems with drinking water, with the agricultural water supply, and with heating and electricity in schools, hospitals, and kindergartens present just a short list of the issues faced by local communities. The absence of a dependable line of communication between the southern oblasts and the central government only adds to the social tension caused by these problems. The geographical isolation of the south compounds a sense of abandonment and hopelessness.

The main goal is to help the local population take greater responsibility for fulfilling its own needs. One of the main objectives of the Ferghana Project is to help the local population understand that the only way out of crisis is creative activity, not a return to totalitarian systems of governance or radical religious movements.

Thus, within the framework of this part of the program, local initiatives will be supported in these areas:

- Drinking water supply.

- Renovation of the agricultural water-supply system.

- Renovation of the thermal network (heating supply).

- Other social projects.

As mentioned above, the support of the Ferghana Project should be implemented, as a minimum, on a parity basis with the local communities. The main factors in the selection process will be the involvement of the population, social effectiveness and importance of the proposed projects, and support and participation of the local government. Taking into consideration that the water supply issue is one of the most significant problems of the region, this issue will be the main emphasis of this part of the Ferghana Project.

To help coordinate these efforts, technical support will be provided to the local communities, and a series of educational and analytical workshops for local government officials will be provided on the basis of guidelines set forth by the Agency for Development of Local Government. This will make it possible to evaluate the impact of the programs on local communities and to make corrections to the developed plans as necessary.

SUPPORT FOR LOCAL ADMINISTRATIVE REFORM

Strengthening contacts with the local administration of the southern region is essential for ensuring the ultimate efficacy of any program. Local administration, responsible for the main issues of social and economic conditions of the territories, carries the main burden for solving these problems and is the only competent structure for communicating the needs of the local population to the central government. Taking into consideration the financial crisis faced by local government officials and the strain of social crises in southern Kyrgyzstan, the work of these programs will embrace a wide spectrum of issues.

Work with the administration of the southern oblasts will focus on three main areas—educational workshops, research into programs that would benefit most from joint cooperation between the foundation and the local government administration, and support for local government programs dealing with social and economic issues. Particular attention will be paid in all three areas to the problems of ethnic minorities in the region.

1. At present, workshop proposals include the following issues:

    ◆   Social issues, social guarantees, and protection of underprivileged populations;

    ◆   Legal basics of market economy and entrepreneurship;

    ◆   Legal issues of administrative and economic activity;

    ◆   Legal issues of social policy implementation;

    ◆   New tax legislation;

    ◆   Business planning; and,

    ◆   Development of investment practices.

Workshops will be based on the Agency on Local Government Development established by SF–Kyrgyzstan and the city administration of Bishkek. The plan is to hire experienced trainers who have attended special workshops conducted by foreign experts.

2. Research into programs which would benefit most from joint cooperation between the Foundation and the local government administration will be assisted by a number of round-table discussions with representatives from the local administration as well as local research groups. The subjects of these meetings will be issues of social policy and the most effective means of participation of the Foundation in the implementation of these goals.

3. Financial support for local government programs dealing with social and economic issues will help make it possible for them to implement much-needed social change in addition to establishing new business contacts, taking into account the existence of a micro credit program currently being developed by the Foundation in this region.

Monitoring and evaluating the administrative development programs of the Ferghana Project will be combined with that of the local community development programs, as these components of the project will overlap and supplement each other. Evaluation of the results of the administrative development programs will be conducted by a group of experts together with Foundation employees as part of a round-table discussion after all of the activities for this part of the program have taken place. Elements of this program that have proved to be the most effective will be continued after the project has been implemented.

SUPPORT FOR TB-PREVENTION PROGRAMS

The spread of tuberculosis is a particular threat to the population of southern Kyrgyzstan. Special alarm is being caused by the fast spread of TB among children: in the last two years incidence of the disease has exceeded 200 percent.

Coefficient of the TB incidence among the population:

In Jalal-Abad Oblast—383.5

In Osh Oblast—215

Among children:

In Jalal-Abad Oblast—43.6

In Osh Oblast—22.4

Implementation of a TB-prevention program will be conducted jointly with the Kyrgyz Research Institute of TB and regional anti-TB institutions. Tuberculosis sanitariums and special schools within sanitariums will be actively supported in the implementation of this program.

The Soros Foundation–Kyrgyzstan will put special emphasis on the following aspects of the program:

1. Provide regional tuberculosis clinics with hematological analyzers, urine analyzers, biochemical computer photometers with one-canal coagulant, binocular microscopes, and other necessary lab equipment.

2. Establish two regional training centers for providing equipment training for the staff of tuberculosis clinics and educational workshops for physicians of the region on prophylactics and treatment of medication-resistant forms of TB.

3. Support of children's educational programs in schools within tuberculosis sanitariums, including purchase of textbooks and the provision of office equipment for the demonstration of physical rehabilitation exercises.

Implementation of the TB-prevention program will help physicians learn state-of-the-art treatment methods, making it possible to cut down on the time necessary for them to make a diagnosis and thus allow starting treatment at an earlier stage in the disease. Professional training seminars will make it possible to improve work with the patients suffering from chronic forms of TB, and the creation of a TB database will help systematize the statistical information to be submitted to the Research Center for TB. The regular submission of reports required during the first year of project implementation will demonstrate the level of success in conducting these activities.

SUPPORT FOR NGO DEVELOPMENT

NGOs, often open to new, relatively untraditional ideas, are organizations which can be far more effective in dealing with local problems than groups solely from the outside trying to influence the region.

The Ferghana Project's work with NGO development will focus on these areas:

◆ Train representatives of NGOs both on general issues and in accordance with specific activities of their organizations;

◆ Hire experts for holding consultations with local NGOs to help in planning the work of their organization;

◆ Publish reference books and practical recommendations for NGOs of the southern region specifically based on the local situation;

◆ Conduct interim workshops for the exchange of experience between NGOs and determine the effectiveness of the Ferghana project implementation stage-by-stage.

Additional assistance will be given in the form of financial and material support for NGO projects to develop the existing NGO network in the south and to create new NGOs based on the immediate needs of the population.

A new approach to work with NGOs will be to establish a connection between NGOs and the local administration for the coordination of activities to address social problems in the region. In addition, special care will be taken to work with organizations representing the Tajik and Uzbek populations in the area. For this purpose, a number of joint meetings and workshops will be held to bring together members of the Soros Foundation–Kyrgyzstan, NGOs, and the local administration.

Taking into consideration the relatively short period of project initialization, it will be necessary to initialize operational work strengthening what has been achieved in the south in the field of NGOs.

Given the remoteness of the region and the fact that the Ferghana Project will be implemented by a number of organizations who have never worked with SF-Kyrgyzstan before, stricter requirements for financial reporting will necessarily be imposed. Quarterly reports on the use of the grant, as well as periodic trips of program coordinators to the region and their familiarization with the NGO work, should guarantee the proper utilization of grants. This process, in addition to a number of workshops and training sessions, will make it possible to successfully evaluate the NGOs and select the most suitable organizations to continue working in the region in the future.

SUPPORT FOR SECONDARY AND HIGHER EDUCATION

Of Kyrgyzstan's 1887 schools, 1070 are located in the South. Although SF–Kyrgyzstan has established several highly effective programs for the support of education in Kyrgyzstan, schools in the southern region need special help, both because of their relative isolation and because of the added pressures of drugs and militant sectarian groups operating in the region. Programs of the Ferghana Project will focus on support of extracurricular activities, development of creative critical thinking skills, and school self-governance. Education support will cover the following areas:

1. Grant support for remote schools. Schools in remote areas suffer greatly from a lack of classroom materials. Support will be provided for these schools in the form of law textbooks and English, Russian, and Kyrgyz language textbooks, as well as works of fiction. The plan is to provide support to 50 remotely located schools.

2. Regional workshops. In order to involve even the most remote regions of southern Kyrgyzstan in the dialogue about education reform, a series of workshops for school administrators and teachers will be held to help identify and discuss the most significant problems facing the region in terms of school management and the survival of the schools in the contemporary situation. The workshops are being organized by a group of representatives from pilot schools in the region.

3. Establishment of an educational resource center. In 1998 the program "Transformation of the Humanities" in Bishkek will establish a methodological center for educational programs to support coordination of activities of the programs, their adaptation to the existing educational system, and the use of methodological and normative resources for innovations. A southern branch of this Resource Center will help implement innovative programs in the schools of the southern region and will help bring the schools of the region together into an educational network. The establishment

of this resource center will not require a huge expense, because it will be based in one of the schools which already has most of the necessary resources.

4.   Grant support for colleges. Support for colleges in southern Kyrgyzstan should combine support of colleges with the task to bring them to the attention of the local administration and NGOs. When implementing the Ferghana Project, it should be understood from the beginning that the goal is NOT to act as a substitute to the government in its activities. Taking into consideration that the situation with the Uzbek minority is a vital issue in the region, some attention will be focused on the problems of Uzbek departments at colleges and secondary schools in the regions where Uzbeks form a majority.

Monitoring and evaluating the education support programs will be aided by the establishment of educational centers in the region. Since these centers will be based on the model of SF-Kyrgyzstan's Resource Centers and will benefit from added staff from the Foundation, it will be possible to monitor the progress of the educational programs and obtain results which can be applied to schools throughout the region and in the rest of the country as well. The Resource Centers will be tested for the first time within the framework of this project.

Support for Cultural Programs

Given an almost total lack of financing by the government for cultural institutions over the past ten years, the number of such organizations has been dramatically reduced, with the few remaining institutions currently on the brink of closure. With the growing influence of religious sectarianism in the region, support for the preservation of secular culture is a high priority for the Ferghana Project. Participation of the local administration in the cultural support programs will help stimulate cooperation between cultural institutions and the local administration and help these institutions to continue operating.

Apart from the organizational work which will be the essence of this program, the project will provide support to such traditional cultural organizations as theaters, museums, music schools, and colleges of the towns of Osh and Jalal-Abad, particularly organizations involving the culture of the Tajik and Uzbek ethnic minorities:

1. Support of theaters and theatrical productions.

2. Work with museums and organization of expeditions to the remote areas of the South to obtain antique pieces for museum collections.

3. Support for music schools and colleges, including instruments and methodological assistance.

4. Support for talented children of the South through exhibitions and competitions in music, painting, and applied art.

5. Library support is of special importance, since libraries are the only cultural institutions aside from schools in the provincial areas.

Monitoring and evaluating the cultural programs of the Ferghana Project will be conducted by cultural program coordinators together with the financial department of the Foundation and employees of the regional resource centers.

MONITORING AND EVALUATION OF PROJECT RESULTS

Effective monitoring of the progress of this project will depend on the cooperation of many different groups and organizations. A responsible attitude towards the work at hand will in part be insured by the variety of interests and backgrounds represented by the participants, but frequent field trips by program coordinators and periodic reports from grant recipients will offer further input in assessing progress in the region. Regional seminars and round-table discussions will provide project participants with a forum for discussing problems as they are encountered and for proposing possible solutions.

Evaluating project results is a more complicated process. The most important goal of this project is to have a long-term impact on the growth of democratization in the region. However, measuring this impact is a task limited both by budget parameters and by the extremely broad spectrum of programs involved.

The effectiveness of this project will in part be measured by the degree of openness and readiness to cooperate expressed by project staff, staff of higher and secondary education institutions, and staff of medical and cultural institutions; the active participation and initiative of

NGOs, mass media, and local government bodies; and the frequency and level of interactions between all of these elements. While this indicator will not give an exact assessment of progress, it is to a certain extent the most effective indicator that is available, and it can be used both during the process of project implementation and after project completion.

— Appendix C —

CENTER FOR PREVENTIVE ACTION
FERGHANA VALLEY WORKING GROUP

RICHARD E. COMBS, JR.
ASSOCIATE DIRECTOR, CENTER FOR RUSSIAN AND EURASIAN STUDIES,
MONTEREY INSTITUTE OF INTERNATIONAL STUDIES

Richard Combs has been director of nonproliferation programs in the former Soviet Union at the Center for Nonproliferation Studies, Monterey Institute of International Studies, since December 1995. In 1996, he was also appointed associate director of the Institute's Center for Russian and Eurasian Studies and designated as research professor of international policy studies. Prior to joining the Monterey Institute, Dr. Combs served as a professional staff member of the Senate Armed Services Committee following a twenty-three-year career as a U.S. diplomat. He also served as Senator Sam Nunn's designee on the staff of the Senate Select Intelligence Committee from 1989 to 1991.

ARNOLD L. HORELICK
VICE PRESIDENT FOR RUSSIAN AND EURASIAN AFFAIRS,
CARNEGIE ENDOWMENT FOR INTERNATIONAL PEACE

Arnold Horelick is vice president for Russian and Eurasian affairs at the Carnegie Endowment. Previously, he was resident consultant in the International Policy Department at RAND and professor of political science at UCLA. In 1983 he became the first director of the RAND/UCLA Center for Soviet Studies. Prior to joining the UCLA faculty, he was visiting professor of political science at Columbia University, City University of New York, California Institute of Technology, and Cornell University. From 1977 to 1980 Mr. Horelick served in Washington, D.C., as the national intelligence officer for the Soviet Union and Eastern Europe.

R. Scott Horton
Partner, Patterson, Belknap, Webb, and Tyler

Since 1990 Scott Horton has been a partner at Patterson, Belknap, Webb, and Tyler, where he has focused on commercial transactions in Europe and the former Soviet Union. He has been involved in many commercial, infrastructural, and agricultural projects in Central Asia and elsewhere in the former Soviet Union. Mr. Horton is the associate editor for Central Asia and Transcaucasus, *Survey of Eastern European Law*, and associate editor for legal affairs at *Central Asia Monitor*, and has written extensively about legal issues in the region. He is also the president of the International League for Human Rights.

Charles R. E. Lewis, III
Executive Director, Center for Public Integrity

Charles Lewis is the founder and executive director of the Center for Public Integrity, a research organization that concentrates on ethics and public service issues. Mr. Lewis has guided more than thirty investigative studies on corruption and ethical conduct among public officials, most recently, *The Buying of the Congress*, published in 1998. Previously, he was an investigative reporter at ABC and CBS and was a producer of *60 Minutes*. He is a current recipient of a MacArthur Fellowship of the John D. and Catherine T. MacArthur Foundation (the so-called genius award).

Nancy Lubin
President, JNA Associates, Inc.

Nancy Lubin, the principal author of this report, is president of JNA Associates, Inc., a consulting firm that conducts assessments and projects concerning the newly independent states of the former Soviet Union. Previously, she was associate professor of political science at Carnegie Mellon University and project director for the congressional Office of Technology Assessment. She has been a Fellow at the U.S. Institute of Peace, the Woodrow Wilson Center, and Harvard's Russian Research Center. Dr. Lubin has traveled to Central Asia for twenty years and is the author of scholarly and popular books and articles.

*G. KEITH MARTIN
SENIOR RESEARCH ASSOCIATE, JNA ASSOCIATES, INC.

Keith Martin is a program specialist at the Overseas Private Investment Corporation in Washington D.C. He is also a Ph.D. candidate at McGill University focusing on Central Asia and has been a research associate at Radio Free Europe/Radio Liberty Research Institute. He founded "CenAsia," the Central Asia Internet discussion group. He is a co-author of this report.

*SAM A. NUNN
PARTNER, KING & SPALDING

Senator Sam Nunn, chair of the Ferghana Valley Working Group, was elected to the United States Senate from Georgia in 1972 and served four terms. He is now a senior partner in the Atlanta law firm of King & Spalding. During his tenure on Capitol Hill, Senator Nunn served as chairman of the Senate Armed Services Committee and the Senate Permanent Subcommittee on Investigations. Among other initiatives, he coauthored legislation creating the Cooperative Threat Reduction Program, also known as the Nunn-Lugar Program.

*OLARA OTUNNU
UNDER SECRETARY GENERAL OF THE UNITED NATIONS, SPECIAL REPRESENTATIVE OF THE SECRETARY GENERAL FOR CHILDREN AND ARMED CONFLICT

Before taking up his present position at the United Nations, and during the period of his participation in the working group, Olara Otunnu was president of the International Peace Academy, an independent, international institution affiliated with the United Nations. He was Uganda's permanent representative to the United Nations from 1980 to 1985. In 1985 he returned to Uganda and served as minister of foreign affairs, playing a leading role in the Uganda peace talks. From 1987 to 1989 he was a visiting fellow at the Institut Français des Relations Internationales and a visiting professor at American University in Paris.

ANTHONY H. RICHTER
DIRECTOR, CENTRAL EURASIA PROJECT, OPEN SOCIETY INSTITUTE

Anthony Richter directs the Central Eurasia Project within the Soros Foundations Network. The goal of the project is to promote the development of open societies in the former Soviet republics of Armenia, Azerbaijan, Mongolia, Tajikistan, Turkmenistan, and Uzbekistan. The project also seeks to foster more informed debate about issues in and around the Caspian basin through its website, www.soros.org/cep, its Open Forum meeting series, and the publication of occasional papers. Richter has previously served as special adviser to the president of the Soros Foudnations and as executive director of the Soros Foundation—USSR.

*Rozanne L. Ridgway
Chair, Baltic-American Enterprise Fund

After retiring from a thirty-two-year career in the Foreign Service in 1989, Rozanne Ridgway became president of the Atlantic Council and served as its cochair from 1993 to 1996. Ambassador Ridgway served as assistant secretary of state for European and Canadian affairs during the period 1985–89. She continues to be called upon for public service and is currently chair of the Baltic-American Enterprise Fund.

Barnett R. Rubin
Director, Center for Preventive Action, Council on Foreign Relations

Barnett Rubin is the director of the Center for Preventive Action at the Council on Foreign Relations. He was associate professor of political science and director of the Center for the Study of Central Asia at Columbia University during the years 1990–96. Previously, he was a peace fellow at the United States Institute of Peace and assistant professor of political science at Yale University. Among other works, Dr. Rubin is the author of three books on Afghanistan. He is a coauthor of this report.

Anya Schmemann
Communications Officer
Robert and Renée Belfer Center for Science and International Affairs
John F. Kennedy School of Government, Harvard Universtiy

Before taking up her post at Harvard, Anya Schmemann was a project manager in the international security department of the EastWest Institute in New York. Previously, she was assistant director of the Center for Preventive Action at the Council on Foreign Relations and a research associate with the Council's Project on East-West Relations.

ADAM N. STULBERG
SENIOR RESEARCH ASSOCIATE, MONTEREY INSTITUTE OF INTERNATIONAL STUDIES

Adam Stulberg is a senior research associate at the Monterey Institute and a political consultant to the RAND Corporation. He has held several research positions including terms at Radio Free Europe/Radio Liberty in Munich and at the Institute of World Economy and International Relations in Moscow.

———————

An asterisk (*) denotes those who did not participate in the study mission to Central Asia in March 1997.

— Appendix D —

CENTRAL ASIAN RESOURCES ON THE INTERNET

GENERAL INFORMATION AND LINKS

There are a number of sites with information about Central Asia on the Internet. Some sites with extensive links to Central Asian studies resources are listed below.

Ferghana Valley Development Programme (FVDP)
(http://www.ferghana.elcat.kg)
Still under construction as this report goes to press, this is the official website of the UN's FVDP (see Appendix A). The website contains an updated mission statement and contact information. Under construction is a full information resource, including social and economic data, program information, references, links to other sites, and a directory of experts.

Central Eurasia Resource Pages
(http://www.soros.org/cep)
This page is by the Central Eurasia Project of the Open Society Institute. It provides links to pages on Armenia, Azerbaijan, Georgia, Kazakstan, Mongolia, Tajikistan, Turkmenistan, and Uzbekistan, and also to some other general sites on Central Eurasia.

Interactive Central Asia Resource Project (ICARP)
(http://www.rockbridge.net/personal/bichel/welcome.htp)
ICARP boasts the "most comprehensive collection of descriptive links to Central Asia on the Internet," with more than 550 independent links.

Eurasia Research Center
(http://eurasianews.com/erc/0main.htm)
This site contains links to websites with news sources, documents, and other resources on a variety of areas including Central Asia.

Asian Studies WWW Virtual Library
(http://coombs.anu.edu.au/)
This is the main site of the Asian Studies World Wide Web Virtual Library and is a repository of online documents and articles relating to Asian Studies.

Center for Political and Strategic Studies (CPSS)
(http://www.cpss.org/)
This website includes pages with links related to Central Asia and each of the republics. It also provides access to CPSS's monthly newsletter, "Perspectives on Central Asia."

Harvard Forum for Central Asian Studies
(http://www.fas.harvard.edu/%7Ecentasia/)
This site provides information about the Forum and has links to other institutional sites and listservs.

SOTA Turkic World
(http://www.turkiye.net/sota/homepages.html)
This site provides links to pages related to Turkic countries and communities, including Kazakstan, Kyrgyzstan, Turkmenistan, and Uzbekistan.

LISTSERVS

There are a number of information sources that are distributed to subscribers via e-mail. Many list servers for discussion and announcements about Central Asian studies can be found on the sites listed above. Two popular lists are:

Central Asia Discussion Group: CENASIA
This e-mail discussion list is dedicated to all things Central Asian. To subscribe to CENASIA, send an e-mail message to: listserv@vm1.mcgill.ca. The text of the message should read: subscribe CENASIA YourFirstName YourLastName.

Central Asian Studies Announcement List: CentralAsia-L
This e-mail list is for announcements about publications, events, resources, and so forth about Central Asia. To subscribe to CentralAsia-L, send an e-mail message to: majordomo@fas.harvard.edu. The text of the message should read: subscribe CentralAsia-L YourFirstName YourLastName.

— Appendix E —

CENTER FOR PREVENTIVE ACTION
ADVISORY BOARD

Chair:
JOHN W. VESSEY
United States Army (ret.)

Vice-Chairs:
FRANCES FITZGERALD
The New Yorker

SAMUEL W. LEWIS
American Academy of Diplomacy

Members:
MORTON I. ABRAMOWITZ
The Century Foundation

GRAHAM T. ALLISON
Harvard University

CRAIG B. ANDERSON
St. Paul's School

JAMES E. BAKER
Long Island University

DENIS A. BOVIN
Bear, Stearns & Company

ANTONIA HANDLER CHAYES
Conflict Management Group

VIVIAN LOWERY DERRYCK
United States Agency for
International Development

ROBERT P. DEVECCHI
Council on Foreign Relations

LESLIE H. GELB (ex officio)
Council on Foreign Relations

LOUIS GERBER
AFL-CIO

ANDREW J. GOODPASTER
The Eisenhower Institute

ERNEST G. GREEN
Lehman Brothers

RICHARD N. HAASS
The Brookings Institution

SIDNEY HARMAN
Harman International Industries

BERNARD E. TRAINOR
Harvard University

ROBERT C. WAGGONER
Burelle's Information Services

MICHAELA WALSH
Women's Asset Management, Ltd.

H. ROY WILLIAMS
U.S. Agency for
International Development

R. JAMES WOOLSEY
Shea & Gardner

ARISTIDE R. ZOLBERG
New School for Social Research

— NOTES —

EXECUTIVE SUMMARY

1. Strobe Talbott, "A Farewell to Flashman: American Policy in the Caucasus and Central Asia," speech delivered at the Central Asian Institute, Johns Hopkins University School of Advanced International Studies, Washington, D.C., July 21, 1997, http://www.state.gov/www/regions/nis/970721talbott.html.

1

1. The term "Kalashnikov" refers to the assault rifles (AK–47 and AK–74) designed by Soviet engineer Mikhail T. Kalashnikov. Kalashnikov automatic and semiautomatic weapons are now produced in many countries, including Russia, China, Egypt, and Bulgaria. They were the standard infantry weapons of the Soviet Army, are used by the militaries of all former Soviet republics, and are prized by guerrillas around the world for their power, lightness, and durability.

2

1. Talbott, "Farewell to Flashman."
2. Barnett R. Rubin with Susanna P. Campbell, "Introduction: Experience in Prevention," in Barnett R. Rubin, ed., *Cases and Strategies for Preventive Action* (New York: The Century Foundation Press, 1998), pp. 1–22.
3. Talbott, "Farewell to Flashman," p. 1.
4. See, for instance, the report of another CPA project: Peter M. Lewis, Pearl T. Robinson, and Barnett R. Rubin, *Stabilizing Nigeria:*

Sanctions, Incentives, and Support for Civil Society (New York: The Century Foundation Press, 1998), especially pp. 3–13.

5. Olivier Roy, *La Nouvelle Asie Centrale, ou La Fabrication des Nations* (Paris: Editions du Seuil, 1997), pp. 141–62.

6. U.S. Agency for International Development, "FY 1999 Congressional Presentation," http://www.info.usaid.gov/pubs/cp99/eni/y-carreg.htm, 1.

7. UN Development Program, "Ferghana Valley Development Programme: Draft Programme Outline," n.p., 1996.

8. "Crackdown in the Farghona Valley: Arbitrary Arrests and Religious Discrimination," Human Rights Watch, New York, May 1998.

9. "Gang Leader Gets Death Penalty in Moslem Sect 'Show Trial,'" Agence France-Presse (Tashkent), July 6, 1998.

10. Thomas Carothers, "The Rule of Law Revival," *Foreign Affairs* 77, no. 2 (March/April 1998): 95–106.

11. Nancy Lubin and Monica Ware, *Aid to the Former Soviet Union: When Less Is More* (Washington, D.C.: JNA Associates, 1996).

12. See Lewis, Robinson, and Rubin, *Stabilizing Nigeria*, esp. pp. 3–13.

3

1. Many locals use shorthand references for different parts of the Valley. With respect to Kyrgyzstan, this reflects the general division between the "north," around the capital, Bishkek, and the "south," which includes Kyrgyzstan's part of the Valley. In Tajikistan, the terms "north," "Leninabad," and "Khujand" are often used interchangeably to refer to the Tajik part of the Valley.

2. *Asia-Plus* (Dushanbe), bulletin no. 10, December 1996, http://www.internews.ras.ru/ASIA-PLUS.

3. *Osh Regional Economic Strategy* (Bishkek: State Commission on Foreign Investment and Economic Assistance, Republic of Kyrgyzstan, June 1996); *Jalal-abad Regional Economic Strategy* (Bishkek: State Commission on Foreign Investment and Economic Assistance, Republic of Kyrgyzstan, March 1997).

4. According to the 1991 statistical yearbook for Uzbekistan's economy, the three Ferghana Valley regions together produced about 24 percent of Uzbekistan's cotton and 23 percent of its fruit and vegetables. *The National Economy of Uzbekistan in 1991* (*Narodnoe khoziaistvo respubliki Uzbekistan v 1991g*) (Tashkent: State Committee for Statistics, Republic of Uzbekistan, 1992), pp. 226–27.

5. None of these, it should be noted, is anywhere near the size or importance of the Nagorno-Karabakh region, which led to fighting between Azerbaijan and Armenia.

6. Mehrdad Haghayeghi, *Islam and Politics in Central Asia* (New York: St. Martin's Press, 1994), pp. 17–18.

7. Immediately after independence, the Central Asian states continued to use the ruble, controlled by the central bank of Russia, now a foreign state. Kyrgyzstan introduced a national currency in May 1993, leading to trade blockades and other measures by Uzbekistan and Kazakstan. The Russian central bank virtually forced the latter two states to follow suit under much less favorable conditions in November 1993. Tajikistan adapted the Tajik "ruble" in May 1995.

8. In one year alone—1979—11,000 antireligious lectures were held in the city of Namangan. See Haghayeghi, *Islam and Politics in Central Asia*, p. 37.

9. At the time of the riots, about 15,000 Meshketian Turks lived in the Ferghana Valley; they were part of the 60,000 resettled by Stalin from Georgia to Uzbekistan in 1944; ibid., pp. 192–93.

10. Daria Fane, "Ethnicity and Regionalism in Uzbekistan," in Leokadia Drobizheva et al., eds., *Ethnic Conflict in the Post-Soviet World: Case Studies and Analysis* (London: M. E. Sharpe, 1996), pp. 271–302; and Haghayeghi, *Islam and Politics in Central Asia*, p. 192.

11. Haghayeghi, *Islam and Politics in Central Asia*, p. 193.

12. Richard Dobson, "Kyrgyzstan in a Time of Change," *Central Asia Monitor* (Fair Haven, Vt.) 3, no. 1 (January–February 1995): 21–22.

13. Haghayeghi, *Islam and Politics in Central Asia*, p. 194.

14. Ibid.

15. For a discussion of the Osh events, see also Valerii Tishkov, "'Don't Kill Me, I'm a Kyrgyz!': An Anthropological Analysis of Violence in the Osh Ethnic Conflict," *Journal of Peace Research* 32, no. 2 (1995): 133–149.

16. Dobson, "Kyrgyzstan in a Time of Change."

17. For a brief account of Adolat, see William Fierman, "Political Development in Uzbekistan: Democratization?" in Karen Dawisha and Bruce Parrott, eds., *Conflict, Cleavage, and Change in Central Asia and the Caucasus* (Cambridge: Cambridge University Press, 1997), p. 382.

18. Haghayeghi, *Islam and Politics in Central Asia*, p. 93.

19. Ibid., p. 94.

20. Ibid.

21. For one account, see "Tajikistan, Leninabad: Crackdown in the North," Human Rights Watch, New York, April 1998.

22. See Bruce Pannier, "Tajikistan's Last Safe Haven," *OMRI Analytical Brief*, Open Media Research Institute, Prague, May 15, 1996.

23. "Former Tajik Leader Offers Alternative to the Regime," *Jamestown Monitor: A Daily Briefing on the Post-Soviet States* 2, no. 149 (July 31, 1996), Jamestown Foundation, Washington, D.C., http://www.jamestown.org/pubs/view/mon_002_149_011.htm.

24. *Novoe Vremya*, no. 51 (December 1996): 20–21.

25. "Tajik Opposition Criticizes Suppression of Prison Revolt," Interfax (Moscow), April 21, 1997; "Voice of Free Tajikistan," Foreign Broadcast Information Service, *FBIS Daily Report, Central Eurasia*, FBIS-SOV-97-109, April 19, 1997; a well-placed U.S. government official confirmed these reports.

26. "Tajik President Injured, Assailant Detained," Interfax (Dushanbe), April 30, 1997.

27. For example, Dushanbe mayor Makhmadsaid Ubaidullayev, said to be as important politically as President Rakhmonov, openly accused Abdullajanov of plotting the assassination attempt. He insisted that Abdullajanov be detained, brought to Tajikistan, and tried; "Mayor of Dushanbe Blames Ex-PM for Plotting Against Rakhmonov," Interfax (Dushanbe), May 1, 1997.

28. "Violent Confrontation in Tajikistan over Investigation into Presidential Assassination Attempt," *RFE/RL Newsline*, Radio Free Europe/Radio Liberty, May 5, 1997.

29. "...But Opposition Accuses, Advises Government," *RFE/RL Newsline*, Radio Free Europe/Radio Liberty, May 27, 1997.

30. Najam Abbas, "Tajik Fingers Pointing North: Rakhmanov's Rare Display of Resentment over 'Uzbek Interference,'" *Eurasia News*, Eurasia Research Center, November 13, 1998, http://eurasianews.com/erc/homepage.htm.

31. Voice of the Islamic Republic of Iran (Mashhad), February 18, 1999, 0230 GMT, BBC Monitoring, Central Asia, February 19, 1999 (electronic version).

32. Reuters (Tashkent), May 2, 1998.

33. "Gang Leader Gets Death Penalty in Moslem Sect 'Show Trial,'" Agence France-Presse (Tashkent), July 6, 1998.

34. Displaying the heads of enemies is an ancient Central Asian custom, practiced by Amir Timur and Genghis Khan before him. Its use may imply that the killing was political.

35. "Crackdown on the Farghona Valley: Arbitrary Arrests and Religious Discrimination," Human Rights Watch, New York, May 1998.

36. Ibid.

37. Ibid. Appendix C of the Human Rights Watch report reproduces the text of the decree banning megaphones on mosques.

38. Interfax (Moscow), February 16, 1998; Interfax (Tashkent), March 26, 1998.

39. "Tashkent, Moscow to Coordinate Policy on Fundamentalism," *RFE/RL Newsline*, Radio Free Europe/ Radio Liberty, May 6, 1998; "More on Karimov Visit to Moscow," *RFE/RL Newsline*, Radio Free Europe/Radio Liberty, May 7, 1998.

40. Uzbek Television, Channel 1 (Tashkent), 1225 GMT, February 16, 1999, BBC Monitoring, Central Asia, February 20, 1999 (electronic version).

41. Ibid.

42. Voice of the Islamic Republic of Iran (Mashhad), 1530 GMT, February 19, 1999, BBC Monitoring, Central Asia, February 17, 1999 (electronic version).

43. Uzbek Television, Channel 1 (Tashkent), 1225 GMT, February 16, 1999, BBC Monitoring Central Asia, February 20, 1999 (electronic version).

44. "Voice of Free Tajikistan," Foreign Broadcast Information Service, *FBIS Daily Report, Central Eurasia*, FBIS-SOV-97-033, February 19, 1997, quoted a stern warning from the Uzbekistan foreign ministry to the Tajikistan government to "take more serious steps to prevent such events."

45. Dr. Rafik Saifulin, "The Fergana Valley: A View from Uzbekistan," *Perspectives on Central Asia: Examining Conflicts in the Fergana Valley and Caspian Sea Region*, (Center for Political and Strategic Studies, Washington, D.C.) 1, no. 1 (April 1996), http://www.cpss.org/casianw/canews.htm.

4

1. Saifulin, "The Fergana Valley: A View from Uzbekistan"; *The National Economy of Uzbekistan in 1991*.

2. *Jalal-abad Regional Economic Strategy*, p. 6.

3. A UNDP-assisted economic strategy report notes that in August 1993 the average monthly wage in Osh oblast was 62.9 som, compared to the national average of 84.3 som and 120.3 som in Bishkek. Average wages in agriculture were only 32.1 som, the lowest of all regions in Kyrgyzstan. At this time the exchange rate was about 6 som per U.S. dollar. See *Osh Regional Economic Strategy* (Bishkek: State Commission

on Foreign Investment and Economic Assistance, Republic of Kyrgyzstan, June 1996), p. 15.

4. *Jalal-abad Regional Economic Strategy*, p. 31. According to this report, the rate of those receiving social assistance was high, at 30 percent, with the government three to four months behind in payments.

5. "Socioeconomic Situation in Tajikistan in the Period from January to September of 1996," *Asia-Plus* (Dushanbe), bulletin no. 14, November 1996, http://www.internews.ru/ASIA-PLUS/bulletin_14/statistics.html. There are two *Asia-Plus* bulletins dated November 1996, no. 11 and no. 14.

6. Data are from the Expert Center, Tashkent.

7. UN Development Program: "Ferghana Valley Development Programme: Draft Programme Outline," n.p., 1996.

8. "Leninabod Business and Politics: Touring the Economic Engine of Tajikistan—Beyond Khojand," U.S. embassy report, BISNIS (Business Information Service for the Newly Independent States), Dushanbe, May 7, 1996, http://www.itaiep.doc.gov/bisnis/cables/960507ti.htm.

9. *Jalal-abad Regional Economic Strategy*, p. 35.

10. UN Development Program, "Ferghana Valley Development Programme."

11. Information provided by Arsalan Zholdasov of the Expert Center, Tashkent.

12. For a fuller description, see Nancy Lubin, *Labor and Nationality in Soviet Central Asia: An Uneasy Compromise* (Princeton, N.J.: Princeton University Press, 1984), chapter 6.

13. See, for example, Nancy Lubin and Arsalan Zholdasov, *Central Asians Take Stock: Reform, Corruption and Identity* (Washington, D.C.: U.S. Institute of Peace, 1995).

14. "Strengthening Law Enforcement Capacities and Cross Border Cooperation in the Central Asian Subregion," project document, UN International Drug Control Program, May 25, 1996. According to another UN report, it is believed that as much as half of the opium leaving Afghanistan now leaves through Central Asia. See *UN Information Service*, September 25, 1996.

15. Graham Turbiville, "Drug Trafficking in Central Asia," presentation at the U.S. Institute of Peace, Washington, D.C., May 16, 1997.

16. Ibid.

17. Ibid.

18. As reported in *Jalal-abad Regional Economic Strategy*, p. 38: "Since 1990, the education sector has had to cope with a severe cutback in financing. There have been virtually no allocations from the domestic budget for textbooks, school equipment or building maintenance.

Teachers' salaries have fallen dramatically in real terms. Teacher morale and performance has been further undermined by the substantial delays in salary payments which are typically 2–4 months in arrears. In addition, several schools in Toktogul and Nooken raions still suffer significant damage from the earthquake and mudslides which occurred between 1992 and 1994."

19. ITAR-TASS, August 31, 1996.

20. *Osh Regional Economic Strategy*, pp. 46–47.

21. "Leninabod Business and Politics."

22. M. A. Olimov and S. K. Olimova, "Regionalism in Tajikistan: Its Impact on the Fergana Valley," *Perspectives on Central Asia: Examining Conflicts in the Ferghana Valley and Caspian Sea Region*, (Center for Political 'and Strategic Studies, Washington, D.C.) 1, no. 3 (March 1996), http://www.cpss.org/casianw/canews.htm.

23. *Biznes Vestnik Vostoka*, April 26, 1996, translated in Foreign Broadcast Information Service, *FBIS Daily Report, Central Eurasia*, FBIS-SOV-96-085, p. 16.

24. In southern Kyrgyzstan, for example, the Osh silk factory was reportedly sold for 1.5 million som, not even 2 percent of its estimated value of 93 million som.

25. For example, see *Nezavisimaya Gazeta* (Moscow), March 10, 1992, noting that people from the south were much more opposed to President Akaev's economic reforms (support was two-thirds lower in Jalalabad than the national average). As of today, much of the privatization in the south has been on paper only, and those enterprises would be bankrupt without state support.

26. Scott Horton and Tatyana Geller, "Currency Convertibility in Uzbekistan," *Central Asia Monitor* (Fair Haven, Vt.), no. 6 (1997): 10–14. Owing to various economic problems, however (ironically including the drastic increase in foreign trade, as well as lower world prices for cotton and high prices for imported grain), the Uzbek government had a trade deficit of $348 million in 1996. This meant that Uzbekistan, which has only small reserves of hard currency and which in any case wanted to decrease the volume of imports, was facing an increasingly difficult task in meeting the demands of local and foreign companies with the (already restricted) right to exchange foreign currency.

27. According to President Karimov, as reported in Interfax (Tashkent), February 26, 1997, 1996 saw a breakthrough in privatization, with 70 percent of the workforce working in the nongovernment sector, which produced 53.5 percent of industrial output and 97 percent of farm produce. By contrast, one study of the Uzbek economy reveals that although only 25.4 percent of state enterprises remained in state ownership, those

companies were producing 49.8 percent of domestic goods and services. See Michael Kaser, *The Economies of Kazakstan and Uzbekistan* (London: Royal Institute of International Affairs, 1997), p. 32.

28. "Privatisation: Firsthand Information," *Asia-Plus* (Dushanbe), Bulletin no. 11, November 1996, http://www.internews.ru/ASIA-PLUS/bulletin_11/economy.html.

29. "Leninabod Business and Politics."

30. For instance, according to one account, the May 1996 riots in Khujand were set off by an incident where Kulabi mafia members killed a Leninabadi restaurant owner associated with the Leninabadi mafia as the Kulabis tried to seize control of profitable businesses in the north.

31. Significant problems in October 1996 led to the temporary closing down of the operation, as members of the Tajik government insisted that the gold alloy be refined at the Vostokredmet refinery in Chkalovsk (in the Ferghana Valley) rather than be exported for refining. It is unclear at this time if those problems have been resolved. See "JV Zarafshon Is Trying to Solve its Problems with the Government of the Republic," *Asia-Plus* (Dushanbe), Bulletin no. 14, November 1996, http://www.internews.ru/ASIA-PLUS/bulletin_14/conflict.html. The report states that, while the Tajik prime minister, Yahya Azimov, claimed that work had not stopped, representatives of Nelson Gold said that work was suspended at the joint venture on November 1, 1996.

32. Examples are cited in "Leninabod Business and Politics."

33. This is corroborated by an American who worked on a *sovkhoz-*turned-collective farm for three years in the 1990s. His comments reflect the extent of state control: "The state, through the kolkhoz, still owns the land, sets crop targets and production quotas, controls capital, and distributes field additives. The state weighs and buys the product (cotton), sets all prices (for inputs and outputs), and controls processing, distribution, and exports. And the rural elite—kolkhoz management, RayVodKhoz, OblVodKhoz, Hakimiyat staff—has profitable reasons to stall reforms. After all, centralized cotton farming, with its complicated array of inputs and elaborate structure of consumers, naturally facilitates the concentration of power." See Tom McCray, "Complicating Agricultural Reforms in Uzbekistan: Observations on the Lower Zaravshan Basin," Part 1, *Central Asia Monitor* (Fair Haven, Vt.), no. 1 (1997): 7–14.

34. *Delovoy Mir* (Moscow), July 8, 1995.

35. *Osh Regional Economic Strategy*; *Jalal-abad Regional Economic Strategy*.

36. *Jalal-abad Regional Economic Strategy*, p. 55.

37. Ibid., p. 35.

38. Ibid.

39. Ibid.

40. *Osh Regional Economic Strategy Report*, p. 49.

41. *Delovoy Mir* (Moscow) July 8, 1995.

42. For a full description of this project, see "Strengthening Law Enforcement Capacities and Cross Border Cooperation in the Central Asian Subregion."

43. One complicating factor is that Kyrgyzstan and Kazakstan are also members of a customs union that includes Russia and Belarus, which Uzbekistan is unwilling to join. How this will affect the Central Asian Union is still ambiguous.

5

1. Nancy Lubin, *Central Asians Take Stock: Reform, Corruption, and Identity* (Washington, D.C.: U.S. Institute of Peace, 1995).

2. This is somewhat surprising since the protests leading to self-rule in Namangan were precipitated by local mullahs' public pronouncements in favor of Karimov (see the "Past Conflicts" section).

3. Since the government has agreed to register those political parties that form the United Tajik Opposition (UTO), Tajikistan is poised to become, once again, the only country in Central Asia with a legal Islamic political party. The party, led by the head of the UTO, Said Abdullah Nuri, and the country's former religious leader, Qazi Akbar Turajonzoda, is the direct successor of the Islamic Renaissance Party, whose participation in a coalition government was one of the triggers of the civil war in 1992–93.

4. "Uzbekistan: Persistent Human Rights Violations and Prospects for Improvement," Human Rights Watch/Helsinki, New York, May 1996, particularly the section entitled, "An Alarming New Trend: The Crackdown against 'Independent' Muslims"; "Crackdown in the Farghona Valley, Arbitrary Arrests and Discrimination," Human Rights Watch, New York, May 1998.

5. On the November incident, see William Fierman, "Political Development in Uzbekistan: Democratization?" in Karen Dawisha and Bruce Parrott, eds., *Conflict, Cleavage, and Change in Central Asia and the Caucasus* (Cambridge: Cambridge University Press, 1997), p. 382.

6. Abdumannob Polat, "Trying to Understand Uzbekistan's Dilemma: The Need for a 'New Marshall Plan' for Central Eurasia," *Central Asia Monitor* (Fair Haven, Vt.), no. 1 (1998): 16.

7. "Crackdown in the Farghona Valley."

8. Mehrdad Haghayeghi, *Islam and Politics in Central Asia* (New York: St. Martin's Press, 1994), p. 95.

9. "Uzbekistan Criticized for Putting Islamic Sect on Trial," Agence France-Presse (Tashkent), June 22, 1998; "Uzbek Opposition Denial," BBC World Service, January 6, 1998, http://www.bbc.co.uk.

10. "Crackdown in the Farghona Valley."

11. Ibid.

12. "Uzbekistan Politics: Power Struggle," *EIU ViewsWire*, Economist Intelligence Unit, October 22, 1998, http://www.viewswire.com.

13. See Daria Fane, "Ethnicity and Regionalism in Uzbekistan," in Leokadia Drobizheva et al., eds., *Ethnic Conflict in the Post-Soviet World: Case Studies and Analysis* (London: M. E. Sharpe, 1996), pp. 271–302.

14. *Human Rights Watch World Report* 1998 (New York: Human Rights Watch, December 1997), pp. 265–67.

15. "Uzbekistan: Persistent Human Rights Violations."

16. *Human Rights Watch World Report* 1998, pp. 294–97.

17. *Human Rights Watch/Helsinki Report on Uzbekistan* 9, no. 7 (July 1997): 3, quoting Uzbekistan Television.

18. Personal observation of Barnett R. Rubin, Khujand, June 1993.

19. "U.S.-Uzbek Military Exercises Finish," *RFE/RL Newsline*, Radio Free Europe/Radio Liberty, June 10, 1997.

20. Personal observation of Barnett R. Rubin, Khujand, June 1993.

6

1. William Maley, ed., *Fundamentalism Reborn? Afghanistan and the Taliban* (New York: New York University Press, 1998).

2. "Proof of Tajik Aid to Anti-Taliban Forces?" *RFE/RL Newsline*, Radio Free Europe/Radio Liberty, March 13, 1997, quoting the same day's edition of *Nezavisimaya Gazeta* (Moscow). The Taliban had claimed, two days earlier, that General Massoud had a "safe haven" in the southern Tajikistan city of Kulab, home of Tajikistan's president, Imomali Rakhmonov.

3. "Tajik Peace Agreement Signed," *RFE/RL Newsline*, Radio Free Europe/ Radio Liberty, June 27, 1997. Russian pressure on the Tajik government, in particular, must have been intense, as the government agreed to major concessions, especially on power sharing, that it had previously consistently rejected.

4. In August 1997 the former interior minister, Yakub Salimov, joined Khudoiberdiyev in an attempt to take Dushanbe that threatened

President Rakhmonov. While these attacks were repulsed, Khudoiberdiyev, an ethnic Uzbek, was reportedly given refuge—and possibly assistance—by Uzbekistan and by General Dostum, who returned to Afghanistan with Uzbekistan's assistance in September 1997. *RFE/RL Newsline*, Radio Free Europe/Radio Liberty, "Renewed Fighting in Tajikistan," August 11, 1997; and "Mutinous Troops Exposition in Southern Tajikistan . . . ," August 18, 1997.

5. For a review of arguments on the causes of the war in Tajikistan, see Barnett R. Rubin, "State Breakdown in the Periphery: Causes and Consequences of the Civil War in Tajikistan," in Barnett R. Rubin and Jack Snyder, eds., *Political Order in the Former Soviet Union: State Building and Conflict* (London: Routledge, 1998), pp. 162–79.

6. "Tashkent, Moscow to Coordinate Policy on Fundamentalism," *RFE/RL Newsline*, Radio Free Europe/Radio Liberty, May 6, 1998; "More on Karimov Visit to Moscow," *RFE/RL Newsline*, Radio Free Europe/ Radio Liberty, May 7, 1998.

7. Interfax (Moscow), December 5, 1996.

8. During the visit of the UN High Commissioner on Refugees to Tajikistan, President Rakhmonov thanked the UNHCR for its help in the return and accommodation of more than 41,000 Tajik refugees from Afghanistan and more than 680,000 displaced persons. Interfax (Moscow), May 31, 1997. Other sources have suggested the number of those who fled the fighting exceeds 1 million.

9. Bruce Pannier, "Tajikistan's Last Safe Haven," *OMRI Analytical Brief*, Open Media Research Institute, Prague, May 15, 1996.

10. Resul Yalcin, "Uzbeks of Tajikistan," on CenAsia listserv (see Appendix D), June 11, 1997.

11. Uzbekistan Television, May 29, 1997, as quoted in Foreign Broadcast Information Service, *FBIS Daily Report, Central Eurasia*, FBIS-SOV-97-149.

12. Interfax (Moscow), May 26, 1997.

13. While the border is on the other side of the mountains from Osh (and therefore quite remote from the Valley), all of the regional administrative links with the border are centered in Osh itself.

14. "Border Agreements Ratified," *RFE/RL Newsline*, Radio Free Europe/ Radio Liberty, May 15, 1997.

15. Interfax (Moscow), June 11, 1997; communication from embassy of Kyrgyzstan, Washington, D.C.

16. "ECO Summit Ends," *RFE/RL Newsline*, Radio Free Europe/ Radio Liberty, May 15, 1997.

17. "Kyrgyz President Comments on ECO," *RFE/RL Newsline*, Radio Free Europe/ Radio Liberty, April 4, 1997.

18. Talbott, "Farewell to Flashman."
19. Lubin, *Central Asians Take Stock.*

Appendix A

1. The Working Group received this draft in the region in March 1997. The preparatory phase of the Ferghana Valley Development Programme (FVDP) began in August 1998 with headquarters in Osh. It is working with the cooperation of Kyrgyzstan and Tajikistan while continuing discussions with Uzbekistan. For more information and an updated program statement, see the FVDP website, www.ferghana.elcat.kg.

— INDEX —

Note: Page numbers followed by *italicized* letter *t* indicate material presented in tables.